EDITORS AS
GATEKEEPERS

EDITORS AS GATEKEEPERS

Getting Published in the Social Sciences

Edited by

Rita J. Simon
and
James J. Fyfe

Rowman & Littlefield Publishers, Inc.

ROWMAN & LITTLEFIELD PUBLISHERS, INC.

Published in the United States of America
by Rowman & Littlefield Publishers, Inc.
4720 Boston Way, Lanham, Maryland 20706

3 Henrietta Street
London WC2E 8LU, England

British Cataloging in Publication Information Available

Library of Congress Cataloging-in-Publication Data

Editors as gatekeepers : getting published in the social sciences /
edited by Rita J. Simon and James J. Fyfe.
p. cm.
Includes index.
1. Social science literature—Editing. 2. Social sciences—
Authorship. I. Simon, Rita James. II. Fyfe, James J.
H91.E35   1994   808'.0663—dc20   94-8978   CIP

ISBN 0–8476–7912–8 (cloth: alk. paper)
ISBN 0–8476–7913–6 (pbk.: alk. paper)

Printed in the United States of America

∞™   The paper used in this publication meets the minimum requirements of
American National Standard for Information Sciences—Permanence of
Paper for Printed Library Materials, ANSI Z39.48–1984.

Contents

Introduction

Editors as Gatekeepers

✳

Rita J. Simon and James J. Fyfe

The essays in this volume explain how and why some scholarly manuscripts gain publication and others do not. They discuss the kinds of manuscripts editors are looking for; the extent to which editors' tastes and preferences influence the decision-making process; the kinds of relationships that develop between successful editors and authors; and how university presses and commercial publishers differentiate their roles. They also provide advice to prospective authors about how to convert a promising manuscript that has received encouraging reviews into a successful publication, offer guidance about where to submit a manuscript, and how long to wait for a decision.

All of the authors are currently, or have been, either editors of major scholarly journals, mostly in the social sciences, or editors and directors of university presses. Each writes from his or her unique experiences as well as from observations of colleagues in other editorial roles. Some of the authors are "professionals"; they have devoted their careers to editing other people's scholarship; most have assumed the editor's role temporarily. They are authors and researchers who serve as editors of journals in their own field for a limited term, usually between three and five years.

To outsiders, an editor is an editor. Those more involved in the business know that the editor's role is played in a wide variety of ways. Some editors have a relatively free hand. Their tastes, interests, and ideas determine what and who get published. Other editors are more likely to reflect a "board's" consensus. Their editorial "we" actually represents the composite views of reviewers, deputy and associate editors, and their own opinions. Their voice is one of many. It may not even be the dominant one. Editors of scholarly journals in the social sciences, especially, when the journal is the "official one" for an association (e.g., American Sociological Association, American Political Science Association, Academy of Criminal Justice Sciences) are expected to submit manuscripts to peer review, and to be heavily guided by the reviewers' evaluations. As the authors in several of the forthcoming chapters explain, they are not completely hamstrung by this process. They do have some degrees of freedom; but it is clearly not "their journal," and cannot be run primarily by their tastes, biases, or inclinations.

In large measure, the extent to which editors sit back and wait for manuscripts to come in as opposed to actively soliciting them is a function of the status of the journal. Editors of "official" journals are especially constrained in this area, as well. It is risky for editors of official journals to solicit papers because they cannot promise authors that their manuscripts will be published. Typically, the editor is obligated to send out solicited manuscripts for review; if the reviewers turn thumbs down, the editor will probably have to reject the piece. Editors of independent journals or of "special series" have more freedom. They have greater power to shape and mold blank pages so that the printed words reflect their interest and their discipline, as well as their sense of what is cutting edge, provocative, and important. Editors of journals that represent more than one discipline have to worry about balance and fairness. They must be concerned about the scholarly integrity of each discipline. Disagreements about method and substantive emphasis within the same discipline (e.g., quantitative versus qualitative methods, basic versus applied research) are magnified dramatically when journals try to bridge two or more disciplines or fields. These issues also are discussed in the forthcoming chapters.

Official journals are pretty much removed from the sordid affairs of the market. They are subsidized by the association they represent. The membership's dues pay most of the costs, and the university at which the editor is employed is expected to make a contribution in the form of space and equipment, released time for the editor, and the hiring of an editorial support staff. Of course, rarely is an editor of a scholarly journal paid for his or her work; it is all honorific. But staying in the black is something that editors of independent journals have to worry about; and what and whom they publish influence whether they stay afloat. Big name authors of articles that are not on the cutting edge may have more reader interest than abstract, theoretical, or highly quantitative pieces by assistant professors with new ideas, new techniques, and new ways of looking at their field. How editors handle these dilemmas is also discussed in this collection.

The various missions that different university presses assume are reflected in the chapters that have been contributed by editors and directors. Each discusses the thematic and disciplinary emphasis he or she wants the press to assume. Should a press try to cover as many fields and disciplines as a university represents or should it have more of a focus or emphasis on certain areas in the social sciences, the humanities, the natural or physical sciences, or the professions? Within fields or disciplines, is there still room for emphasis on, for example, "women's studies," or works about racial and ethnic minorities, or research monographs versus more popular types of offerings?

With what kinds of authors is the press most likely to work? Are they likely to be the big name, established scholars who contribute on a regular basis, or younger, newer scholars who the press brings to the attention of colleagues with the publication of first works? Is the editor of the press more likely to perform as the author's mentor, guiding and directing her or him, making substantive as well as formatic suggestions; or as the author's associate, clearing the way for uncomplicated movement of the author's manuscript from submission through reviews, revisions, and copyediting, to publication?

All of the chapters provide insights into each editor's definition of his or her role; her or his major pleasures and pains; the disappointments and successes each has experienced. They tell how different editors have resolved problems with authors, reviewers, readers, and publishers. Standing back and observing their fields, they offer advice about where to submit, how to read editors' letters about revising and resubmitting manuscripts, and when to complain. They describe what they hoped they would accomplish when they began their editorship, and the extent to which they have realized their goals.

For readers who see themselves as future editors, this book will be good preparation. For readers who are active scholars, it offers broader explanations about how and why your manuscripts fared as they did; and the changes you might make that would convert rejections into opportunities to revise, and revised manuscripts into published articles or monographs. For the neophytes, those readers who are just beginning to write for publication, the book can save you time and pain.

The book has three major sections. Part one includes eight chapters authored by former and current social science journal editors, most of whom were or are editors of the official or flagship journal of an academic association. Part two includes chapters by editors of special series and an editor of a commercial law journal. Part three reports the work of current and former editors and directors of commercial and university presses. All together then, the volume describes the varied experiences of professional and "amateur" editors of journals in different disciplines within the social sciences, and of editors and directors of research annuals, monographs, and books from commercial and university publishing houses.

Part I

Social Science Journal Editors

1

The Itch to Publish in Political Science

*

Samuel C. Patterson

A scholarly discipline is a remarkable thing to behold. Those who view it from outside the academy commonly find it baffling and sometimes even a little bit annoying. Students seeking to commission themselves to the ranks of the chosen usually find the process of taking on a scholarly discipline both exacting and exasperating. Communicants and practitioners mainly accept it as given, a cocoon protecting the pursuit of discovery, explanation, invention, or restoration.

Political science is one of the oldest of systematic intellectual or scholarly endeavors. It is rooted in ordered observations from very ancient times about the constitution of the state. But political science as an organized discipline, based in the colleges and universities of the land, is a fledgling (a good history is Somit & Tanenhaus, 1967). The first political science department was established at Columbia University in 1880, founded by John W. Burgess; Johns Hopkins University followed on Columbia's heels. Columbia and Johns Hopkins supplied the first three dozen Ph.D.s for the burgeoning discipline. Both nascent departments laid a very heavy emphasis on research and publication, requiring all doctoral candidates to have their dissertations published (at their own expense, if necessary).

From the beginning, scholarly publication in the form of journal articles was an integral part of the research process in American political science. Columbia University launched the *Political Science Quarterly* in 1886, and that journal served as the principal outlet for the scholarly articles mainly of political scientists for the next quarter-century. Then, in 1903, the American Political

3

Science Association was created at a founding meeting in New Orleans. Its official journal, the *American Political Science Review*, came into existence in 1906. In its earliest years, the *Review* was mostly a newsletter, its pages filled with news of legislation, court decisions, trends in governments abroad, and information about association activities. The *Review* really did not become the flagship journal of American political science until 1914, when the association discontinued the practice of publishing the learned papers given at its annual conventions in volumes of *Proceedings of the American Political Science Association*.

The numbers of journals in political science grew in the years following World War II. Regional political science associations established new general journals—the *Journal of Politics*, the *American Journal of Political Science*, the *Western Political Quarterly*, *Polity*. A wide variety of specialized journals was established, as well. But the prestige of the national association's *Review* has always outdistanced the other journals. Today, it is true to say that publication in the *APSR* is a major event in the career of American academic political scientists. Because great professional prestige derives from authorship in the *Review*, its processes of evaluation and judgment require thoughtful reflection on the part of its managing editor, and in the profession generally.

Institutionalized Skepticism

A scholarly, scientific discipline is denoted by the relentless, systematic, rigorous, universalistic standards it applies to the scholarly product. Such a discipline recognizes that upholding high standards of scientific work is a collective responsibility. The process of evaluation of the quality of scholarly work that has evolved in the scientific disciplines is their "referee system." This involves the trenchant assessment of scholarly work, books or journal articles, by the author's peers as a basis for judgment of their publishability.

Such a system of peer review provides an organized, institutionalized skepticism about a scholar's research and writing. Is the research important? Is the methodology sound? Are the findings significant? Is the analysis logically and coherently written? Is the craftsmanship of the presentation up to high standards of quality?

Organized skepticism, institutionalized as a system of peer review, directly addresses issues of quality control in scholarship.

Research findings, in order to acquire the mantle of authority and prestige, must pass through the screen of peer evaluation and judgment. But peer review also has an indirect effect on the control of the excellence of scholarly work. A peer review system contributes to quality control of scholarly communication by anticipation. As sociologist Robert K. Merton observed, "Knowing that their papers will be reviewed, authors take care in preparing them before submission, all the more so, perhaps, for papers sent to high-ranking journals with a reputation for thorough refereeing" (Merton, 1973, p. 495).

The scientific journal, and its attendant practice of peer review of contributions, has a rather long history in the natural and physical sciences. The modern scientific journal was first conceived about three hundred years ago. The first such journal was *Philosophical Transactions*, founded in 1665 and in 1753 adopted as the official publication of the British Royal Society, whose fellows included the most important scientists of the day. Prompt publication in the journal helped to curb the widespread plagiarism in the science of the time, called "philo-sophicall robbery" by Robert Boyle (1627-91), the founder of modern chemistry. To protect the integrity of its implicit endorsement of articles published in *Transactions*, the Royal Society insisted that articles be published only after "being first reviewed by some of the members of the same" (Merton, 1973, p. 463). Thus, the practice of peer review was invented.

Scholarly skepticism incorporates a large measure of judgment and doubt, making the application of standards both changeable and, to some degree, intangible. Obviously, the standards of scholarly evaluation and judgment change with time. We are applying much more exacting standards today than were generally applicable a century ago, or even thirty years ago. The element of doubt is, perhaps, more constant. Being in doubt is endemic to a system of organized skepticism, and an occupational hazard for scholars, especially journal editors.

Editors and the referees who advise them, at least in the social sciences, generally seem to resolve doubt on the side of avoiding what we might call a type 1 error: publishing a paper that should not have been published, rather than eschewing a type 2 error: failing to publish a paper that should have been published. This conservative aroma of editorial decision making usually is prudent and workable, as long as there remains room for recognizing genuinely innovative work of genius. But, resolving doubt and making judgments is unavoidable in the course of peer review in political, or any other, research.

In American political science, systematic peer review is, in fact, a recent development. There is no record of editorial practices at the APSR in the early days of this century. Frederic A. Ogg of the University of Wisconsin, the third managing editor, controlled the *Review* from 1925 until he relinquished the editorship in 1949. It appears that he alone read and passed judgment on all submitted manuscripts, although he may, of course, have consulted his colleagues at Wisconsin from time to time. A publications committee of the American Political Science Association reported in 1935 that the "Managing Editor . . . handles almost alone the reading and evaluation of manuscripts" (Somit & Tanenhaus, 1967, p. 96). In political science, peer review appears to have been a development of the 1950s. Ohio State University's Harvey Mansfield is reputed to have regularly consulted one or more specialists in evaluating manuscripts for the *Review* during his decade as managing editor beginning in 1955. A fully established system of peer review came when Austin Ranney, then at Wisconsin, became managing editor in 1965 (for a historical analysis, see Patterson, Ripley & Trish, 1988).

As a scientific discipline, complete with the scholarly trappings of peer review, American political science is a johnny-come-lately discipline. But its practice of institutionalized skepticism is neither more casual nor less embedded in disciplinary norms than is true for other sciences. Like them, political science has familiar and equally fascinating peculiarities.

The Itch to Publish

In political science, as in other realms of inquiry, publication, especially in the leading journals, has always been tied to academic career success. Young, ambitious scholars exhibit an "itch to publish" that "malignant disease known, since the days of Juvenal, as the *insanabile scribendi cacoethes*" (Merton, 1965, p. 83). "There are," says Robert Merton in his delightful treatise *On the Shoulders of Giants*, "indications that the frequency of the 'itch to publish' increases steadily in those educational or research institutions which lavish rewards upon the prolific author of scientific papers or scholarly books" (1965, pp. 83-84).

Journal editors bear the brunt of the "itch to publish." In Ogg's halcyon years, some thirty to forty manuscripts were submitted to the *Review* each year; today, the managing editor receives about ten times that amount, or two manuscripts in the mail each working day.

It seems the original cure for the scholar's itch to publish was invented by Reverend Thomas Fuller (1608–61), that puckish royalist preacher, wit, lay historian, and prolific author of books of the mid-seventeenth century. There was, says Merton, no great mystery as to how Fuller satisfied his itch to publish—"he had hit upon an admirable device which more of us could put to the same ingenious use: he would simply write the first word on every line on a sheet and then fill up all the remaining space, a most infectious method for rapid composition" (Merton, 1965, p. 83).

Some political scientists forsake the cure; they write so much, and so often, that they lose credibility. They have neither counsellor, like the friend of molecular biologist Seymour Benzer, who "wrote to my wife to tell me to stop writing so many papers. And I did stop," nor referee who advised a prolific physicist: "If [he] would write fewer papers, more people would read them" (Merton, 1973, p. 455).

The itch to publish can contribute to the perversities of scholarly communication. In this technotronic age, writers of scholarly papers can learn to communicate in computer acronyms, comforting their readers that PROBIT, LOGIT, LISREL, and other remedies have been at work. More distressing is that contrived obscurity or predestined abstractness forewarned by English scholars lately absorbed in the future of social research in their country. In the words of Sir Ernest Gowers "some [social scientists] strain after 'expert' language because they are afraid that if their manner is lucid their matter will be despised as elementary." In this vein, Lord Rothschild "described social scientists as notorious sufferers from the 'succulent bivalve' syndrome (the inability to call an oyster merely an oyster)" (*SSRC Newsletter* [U.K.], Vol. 50, November 1983, p. 29).

The Wages of Peer Review

The *American Political Science Review* receives well over four hundred manuscripts a year, and has since the early 1970s. Figure 1 shows the trace line of submissions since 1962. The *Review*, like most journals in the social sciences, publishes less than a fifth of the manuscripts submitted to it. The authors of these, the chosen, often harvest the rewards of prestige publication. They take their wages in status, promotion, pay raises, and that final blessing, tenure. For those senior scholars who have not conquered the itch to publish, publication in the *Review* can reaffirm; for the young, just lately infected with the itch, the article can anoint prospects

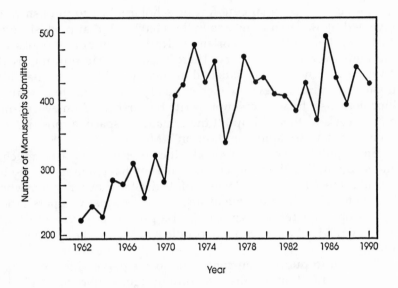

Figure 1. Number of papers submitted to the *American Political Science Review*, 1962–1990.

for a lifetime. The system of peer review bears a heavy responsibility.

As its managing editor from 1985 to 1991, I observed the referee system of the *Review* with considerable devotion and fascination. At a given time, the *Review* draws from a pool of about one thousand scholars who serve as referees for the journal (this number roughly represents the number of highly active research scholars in the discipline). But in political science more generally, participation in the referee system is widespread, an empirical claim handsomely supported by the results of a survey conducted in 1985 by the American Council of Learned Societies (ACLS). Of 577 political scientists in the ACLS sample, 77 percent reported they had published an article in a refereed journal, and 72 percent indicated they had served as a referee for a scholarly journal article (*Chronicle of Higher Education*, Vol. 32, August 6, 1986, pp. 1, 21–23). The unusually wide engagement of political scientists in the referee system indicates broad agreement in the discipline that maintaining scholarly standards truly is a collective responsibility.

But there is, in Max Weber's sense, a status hierarchy in academic political science. The large graduate programs of the elite private universities—Yale, Harvard, Stanford, Chicago, the Big Ten, and the University of California, Berkeley—embrace the most prestigious academicians, and the research progeny of their faculties frequents the pages of the scientific journals. Indeed, over half the political science respondents to the 1985 ACLS survey agreed that "the peer review system for scholarly journals in my field is [frequently] biased in favor of established researchers in a scholarly speciality," and 42 percent said the system was, they thought, "frequently biased in favor of scholars from prestigious institutions."

Students of the behavioral proclivities of the scientific establishment have observed the tendency for renowned scholars to be advantaged in publication, and in the credit given to their research and discoveries. Robert K. Merton has dubbed this phenomenon "the Matthew effect in science"; according to the Gospel of St. Matthew, "For unto every one that hath shall be given, and he shall have abundance: but from him that hath not shall be taken away even that which he hath." It is, therefore, important to be sensitive to the possiblity that contributions made by highly visible, prestigious scholars are "the most likely to enter promptly and widely into the communication networks of science, and so to accelerate its development" (Merton, 1973, p. 450).

In its infancy, the *Review* apparently published "commissioned" papers and reports with considerable frequency; today, who publishes in the journal is a function of who submits. When we examined submissions to the *Review* during the 1986-87 period for our own study of potential biases in the referee system, we found that as many papers were submitted by assistant professors as by full professors, and, beyond that, the proportions of papers accepted for publication were the same for scholars in both ranks (Patterson, Bailey, Martinez, & Angel, 1987). Although we have not taken into account the relative total numbers of scholars in each academic rank, our analysis at least indicates that publication in the *Review* is more a consequence of submission than of status.

The APSR did publish work of scholars in the twenty most prestigious departments at a greater rate than papers submitted by scholars in less prestigious departments. Our 1986–87 study of submissions and acceptances showed that 28 percent of our manuscripts came from scholars in the "top twenty" departments, but 51 percent of those we published came from the high status departments. At the same time, 55 percent of the manuscripts received, and 40 percent of the manuscripts accepted for publication came from scholars in departments rated below the top forty in prestige. That *Review* authors tend to come from prestigious political science departments is no suprise; these are the larger, more research-oriented departments, and they tend to attract and support the most active research scholars.

But how fair and professional is the system of peer review? Many political scientists apparently feel dissatisfied with the system; in the 1985 ACLS study, 43 percent of the political science respondents agreed that the peer review system was in need of substantial reform. This worrisome result prompted the staff of the *Review* to conduct an analysis of the professional effectiveness of our referees. We content-analyzed a sample of two hundred written peer evaluations drawn from 1,323 reviews in the APSR files (as of December 1986). Each peer evaluation was coded in four areas: (1) manuscript properties (e.g., did the review deal with the theory presented or the methodology used?); (2) referees' evaluative criteria (e.g., did they look at logic, importance, suitability, organization, etc.?); (3) the positivity or negativity of the evaluation; and (4) interreviewer agreement.

The main findings of our study indicate a system remarkably free from inappropriate biases. No one aspect of manuscripts was systematically singled out for criticism. We thought a major reason for rejection of manuscripts might be that they were fundamentally flawed methodologically; but methodological criticism was no more likely than criticism of the theory advocated, the results presented, or the conclusions advanced in submitted papers. There simply did not appear to be a "methodological bias" in the review process. More generally, in investigating a range of criteria that referees employed to evaluate manuscripts, we found universalistic standards vastly predominating, with only a faint trace of what we called "author" or "reviewer" bias. We found that it was the general importance of a paper and its general interest value that were most highly correlated with the decision to accept or reject it for publication in the *Review*.

A further objective of the APSR peer review study was to estimate the extent of agreement among referees. Our sample included fifty-three pairs of referees for the same manuscript, a result determined by our sampling procedures. Publication decisions recommended by referees were coded into three categories: publish, revise, and reject. Each pair of referees was in "high agreement" if they fully agreed (publish/publish, revise/revise, or reject/reject); in "moderate agreement" if there were disagreement by only one category (publish/revise or revise/reject); and in "low agreement" if they substantially disagreed (publish/reject). High agreement accounted for 43 percent of the referee pairs, moderate agreement for 42 percent, and low agreement for 15 percent of the pairs of referees. We were happy to conclude that there was very substantial agreement among referees regarding the publishability of APSR manuscripts.

We could find no pathologies in the *Review*'s referee system. The system embodies human error, and embraces at least a standard deviation in professional competence. But the overwhelming impression of editors like me is that anonymous referees produce professionally competent, thoughtful, critically constructive, well-balanced, altogether admirable assessments of the scholarly papers entrusted to them.

Variations among Political Science Journals

Do political science journals differ in content? Political science is a diverse and somewhat disorderly field of study, so variations among journals, even among those of more-or-less similar purpose, might be expected. In order to compare the kinds of political science published in various scholarly journals and assay changes over time, in 1989 we coded the articles published in the *APSR* and four other political science journals for five years in the 1960s and five years in the 1980s (Patterson, Adolino, & McGuire, 1989). We chose to analyze the *American Journal of Political Science* (the official journal of the Midwest Political Science Association) and the *Journal of Politics* (the official journal of the Southern Political Science Association) because they are major general journals in the field. In addition, we examined *Comparative Politics* and the *International Studies Quarterly* because they are principal journals in the comparative and international fields.

The histograms of Figure 2 allow comparison of the *Review* with the other two major general journals in terms of substantive contents. We found that in the 1960s, and even more so in the 1980s, all three of the major general journals published more research and scholarship about American politics than about anything else. This was somewhat less true of the APSR, which in both periods carried more articles about comparative politics and normative political theory than the other two journals. And, by the 1980s, the *Review* was publishing a substantial amount of work in the field of international relations, more than it had in the 1960s.

Much of the work of political scientists specializing in international or comparative politics has been drawn to the specialized journals. For instance, the number of articles on international re-

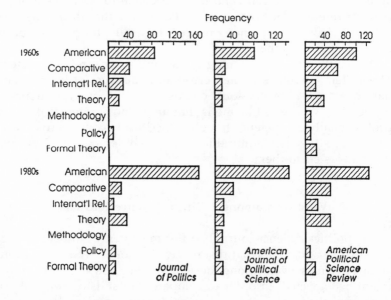

Figure 2. Distribution and number of articles in the APSR, AJPS, and JOP in the 1960s and the 1980s.

lations published in the *International Studies Quarterly* doubled between the 1960s and the 1980s. The research published in the ISQ is mainly international and partly comparative in nature; as might be expected, *Comparative Politics* publishes primarily research on non-U. S. systems.

In addition to appraising the substantive contents of the *Review* and other journals, we contrasted these journals' methodological and data characteristics for the 1960s and the 1980s. The results of this analysis are shown in Tables 1 and 2. In coding the content of journal articles, we focused upon the primary method and data. Where more than one coding category applied to an article, we asked, "what is the primary method? Is this method central to the argument? Where did the bulk of the data come from? Which data do the author rely upon most heavily?"

First, we classifed journal articles on the basis of their "methodological approach." Some we classified as being mainly philosophical, relying on normative or analytical theory; some invoked straightforward statistical inference; some rested on qualitative analysis; and some developed positive, formal theory. Table 1 dis-

Table 1

Methodological approaches of research reported in the APSR and other journals, 1964–68 and 1984–88 (in percentages)

Methodological Approach	American Political Science Review		American Journal of Political Science		Journal of Politics		Comparative Politics		International Studies Quarterly	
	64–68	84–88	64–68	84–88	64–68	84–88	68–73[a]	85–88[b]	64–86	84–88
Normative or analytic theory	21.7	14.6	8.6	8.2	14.5	15.3	22.7	3.4	50.9	17.0
Statistical inference	46.4	55.0	72.4	75.5	41.5	72.5	27.3	21.4	9.1	29.3
Qualitative, nonstatistical analysis	23.2	5.0	18.1	4.1	42.8	5.9	48.2	70.8	38.2	32.1
Formal theory	8.7	25.4	1.0	12.3	1.3	6.4	1.8	4.5	1.8	21.7
Total	100.0	100.0	100.1	100.1	100.1	100.1	100.0	100.1	100.0	100.1
Number of cases	207	240	105	220	159	236	110	89	55	106

[a]First five years of publication.
[b]Vol. 17 (1984–85) was not available for analysis.

Table 2

Types of data used in research reported in the APSR
and other journals, 1964–68 and 1984–88 (in percentages)

Type of Data	American Political Science Review		American Journal of Political Science		Journal of Politics		Comparative Politics		International Studies Quarterly	
	64–68	84–88	64–68	84–88	64–68	84–88	68–73[a]	85–88[b]	64–86	84–88
Gathered by investigator	15.9	12.5	31.4	13.6	15.1	8.9	23.6	31.5	10.9	17.9
Gathered by survey organization	8.7	24.2	—	22.7	3.8	19.1	7.3	10.1	—	9.4
Documentary sources	30.0	19.6	36.2	25.0	21.4	34.3	14.6	14.6	—	1.9
Secondary sources	14.5	15.4	9.5	18.2	13.8	14.4	33.6	37.1	25.5	44.3
No observations	30.9	28.3	22.9	20.5	45.9	23.3	20.9	6.7	63.6	26.4
Total	100.0	100.0	100.0	100.0	100.0	100.0	100.0	100.0	100.0	99.9
Number of cases	207	240	105	220	159	236	110	89	55	106

[a]First five years of publication.
[b]Vol. 17 (1984–85) was not available for analysis.

plays the distributions of journal articles in these methodological types. It is apparent that work published in the *Review* came increasingly to entail statistical inference and formal theory, and relied less on qualitative analysis, from the 1960s to the 1980s. The other journals reflect their special character. The AJPS has been heavily statistical for a long time; the JOP and the ISQ seem to have taken a strong statistical turn in the 1980s; and *Comparative Politics* appears to have turned toward qualitative case study analyses. The development of formal theory was clearly reflected in the *Review* and in the ISQ, less clearly in the AJPS. and even less so in the other two journals.

We also classified journal articles on the basis of the type of data analyzed (See Table 2). In some studies, the data were gathered by the investigator who, for instance, undertook elite interviews, engaged in participant observation, or conducted special surveys.

In other research, the data come from survey organizations, such as the Michigan Survey Research Center. Then, there are studies relying on documentary sources, such as the census, election returns, court opinions, or roll-call records. Yet another category of research derives from secondary data, relying on published work or observations collected by others. Finally, some articles contain little or no data or observations at all, what Joseph Tanenhaus used to call "data free research," and in the 1980s these were often public choice or other formal analyses.

In the general journals, the APSR, the AJPS, and the JOP, inquiry shifted most strikingly toward the use of survey data generated by polling organizations (the NES, the Gallup Poll, etc.). For the *Review,* about 9 percent of the 1960s articles derived from such surveys, compared with nearly 25 percent in the 1980s. In these general journals, data gathered by investigators from elite interviews or participant observation declined in use, although less so in the *Review* than in the AJPS or JOP. In contrast, data of this kind became more prevalent in *Comparative Politics* and the ISQ. Use of so-called documentary sources for example, aggregate election data, or roll-call votes, generally held steady or declined except for the JOP, where substantial increase was evident. In all the journals, the proportion of articles not relying on data declined.

Although our inquiry focused on political science journals, others have uncovered interesting differences in methodology and data among a wider range of journals. University of Wisconsin economist Theodore Morgan compared the nature and use of data in articles published in economics, political science, sociology, chemistry, and physics journals for 1982-86 (Morgan, 1987, p. 9). His analysis showed that 42 percent of the articles in the *American Economic Review* developed mathematical models without any data, compared with 18 percent in the APSR, less than 1 percent in the *American Sociological Review*, zero in the *Journal of the American Chemical Society*, and about 12 percent in *Physical Review*.

Morgan found the remaining published research of economists to be preponderantly based on data published or generated by others, rather than being generated on their own initiative (constituting 39 percent of the AER articles). He classified 41 percent of the APSR and 51 percent of the ASR articles in this category. In contrast, the vast majority of published research in chemistry is based on experiments and simulations, and this is also the case for nearly half of the articles in the physics journal. Our investigation of the nature of research published in the *Review* and other political science journals produced results in general agreement with Morgan's findings. The bulk of political science research is based on data that have not been newly generated by the investigators. Roughly one-fifth of published political science research contains no systematic observations, although most of this work falls under the aegis of normative theory rather than residing in the bailiwick of mathematical modeling.

Seminar by Mail

The system of institutionalized criticism in political research is by no means infallible. Nothing I have said should be taken to suggest that peer review works with unfailing success. The system does help confer authenticity upon political research, and contributes to the confidence scholars can have in the research literature.

In the case of the *American Political Science Review*, and for most journals in social sciences generally, 85-90 percent of the papers submitted are not accepted for publication. The authors of these papers benefit from peer review in a mainly pedagogical way. The system gives them two or three thorough and trenchant critiques of their efforts, often including very detailed suggestions for revising and perfecting the research procedures, the strategy of presentation, the craftsmanship of the paper, or all of these. The journal editor is conducting, thereby, a "seminar by mail" for his or her profession. And, even for authors of published papers the referee system is plainly instructive; most published articles are the finale of a rigorous process of review and revision. Rarely is a paper published without improvement.

In order to learn something about the fate of manuscripts not published by the *Review*, in 1990 we conducted a study of "rejected" authors (Patterson & Smithey, 1990).

We mailed questionnaires to a sample of six hundred rejected authors drawn from the APSR's manuscript files of the previous two years. The response rate was quite high, 64 percent responded, about 380 authors, and the sample appropriately represented the various subfields of the discipline.

The basic evidence is presented in Table 3. Most rejected authors at any one time are "repeaters," only a third of our respondents had never before submitted a paper to the APSR. Of those who submitted to the *Review* previously, two-fifths had been published in the journal. For more than half, the paper had been ex-

---

Table 3

Experience of scholars whose manuscripts are not
accepted for publication in the APSR, 1990

Manuscript history	% of respondents
First submission to APSR	32.6
Submitted a paper in the previous five years	60.3
Previous paper published in APSR (% of those who submitted, N = 229)	40.2
Submission was a convention paper	52.9
APSR was the first journal to which the paper was submitted	90.9
Used comments of referees or managing editor to revise the manuscript	57.4
Resubmitted the paper to APSR	7.9
Submitted the paper to other journals following rejection by APSR	69.2
Paper submitted to other journals was published (% of those who submitted, N = 263)	75.3
Submitted manuscripts to APSR subsequent to rejection	30.8
Subsequent paper submitted to APSR was published (% of those who submitted, N = 117)	31.6
Total number of cases	380

posed to the profession in the form of a convention paper prior to submission to the *Review*. And, fully 90 percent had not submitted their paper to another journal prior to submitting it to the APSR.

A substantial proportion of these rejected authors submitted their rejected manuscript to another journal, and quite a few of these eventually were published. More than 57 percent indicated that the APSR review process had been helpful in strengthening their paper for submission elsewhere. Nearly seven out of ten rejected authors submitted their papers to other journals following rejection by the APSR, and three-quarters of those who submitted elsewhere ultimately got published. Only 8 percent resubmitted to the *Review*. Almost a third of the rejected authors, undaunted by their rejection, subsequently submitted other papers to the *Review*, and about a third of these did so successfully.

Rejected authors appear to fall into three broad groups. About a third are *novices* who have not submitted work to the *Review* before, many of whom are trying out their research and writing skills for the first time in the arena of scholarly journal publication. In contrast, 25–30 percent are *hardcore professionals*, those who submit papers regularly, whose work has been published in the *Review*, and who are salubriously socialized to the professional norms of submission-rejection-revision-resubmission. Not only have these authors published in the APSR in the past, but also they fully expect to do so in the future. Between novices and hardcore professionals lie most research-oriented political scientists, the *working scholars* who try out the *Review* occasionally, but whose work is more often published in other political science journals.

The seminar by mail works especially well in an environment of a plurality of journals. Scholars whose papers are rejected can revise where their critics have uncovered flaws, and then submit their papers elsewhere for a second opinion. Some of the specialized journals serve as "vaudeville" for inexperienced academic novices trying to learn the scholar's trade. What is more, the plurality of journals makes possible the best treatment for rejection— the photocopy machine. The option to photocopy one's paper and submit it to an alternative journal helps to preserve the autonomy of the budding scholar, and it relieves the rejecting editor of a terrifying sense of despair that mistakes could be immutable and irredeemable.

It is, I think, in faithful keeping with these remarks that I may, with consummate serenity, assert with Merton that the system of scholarly authenticity, of which peer review occupies a very umbilical place, "provides an institutional basis for the comparative reliability and cumulation of knowledge" (Merton, 1973, p. 495).

References

Chronicle of Higher Education. August 6, 1986. 32:1

Merton, Robert K. 1965. *On the Shoulders of Giants.* New York: Harcourt, Brace & World.

———. 1973. *The Sociology of Science.* Chicago: University of Chicago Press.

Morgan, Theodore. 1987. "Academic Economics: A Pulse-Taking: Comparisons." Department of Economics, University of Wisconsin, Madison. Typescript.

Patterson, Samuel C., Michael S. Bailey, Velerie J. Martinez, & Susan C. Angel. 1987. "Report of the Managing Editor of the *American Political Science Review,* 1986–87." *PS: Political Science and Politics* 20: 1006–1016.

Patterson, Samuel C., Brian D. Ripley, & Barbara Trish. 1988. "The *American Political Science Review*: A Retrospective of Last Year and the Last Eight Decades." *PS: Political Science and Politics* 21: 908–925.

Patterson, Samuel C., Jessica R. Adolino, & Kevin T. McGuire. 1989. "Continuities in Political Research: Evidence from the *APSR* Since the 1960s." *PS: Political Science & Politics* 22: 866–878.

Patterson, Samuel C., & Shannon K. Smithey. 1990. "Monitoring Scholarly Journal Publication in Political Science: The Role of the *APSR*." *PS: Political Science and Politics* 23: 647–656.

Patterson, Samuel C., John R. Bruce, & Martha Ellis Crone. 1991. "The Diffusion of Research in Political Science: The Impact of the *APSR*." *PS: Political Science & Politics* 24: 765–774.

Somit, Albert, & Joseph Tanenhaus. 1967. *The Development of American Political Science.* Boston: Allyn & Bacon.

SSRC *Newsletter,* November 1983 50: 29.

2

Editing Social Psychology

✳

Leonard W. Doob

First, I would explain that editing the *Journal of Social Psychology* is a somewhat personal enterprise. The journal was founded by John Dewey and the psychologist Carl Murchison in 1929; it has remained independent of the American Psychological Association and, hence, has greater freedom to depart from current convention, although almost without exception as editor I approve of rules and guides set forth in the APA publication manual. Its present owner is a private, nonprofit, educational foundation called HELDREF, which is named after the political scientist Helen Dwight Reid and which aims "to support projects in education, international affairs, and the sciences" through the forty journals and magazines it publishes. The preceding and the present directors have offered me complete freedom in my assessing and editorial role. Another HELDREF psychological journal I coedit states, at my suggestion, that we solicit "outrageous" articles on the assumption of a possible relation between the offbeat and the creative. What I write here is both truthful, I hope, and blunt, so that I may reveal not only to the reader but also to myself my gatekeeping role.

As a hypothetical illustration suppose a paper is submitted to this journal with the title "Right Shoe, Left Shoe" and we must decide whether we have here a contribution to social psychology. The article conforms to our format and that of other psychological journals. It begins with an introduction that states the problem: when "people" are getting dressed, which shoe do they put on first, the right or the left? The author indicates that this topic has not been investigated, although there are studies concentrating on right- versus left-handedness and right versus left sections of the human brain. Hypotheses are then formulated concerning factors that may effect the dependent variable of shoe-priority; and the postulated independent variables are age, gender, parental tendency regarding shoes, and a host of personality factors that are carefully and modestly specified. The study, therefore, seeks (a) to determine whether individuals consistently give priority to one foot rather than the other and (b) to verify the carefully reasoned hypothesis that authoritarian men and women favor the right rather than the left foot.

Under Method we are told that 212 college students were the subjects who thus discharged one of the requirements of the psychology or sociology course in which they were enrolled. Trained observers of the same gender watched them dress after exercising or swimming in the campus gymnasium without telling them the purpose of the investigation; during the observation they interviewed the women and men on an irrelevant topic. When fully dressed, the subjects were asked to complete a standard questionnaire on authoritarianism that has been used frequently in other studies. On a second occasion as many as possible of the same students were observed dressing again; the original number of 212 was thus reduced to 163 (84 females; 79 males) because the others did not appear or could not be located a second time—note the precision. After the subjects who could be located twice were dressed, they were "debriefed," as the ethical standards of the profession demand, by being told the purpose of the exercise, but they were asked not to talk about their experience while the investigation was in progress.

In the Results section, the statistical method is carefully explained before it is revealed that more subjects favored the same foot on the second occasion than the other foot. There was a tendency, moreover, for the consistent subjects to have higher scores on the authoritarian scale than those of the inconsistent ones ($p < 0.05$). There follows a long Discussion section in which the author emphasizes "the pioneering, exploratory" nature of the study, but praises its promising significance in providing new insight into the human condition. Before definitive conclusions can be drawn, however, the final paragraph states, additional research is necessary; that research is outlined in some detail.

As editor of the *Journal of Social Psychology*, I must wonder whether papers like that one should be accepted for publication. Let me review as carefully as I can some of the thoughts that have pervaded me during the two decades and more of my responsibility for this journal. First, I recognize that a human being has submitted every paper I read. He, she, or they have undoubtedly devoted hours of cogitation and labor to the problem and have received a university or foundation grant mentioned in footnote 1. Eventual publication is important, perhaps to satisfy one or more egos, perhaps because tenure is at stake. I really don't want to damage anyone, or almost anyone, which is what a rejection is likely to do. But of course this charitable pang of mine is irrelevant, for then almost every single submission would have to be accepted.

There are other irrelevancies that I have succeeded in ignoring over the years, but not always easily. Do I know that author or is he or she a student of an acquaintance or a respected name in social psychology? Such favoritism is taboo of course. And again of course, from what university or institution does the paper come? Surely a submission from an Ivy League university or its equivalent or especially from a department with a deservedly high reputation should be given some priority not only because its products are likely to be superior but also because "my" journal is competing with other journals in social psychology (some with the very same label as part of their title and some also considered to be more prestigious) and in related fields to maintain its reputation. Nonsense, I whisper loudly to myself: one judges the research, not the place or the person involved in its production.

The reverse situation might also raise another humanitarian quiver: doesn't an author from a less-glamorous, more struggling college or university merit extra consideration, and shouldn't I try to help those who could use the recognition of publication? Again this impulse of mine must be squelched, but perhaps not always for a reason or two having theoretical significance as I shall indicate below.

Finally, what shall I do about an article that, according to the second footnote, is an adaptation of the author's Ph.D. dissertation or of a paper delivered a very short time ago to a regional or national meeting of psychologists or other social scientists? Once more, no, no, and with no exception. There is no guarantee that the father or mother of a dissertation always helps his or her adoring child make a really substantial contribution, and I may have my own doubts about that parent's wisdom. Participants at scholarly meetings may be more intent on displaying themselves and their delivery to secure a job than they are in the paper they have prepared for that occasion.

A final set of irrelevancies pertains to the journal itself. I judge papers on their so-called merits, not whether they will "fit" in a particular issue of the journal. Besides, the central publishing office of HELDREF controls the flow of papers into each issue, not I. Is the backlog of already accepted papers so great that new submissions should be more critically examined lest the publication lag become even greater? This challenge is a bit difficult to resist especially when a copy editor politely drops hints concerning the accumulated backlog of papers and also when I consequently begin to wonder whether my own standards of acceptance have become too lax.

Let me return to the paper on right versus left shoes. I am fairly certain that I would reject this alleged contribution to knowledge, and then carefully provide the author with my reasons for doing so. I could say a number of things—that other problems these days have a higher priority, which is true but could sound only like a polite excuse. That p of only 0.05 and not of 0.01 or 0.00001, indicating a statistically significant but very modest relation between shoe priority preference and authoritarianism, accounts for too little of the variance, may reflect no psychological profundity, but may be a consequence of the sample's large size. Using the usual American undergraduates as subjects provides very uncertain grounds for generalizing even about Americans. The style of the paper is thus misleading in two respects: in the Abstract there is not even a reference to the sample being employed, and the verbs in most of the Results and Discussion sections are in the present tense as if eternal or universally applicable truisms were being unveiled. I might also tell the author that an acceptable paper could possibly emerge when the investigation is repeated with other human samples and with additional psychological variables; yet should I encourage more drivel?

As a gatekeeping editor, I quickly admit that my insecurity about the acceptability of manuscripts reflects my own publicly expressed views concerning social psychology and most but not all of social science. We do follow a scientific tradition and require that our so-called instruments (whether interviews, questionnaires, or simulated or realistic experiments) be reliable and valid; statistical manipulations must be flawless in terms of contemporary, fashionable methods or available computer programs; whenever possible, hypotheses and deductions therefrom must be clearly stated; principles, it is hoped, will emerge. Human interactions, however, are so intricate and complicated that principles almost always are elusive and uncertain. What we have instead are guides that fluctuate from moment to moment, and especially from generation to generation, and that are ever somewhat perilous and likely to be either altered or invalidated with the passing of time. We know very well that doctrines like determinism, idealism, and Marxism did once or do now seem to provide insights; and that the unconscious of psychoanalysis or even concepts like rationalization, projection, and dissonance revive and supplement views and intuitions prevalent in classical times.

And so, with such a weltanschauung, what can I do about that paper on footedness other than reject it? Into the *Journal of Social Psychology*, I have introduced three kinds of "Notes" that summarize an investigation in five hundred words or less, consequently without tables or graphs and with a minimum of footnotes as references. One is called "Repetition and Replications" whose function is exactly specified by its title. Clearly, for many reasons generalizations especially about human beings require substantiation: the soundness of their method or their applicability to other persons under similar or different conditions must be demonstrated. Then there are notes called "Current Problems and Resolutions": social psychologists often seek to be practical as defined currently. Dare one hinder any effort to offer assistance to our struggling world? The third, "Cross-Cultural Notes," are devoted to replications in other societies especially outside the Western spheres of Europe and North America.

The last named notes recall an altruistic impulse mentioned above: accepting a full-length article when I have empathy with its author. I am always somewhat tempted to feel favorably inclined toward a paper, even though its theme and technique are unoriginal, when it concerns a developing country from whose scholars one seldom hears. I am not the least bit troubled by this policy because so many of the Western submissions I must read perforce are ethnocentric: implicitly they assume that what is demonstrated here is also true there. Naturally, I must be cautiously alert in pursuing this cross-cultural policy. Again and again in countries I shall politely leave nameless, authors who have studied and especially who have attended graduate schools in Europe and America seem to be saying, "let's see if that is true in my country and I shall demonstrate my scientific attainment by employing very complicated and involved statistical manipulations; and my prestige at home will increase when I have an article appearing abroad." Somehow, and I am not sure how, I try to discriminate between articles that are mere repetitions elsewhere and those repetitions that strengthen our belief in the theory being tested or add a significant nuance to it.

Not the least timidly do I confess in this context that as a gatekeeper, I tend to look favorably on articles that come from any African country. I have been attached to three English-speaking universities on that continent, I have traveled extensively and frequently in South Africa. Perhaps this is a reasonable prejudice: my experience and contacts there enable me to make better informed judgments concerning papers originating in Africa. In addition, for decades I have been strongly motivated to improve scholarly exchanges with South Africans.

Let me add, both however and immediately, that I am far from being clear about cross-cultural research. Yes, replication overseas always may have potential value, but then you and I must ask, why investigate the problem in one particular society and not in another? What one must do is to select "representatives" of the world's societies and examine among them the relations of the variables of interest. To achieve this objective, I have learned over the years, one must or should obtain a sample from some compendium, such as the human relations area files at Yale University and elsewhere. But then—always a *but* for this harassed editor— such a file provides the data by detaching societies from their determining cultural context. Let contributors to the *Journal of Social Psychology* carry on the good struggle centered on that theoretical issue, and undoubtedly I shall approve of what they write.

In this context, an annoying and practical, challenging addition can be quickly outlined. All of the submitted articles are written in English; our publisher actually has no funds either to obtain translations or improve translations of foreign papers. Those from other English-speaking countries obviously offer no problem except for minor differences in British and American spelling and in idiomatic modes of expression. The English in other countries, however, that is taught—sometimes badly—in local schools, that functions as a lingua franca, or that has been learned by those studying abroad varies considerably in quality and intelligibility. A copy editor and I are then challenged concerning the amount of effort we should expend to translate a paper into acceptable English and otherwise whip it into shape. Usually the effort seems too great; then as diplomatically as possible I ask the author to seek help from a colleague at home or from some person with a keener grasp of English, and later resubmit the study, which I sincerely praise while forwarding that annoying suggestion.

There are some current verbal practices I find stylistically distasteful. Too many psychologists these days say they "run" subjects when what they mean is that they have submitted their subjects to an experimental procedure; others also "generate" (compose or draft) new items for a questionnaire. I hate sentences that begin with "this" that is not followed by a noun or phrase when it is not clear to what the "this" refers. Long ago in a tense moment during World War II, a journalist warned me not to use "due to" as a preposition but only after some form of the verb "to be." The trite expressions, "it is important to note," "I would argue," and "as is well known," accomplish little and hence perish beneath the scratch of my pencil. References to a cited article or book as "classic" or "seminal" I almost always delete because the adjectives are really praising not the reference but the writer's own perspicacity. I usually try to detect and eliminate an author's own jargon or neologism. I keep trying to maintain the methodological distinction between "culture" and "society," concepts that creep frequently into the prose of social psychologists anxious to display their sensitivity to anthropology. The favored phrase, "in our culture," often refers to the society in which a cultural trait transmitted from the past may or may not be exhibited. I give battle against the current fad to propose titles or subtitles of articles that are so smarty or snappy that they look as though they have been deliberately borrowed from the headlines of an American tabloid newspaper. For years I have scribbled changes on the papers I have been reading to correct these and other linguistic usages, but gradually I have largely abandoned the practice and permit our carelessly changing language to evolve. Lately "due to" as a preposition almost sounds correct to me, and I am about ready to accept infinitives that are split, but not "media" followed by a singular verb.

On one linguistic score, I have surrendered completely, even though I still find it awkward, wordy, and stupid to do so, that is, the relatively recent taboo against using "he," "him," or "his" to refer to both genders. Of course there are generic words like "mankind" and "chairman" with similar unrestricted referents; and how can one quote directly and accurately one's precious predecessors who unintentionally belittle all women by writing, for example, "ever since men learned that . . . ?" And what about "human" (hu-man) or even the favored–ugh—"humans?" My argument in favor of customary usage was once impressive, at least to me, even though I have taught a course concerning language's effect on behavior: I prefer to fight the good fight in behalf of women's rights realistically and not grammatically; and I think of other languages whose nouns have unalterable grammatical genders. I am especially fond of German where the word "sie" must be employed to mean the equivalent of our "she," "they," or the formal "you" depending on the verb that follows, or on the use of uppercase or lowercase in the written language; or the word "man" as pronounced by a German means our masculine "man" and sometimes both genders or else is the exact translation of our very ambiguous "one." I am absolutely unable to tolerate "s/he."

Finally, the phrases "as mentioned previously," "to be indicated below," or their equivalent (cf. their earlier appearances in this paper) are usually unnecessary and rarely helpful.

I do advocate and enforce more serious changes than those involving linguistic style. Usually a summary in the Introduction of all the methodological details in the present research serves no useful function; all articles in our journal begin with an abstract and such details need be related only once in the Method section. I try to ban from the Discussion section guesses about the implications of the study for real life: some authors tend to be a bit too reckless and boastful. Also, I almost always delete recommendations for studies that should be conducted as a follow-up to the magnificent research in the paper being concluded. Someone once told me that an efficient way to discourage such research is to propose what should be done because then others know they owe a debt to the author and cannot claim complete originality. I sometimes wonder about the tables and charts that accompany submitted articles. They require additional space and are costly; often, but definitely not always, their high points can be reported by inserting the data within the text of the paper. If they are retained, they may require an explanation in the text. Some of the references at the end of articles may not be essential and perhaps serve only to attract attention to the author's erudition.

Certain factual information is frequently omitted in the abstract at the outset and sometimes even in the Method section of papers we receive, vis., the nature of the subjects or respondents: adolescents, students, adults, a representative sample, the name of the society or section thereof? These items I strongly believe must be at least foreshadowed in the abstract because many readers have the patience or interest to read only the abstract or because an abstract is all they can see in the psychological or sociological abstracts or on computer terminals in libraries. I would thus emphasize that in social psychology, we almost never approach universal truths about human beings everywhere. Then usually, though possibly not always, it is important for the reader to know the year in which the data were collected; the actual date when the study appears in the journal provides a clue, but there may have been delays in analyzing the material, in writing the article, and in having it evaluated and finally published. In addition, it may be important to know precisely where the data were collected; especially where respondents were being interviewed: the site may affect their responses. Likewise it may be valuable to disclose something about who has collected the data, whether the investigator, the experimenter, or a confederate. What people disclose and indeed their behavior can be affected by their surroundings.

The content of the paper, the problem being addressed is obviously the crucial challenge confronting a beleaguered editor. Somehow I must continue to be sensitive to the contemporary state of social psychology, to appreciate and not be dismayed by its apparently unrestricted scope, its reactions to the appalling practical problems of our era. As an editor, I am always truly puzzled as I try, for example, to evaluate the method being employed to investigate the problem at hand. Certainly, paper-and-pencil questionnaires may be the only available method to produce useful—and publishable—data, yet sometimes the procedure is employed because it is just so easy to distribute the schedules to a captive class of undergraduates or to send questionnaires, along with junk mail from other sources, to a sample of potential informants, with the hope that there will be at least a 50 percent return from the men and women whose representativeness can somehow be determined or at least rationalized. Admittedly, data from "real" life are both difficult and costly to obtain. Observing people realistically takes time. Often or usually it is difficult or impossible to manipulate conditions as they exist and, in addition, to have the necessary control group to determine whether it has been the experimental variable or some other condition that has produced a difference. The gate of the *Journal of Social Psychology* is wide open to authors of the few studies that confront these challenges.

As a substitute for some "real" life conditions, social psychologists very frequently perform experiments that simulate those conditions. Actually, experimentation of this sort is a sacred cow within the profession. As editor, I tend to view such experiments with amused if respectful skepticism. I value the ingenuity that is displayed, but I must wonder whether the experimental group, and sometimes the control group, is really behaving sincerely and honestly when the experimenter asks group members to make believe they are doing such-and-such or when in a university laboratory after class they are subjected to the investigator's contrived conditions. We, the editor and our readers, are not always given enough information enabling us to conclude whether or not the subjects have actually behaved genuinely or sincerely. P.S.: one realizes that subjects can become so involved in the contrived situation that they may actually be behaving or displaying "real life" emotions or actions.

As an editor, I do not value facts as such unless they explicitly—not implicitly—are made to contribute to some theoretical proposition. Often papers are submitted that offer polling data that are interesting if not compelling in their own right. Information of this sort obviously is also available in the press or through commercial agencies and is relevant to social psychology, though somewhat remote. Authors do and can maintain that their surveys are longer and subtler than the others and hence more penetrating even with smaller samples, a contention that may or may not contribute to theory building. My frown is less compelling when the identical or very similar survey is repeated over time with or without an intuitive guess or attempt to relate changes in the findings to events within the society.

More generally, I strongly favor longitudinal studies of the same subjects, for thus we obtain histories of individuals and groups. Latitudinal research concerning different persons at different ages in different social groups may have the same objective but may be less impressive as a result of its inability to control essential variables assumed to be "equal" per se or through random selection. Quite naturally, latitudinal studies are more frequently conducted than longitudinal ones because graduate students and professors are unable to or unwilling to await the passing of time: get your Ph.D. soon or add to your list of publications now if you are to achieve that tenure slot.

Space in the *Journal of Social Psychology* obviously is limited and therefore articles without new or original empirical or experimental data are not acceptable. Excluded are summaries of the published literature or straight theoretical expositions, no matter how brilliant. Other journals serve this function. What a pity, I very infrequently think and sometimes make an exception, though I realize doing so sets a bad precedent.

A partial sense of both gratification and self-improvement I have been able only partially to realize: feedback from contributors. Authors whose manuscripts have been accepted with major or minor suggested changes have no reason to express their gratitude. Those receiving tentative acceptance and possible or probably acceptance if changes are introduced then generally respond. What they write is usually a perfunctory letter of thanks that is cautiously expressed since they seek final acceptance. Such letters, let me add, also display cultural variations. Those from some countries, including the United

States and Canada, are almost always factual and to the point; those from other areas, especially Asia and the Middle East, are likely to contain expressions of deep gratitude for the time spent reading their papers and for our positive suggestions. Letters responding to outright rejection are seldom written; the very few I see, aside from expressing regret or frustration, may raise cogent counterarguments with which I may or may not agree—usually the latter.

More genuinely, more painfully, and very impatiently I ask myself from time to time why I continue to remain editor of this journal. Ego aside—but of course that not so fat ego plays some role, I admit—I think I detect two other sources of satisfaction. These days, in my semiretired state, I spend considerable time doing my own research and especially writing books. When you write, you must keep criticizing yourself and what you are writing; it is refreshing and less self-damaging occasionally to turn my critical powers away from myself and apply them to the contributions submitted to the *Journal of Social Psychology*. Then I think, or at least I delude myself into thinking, that by trying to improve this journal I may also be contributing to the improvement of a largely imperfect milieu in which we as social scientists, scholars, and citizens find ourselves *faute de mieux* (author: use only English).

3

An Effective Journal Editor: Insights Gained From Editing the *American Sociological Review*

＊

Rita J. Simon

An effective journal editor publishes important, useful, original work that contributes to an existing body of scientific knowledge and expands knowledge and insights about the discipline in which that editor is working. The editor of a scientific journal, especially an official journal for the discipline (or a major contender), is in a position to perform crucial gatekeeping roles. He or she has the authority to launch a new author or a new work into the field or to hold back the person or the work. Publication, especially in a major journal, can play a crucial role in a young academic's career. It can mean the difference between gaining tenure or losing one's position. Even for older scholars, publication in a major journal can be the key to a promotion, a better job offer, or winning an award.

But the discipline places constraints on the editor's freedom and authority. For official journals, those constraints can be formidable. There is the strong expectation, for example, that every submitted manuscript will be sent out for review; in practice, about 95 percent of the manuscripts are sent out to two readers. Perhaps a third of those manuscripts, including the ones that are clearly unworthy or inappropriate, could be rejected by editor and staff. But "form" requires outside reviews for all.

Other restraints include strong expectations that the journal will not publish manuscripts that receive negative reviews. This is the case even though in the editor's judgment the manuscript would make a contribution and is publishable. Now, this is not to say that the editor has no options. She or he can seek additional reviewers. And if, after receiving a third or fourth review, there are disagreements among the readers, the editor may suggest that the author revise and resubmit the piece; including the proviso, of course, that the revised version would be sent out for review.

What kinds of manuscripts are likely to receive favorable reviews from an editor and negative reviews from readers? Some, perhaps the largest group, are probably technically flawed, not up to snuff by the most recent methodological or theoretical standards. But the category may also contain some of the more imaginative, more pathbreaking pieces. A "gifted maverick" is more likely to fall by the wayside in the process. His or her imagination, innovation, or iconoclasm may not receive positive appraisal from the competent yeomen who are good at catching errors and omissions but might miss a "gem"; or at least the unusual, provocative, or outside the mainstream, submission.

Editors should be encouraged by the system to take more chances. Livelier, brasher issues would be the result. And, yes, there would be more debate, more argument, and not so much on technical issues, as on what contribution the article makes, how it fits into the current state of the discipline, whether it is on the cutting edge, and whether it refutes current schools of thought.

There is also the other side of the coin: reviewers may recommend manuscripts for publication that the editor believes should not be published. Here again, the editor can employ the strategy of sending out the piece for additional reviews and if the third and fourth ones are more critical, ask the author to revise. The editor also has some leeway about which readers receive the revised manuscript. The author may not be able to meet the standards demanded of the more critical readers and the revised manuscript would not be accepted for publication. Of course, the author has read all of the reviews prior to undertaking revisions and, therefore, can properly question the basis upon which the revised manuscript was rejected.

The editor's freedom is restricted also in the realm of comments on articles already published. How much authority does an editor have to decide which comments are worth expensive journal pages? The typical strategy is the same as that employed for regular manuscripts except that usually only one reader is called upon. Again, the editor may get into a bind. The comment does not report a basic flaw in the piece, a mistake in interpretation or design, or an attack on the originality of the article. Rather, the comment is about a matter of emphasis, a failure to cite some relevant study, or a disagreement about which technique to use with no implication that the outcome might be affected. It is a matter of "elegance" and "state of the art technique." Then, does the author of the original piece have an automatic right to a published rejoinder? Who decides: the editor, outside reviewers, or both? On these matters, how limited or how great a role should the editor play?

One innovation that could be introduced in the name of editorial discretion without bringing down the whole structure is to have a portion of the journal set aside for editors' selections, articles about which the editor openly declares: these are my choices; they did not meet peer review or they were not sent out for review. They have been published because they are iconoclastic, irreverent, provocative, and maybe pathbreaking, useful, or important. It is not likely that the editor would take advantage of the pages set aside for him or her in every issue, but they would be there when and if needed, perhaps even accompanied by the readers' critical comments and the author's rejoinder.

Also, in the name of more discretion for the editor, those pages might be used to publish a piece out of order. Let's say there is a manuscript that has been favorably reviewed and that the editor believes is especially worthy. However, there are ten pieces ahead of it, already selected for publication. Should the editor let the new article wait or pull the piece and publish it in the next issue? I would support a decision to publish out of order, when it is made, of course, on the basis of merit and not because the author needs a publication right away.

So, one big theme of this chapter is to give editors—who are, after all, selected because of the work they have done, their standing in the discipline, the respect they enjoy among colleagues—more freedom to exercise judgment and initiative. Do not circumscribe their roles so that they are little more than paper pushers. They were given their positions because of their accomplishments. Let them exercise their talents.

There has been some discussion about whether reviewers should remain anonymous. The practice of having manuscripts reviewed anonymously is a good one. I come down on the side of maintaining the status quo. Yes, there are some dangers that negative readers hide under, and take advantage of, the cloak of anonymity. They express themselves more negatively and with greater virulence than the manuscript deserves; and they would be more circumspect if they thought that their authorship would be made public, or at the very least, made known to the author. I suppose the argument for signed reviews stems in part from a legal paradigm. Authors, like defendants, should have the right to know who their accusers are. On the other hand, I believe a great many competent reviewers would decline the opportunity to critique a manuscript because they would not want to get involved in a dispute with the author should they have a negative reaction to the piece and recommend that it not be published. It would not be worth the hassle to them. Those reviewers who are left might overrepresent hostile, aggressive readers who enjoy the give and take more than they do the scholarly task of carefully reading a manuscript and making helpful suggestions.

What about the subject matter, the content of the manuscripts that are accepted for publication? If a journal is the official one for the discipline, or if it purports to represent the entire discipline, then it should apply the same critical standards for all submissions without regard to specialty or content. It should not, for example, tell authors of a manuscript on religion, crime, education, or law that there are specialty journals to which they should submit the piece before the editor has allowed for the review process to play its role. Journals that purport to represent the discipline should do just that and not chip away at different subspecialties and thereby redefine what is mainstream to the discipline. Neither should such journals arbitrarily exclude or favor some methodological or theoretical orientations over others. Each manuscript should be scrutinized for its validity, usefulness and appropriateness, and not be evaluated on the basis of its political correctness or methodological trendiness. Theoretical, applied, and empirical pieces should all go through the same review process.

How long should the review process take? There are horror stories of authors waiting more than a year to find out the fate of their manuscripts. There is no excuse for that. Even if the two initial readers disagreed and the editor sent the manuscript to a third reader, the author should not have to wait a year. It has been my experience, as the editor of two journals each for a three-year stint, that the delays do not occur in the journal office. They are usually a function of reviewers' tardiness and forgetfulness. Even though the letter that accompanies the manuscript asks the reviewer to send comments within three weeks and if that is not possible, to inform the editor so another reviewer can be found, such deadlines are not honored. They are not honored by the reviewer or by the editor. The reviewer keeps the manuscript, sometimes for months before responding; and hears nothing from the editor about why she or he is holding it so long. The editor allows the time to go by without reassigning the piece to another reader, and often without bothering the reviewer with phone calls or letters.

These long delays are not uncommon even though all social science journals (not law reviews and perhaps not journals in other disciplines) demand exclusive review rights. From the point of view of the journal, an exclusive right of review makes good sense. It takes time, effort, and good will on the part of readers, to reach a decision about whether to accept a manuscript for publication. Imagine the editor's dismay, if after finally arriving at a decision to publish, he or she hears from the author that the piece will be published elsewhere. The dismay is even greater if the editor has counted on that piece to fill a gap in the next issue or to round out a theme that the editor had been developing for a forthcoming issue. But the author had waited and waited, had inquired about the status of her piece and had been told—it takes time—be patient.

I think some changes are called for in this area. I think both authors and editors should have the option of multiple submissions. An author should inform each editor that he or she is submitting the manuscript to more than one journal. The author should also inform each editor as soon as the manuscript has been accepted and she or he has agreed to publish it in the first journal that is willing to do so. An editor, on the other hand, has the right to refuse to consider a manuscript that is under review elsewhere. The editor needs to say so up front and right away.

But, I would urge that the editor not take that tack; he or she could miss out on some good pieces. Why not use the multiple submission ploy as a way of getting faster turn around time from readers? A little competition in the system might make everyone happier. The author would hear results faster; the editor who is on top of things comes off with the best manuscripts and the process would take half the time. It seems to work in book publishing and for some journals as well, law reviews, for example.

So far I have discussed journal editing when the journal is the official or major one in a given discipline. The issues covered and strategies recommended have been: publish the best there is without regard to specialty, orientation, or method. Maintain the practice of anonymous reviewing and reviewers. Loosen up on the exclusive submission rule as a benefit to the authors and as a way of providing editors with greater leverage for turning around manuscripts more quickly. Finally, allow the editors more discretion.

What follows now is a section on the nuts and bolts of manuscript submission and review; first, from the potential author's, and then from the editor's, perspective. "Old hands" can probably skip much of this discussion. The first thing to do is find out as much as you can about all of the journals in your discipline and in allied disciplines: that is social psychology demography, social history, law and society, and so on. What kinds of pieces appear in those journals? Which journal seems to publish pieces that are most similar in subject matter, method, and/or orientation to your piece? You find this out, not by looking at one issue, but by skimming several issues scattered over several years. Look over the list you have put together and find out which journals have the largest readership, are the most prestigious, have the quickest turn around time—whatever criteria are important to you. After you have decided in which journal you would most like your piece to appear, find out the style and format your manuscript needs to follow. Should notes appear at the end, separated or combined with references? What type of cites should you use in the text? Do you need an abstract? How many copies should you send? Are fees required, if so how much? This type of information can usually be obtained by perusing the most recent issue of the journal. If you still have questions, it is worth a phone call to the journal's editorial office.

What are the nuts and bolts that editors need to know about? First, they need to have access to a broad range and large number of potential reviewers. These are the scholars who represent all of the specialties and methodological and theoretical orientations in the discipline. They should also be well spread out geographically so there is no great concentration in any one part of the country. It helps if there is also a broad age spread within the reviewing pool. All of these factors protect against bias in the process. Usually an incoming editor does not have to create this pool anew. She or he is likely to inherit a fat file of names with information about each that includes areas of expertise and track record including the number of reviews sent and returned within a year, and the amount of time spent on the manuscripts. Some files may even contain comments about the quality and style of reviews. For example, is the reader given to making ad hominem attacks on authors, do the reviews provide useful comments about how to improve a manuscript, does the reviewer know and cite the relevant recent work in the field?

Second, the editorial office needs to keep good records and be responsive to the author. It needs to know the status of every manuscript: When did the manuscript arrive in the office? Is it new or a resubmission? How long ago was it sent out for review and to how many readers? Have any readers returned it; when and with what recommendation? If all the reviews have been returned, have the editor and staff acted on the manuscript and with what result? Dates and decisions should be noted. These records need to be constantly updated and available for review. When authors ask about the status of their manuscripts, they have a right to know where it is in the reviewing process.

The records need to be accurate for the editor's use. They alert the editor when reviewer comments are due or when the editor has to decide to send out the manuscript to a new reviewer. They prompt the editor to write to the author about the status of a manuscript before the author calls to complain.

If the editor is not able to make a decision on the manuscript in the expected time period, she or he should write and tell the author there will be a delay. Journals that gain the reputation of holding manuscripts for months (and yes, sometimes even for years) lose out on good pieces. Prestigious as the journal may be, authors of exciting, interesting, or important papers may opt to get into print faster in slightly less prestigious outlets. Plus, of course, the word gets around: "That journal takes forever to make a decision, don't bother submitting to it." The pool of potentially publishable pieces grows smaller.

Third, there is the matter of copyediting. The editor and copy editor should agree on the style they want for the journal. If the editor wants clear English, active verbs, short sentences, the copy editor should operationalize those preferences. If the editor wants each author's style to come through untouched except for grammatical errors, that message should be communicated to the copy editor also. What is important is that the editor and the copy editor work together and share the same vision about how the journal should read.

Some other thoughts about running the editorial office have to do with the division of labor that is worked out between editor and deputy editor(s) and among editorial board reviewers and ad hoc reviewers. On the first point, some editors divide the labor such that deputy editors, with or without regular consultation with the editor, make the decisions about which reviewers should receive what manuscripts. The editor looks over the manuscript when it is received in the office and decides whether to send it out for review or return it to the author as "inappropriate," so poorly done as not to be in the ball park, or whatever. The editor does not see the piece again until the reviews have been completed or there is trouble getting it reviewed. Of course, the work does not have to be divided that way; the editor can choose to be involved at all stages of the editorial process including reading proofs, but I advise against such a strategy. Editors should protect their time and energy. Reading the manuscripts and the reviews, evaluating them, and communicating with the authors are more important ways of spending time.

The second point goes to the matter of how the editor uses, or how extensively he or she uses, the editorial board or associate editors as opposed to ad hoc reviewers. Obviously, the board cannot be used exclusively because, at least for major journals, reviewing would take an inordinate amount of each board member's time. But associate editors or board members should do more than nonassociates. When I edited the *American Sociological Review,* I tried to keep the number of manuscripts I asked associate editors to review to three or four a year. I also tried to use them more often as "third" readers for manuscripts that had received split reviews from the first two readers, and I explained to them that was the role they were playing.

Editors have a responsibility to their boards and to their readers to keep them informed about what is happening on the journal. This may be done in several ways. On the occasion of the annual meeting of the profession or discipline, the editor may invite the board to a lunch during which he or she describes the events of the past year, reports on such matters as the number of manuscripts that were submitted, distribution by subspecialty and theoretical and methodological orientations, the acceptance and rejection rates, and on the average, how long it took to complete the review process. Problems that have arisen in the course of the year are shared with the board, such as what to do about tardy reviewers, complaints by authors, should there be issues devoted to special topics, is the journal catering to the needs of the discipline as a whole, and any other matters that the editor or a board member believes ought to be aired. The editor also reports to the readers of the journal and the members of the discipline in the form of an annual written report in which many of these issues are discussed. Feedback from readers and members in the form of letters or comments should be welcomed by the editor. They tend to see the journal as consumers, and may observe things the journal's producers do not.

I am going to shift the discussion now to the editor's role in nonofficial journals and in specialized journals with smaller readerships. The biggest difference, insofar as the editor's role is concerned, is the greater autonomy and freedom the editor is likely to have. I am not suggesting that such an editor should not consult, or not be held accountable for his decisions, but the process is likely to be less cumbersome, shorter, and involve fewer people. The editor should feel much more comfortable about deciding whether to send out a manuscript for review or make the decision alone. The number of readers need not be adhered to as rigidly: depending on the manuscripts' subject matter, method, length, one or more readers might be asked to review it. In cases of disagreement among reviewers, the editor should feel more comfortable about making the final decision alone or in consultation with editorial associates rather than sending it out to a third reviewer.

But in my opinion the biggest difference between editors of official or major journals and editors of other journals is the proactive role that the latter could and should play. First of all, they should feel comfortable about soliciting manuscripts rather than waiting for pieces to come in over the transoms. They should solicit for special issues that they plan to run or just because they have heard of, or read the work of scholars whom they think well of. Special issues that are organized around substantive themes or methodological or theoretical orientations can be very exciting. Occasionally, such issues should be "guest edited."

The format of the journal does not need to be as rigid as those of official journals. There may be greater variations in the length of articles in each issue. Some pieces might be only four or five pages, others might run to thirty. The editor should feel freer about soliciting comments and rejoinders on pieces she or he decides to run. The opportunity to discuss and debate within the pages of these smaller journals should be taken advantage of using different formats: symposia, dialogues among authors of major pieces, followed by comments. The editor might purposely solicit pieces that represent opposing view points, arrive at different conclusions, recommend different research or social action strategies, and then after they have appeared in print, give the readers, in the form of letters to the editor, a chance to be heard at length.

The editor might be more visible in the pages of such a journal by calling for a new way of looking at some aspect of the discipline; or by calling attention to the need for research on a social problem; or by offering a critical assessment of a major theoretical or ideological orientation currently applied in the discipline; or by asking rhetorical questions about "where" the discipline is headed, "why" it has lost its voice, and "how" it has become so circumscribed. In other words, the irony here is that the editors of smaller, less prestigious journals, may in fact have greater influence, and make more of an impact on the discipline and the world of ideas than editors of the larger official journals, because their roles have become so limited. Should the editors of smaller journals choose to take advantage of their greater autonomy, they can function both as gatekeepers, and initiators of knowledge and ideas. After they have completed their tour of duty, they are more likely to leave their imprint than are editors of the official journals. They will have something that they can point to and say, "I was responsible for that. I made the difference here." The readers are also more likely to remember the journal as being under the editorship of a particular individual during various periods of its history. Editors of official journals are more likely to fade into the woodwork.

So, future editors, if you want to mold, create, and leave your mark, it is the unofficial journals that you should seek to edit. If on the other hand, you crave the gratification and experience of being in the center, at the pulse of a discipline look toward "official" major journals. The opportunities they provide for learning about the ferment that is going on, the type of work that is being done, and how such work is evaluated are much greater. These editors play more passive roles, but they may be actively learning a lot more about where the field is and where it is likely to be going.

The decision about which type of editorship one seeks out might in part be a function of age, especially professional age. The editorship of an official journal may suit older scholars, those who see themselves as having done their major, most creative work; not unlike the decision of some professors to become deans. Taking on the editorship of a smaller and nonofficial journal is more likely to allow the editor to continue to exercise creativity and imagination. The editor has more control and autonomy, and there is greater opportunity to leave a mark. His or her ideas, views of the discipline, notions of the direction in which the field should go permeate the pages of the journal.

There is still another type of editor that should be discussed; that is the editor of a research annual—a special collection of manuscripts with a common theme that is published annually or occasionally. The pieces in these volumes almost always come in unsolicited. From start to finish, they are under the editor's control. The editor decides what theme or connecting thread will bind the manuscripts together and then goes out and solicits them from experts in the field, from recent authors whom he has come across, and from friends or colleagues who have told him of a former student's, or a friend's work.

The research annuals' editor negotiates at a level different from regular journal editors. Quite often this type of editor negotiates at the idea or outline stage. There is no manuscript, there is talk, or there is an outline of what the eventual manuscript will cover. The editor is relying on reputation, or recommendation, or perhaps wishful thinking. Not every potential author comes through. Some never submit a manuscript; some submit a piece that is far off the mark. Even with heavy editing and rewriting, it won't make it. Since the editor can ask the author for an extensive rewrite, she or he can specify which sections need expansion, which can be shortened or cut, and what kinds of additional sections need to be written. And, some manuscripts can be overhauled by the editor and simply returned to the author for approval.

This is the editor's role at its most creative. Not only was the editor the source of the idea or theme for the piece, but he or she has also, in effect, coauthored the final version. Here we have the editor as the invisible hand: creator, organizer, coauthor, and critic. The volume is a reflection of the editor's view of the field or problem, or, of the type of research that needs to be done. These editors might have an editorial board to which they turn for advice on specific manuscripts or indeed for themes or subject matter. They might even send out some of the manuscripts they have solicited for review. But the advice does not usually affect the acceptance or rejection of the piece. It provides help on additional sources, or other forms of improvement. The decision about whether to publish rests almost exclusively with the editor.

Editors of research annuals are free to return to the well many times. Having found an author who has produced one work, the editor is likely to solicit additional work on other topics. Such editors are also likely to turn to former students and friends for work that they are capable of producing or that they have already produced. Editors in this context are likely to see themselves, and to perform, as mentors. They not only go back to the same sources for manuscripts on themes of interest to them, they actively encourage and develop younger scholars to direct their efforts along certain research or scholarly lines. They cultivate, encourage, even manage the careers of these younger scholars. Over time, a few of these authors become coeditors and, over a longer time, a few might

inherit the annual or the series and take over editorial responsibilities. The analogy of the relationship that these types of editors
have with some of their authors is akin to that successful fiction
writers have with editors of established publishing houses. The
consultation begins before a word is written and continues on a
regular and steady basis until publication. Such a relationship is
not established in the more typical journal or indeed in the social
science book-publishing world. It is relatively unusual even in the
annual or special collections context described here, but it does
happen.

Two major types of editors' roles have been described in this
chapter. The first, an editor of an "official" journal may enjoy the
most prestige, but is expected to, and indeed is likely to play a
more passive and more narrowly defined role than are editors of
smaller, unofficial journals or of annuals or special series. The latter
are likely to interact more closely with authors, to exercise greater
influence on the acceptance and rejection of specific pieces, to have
greater say about the general orientation and tone of their journal, and are more likely to leave a longer lasting, personal imprint on those journals. The editor of an official journal, on the
other hand, is more likely to make a greater impact on the discipline and on the careers of younger scholars.

4

Editing the *Policy Studies Journal* and *Public Administration Review*

*

David H. Rosenbloom
and Melvin J. Dubnick

We coedited the *Policy Studies Journal* (PSJ) from 1985 to 1990 and began editing *Public Administration Review* (PAR) in 1990, with David Rosenbloom serving as editor-in-chief and Melvin Dubnick as managing editor. PSJ is a quarterly running about 220 pages per issue, whereas PAR is a bimonthly that typically consists of 96 pages. Although there is some overlap in the substance of the two journals, the editorial arrangements and processes have been quite different. This chapter outlines our experiences and provides a record of how the two journals operated and of what we thought we were about.

Selection As Editors

Sometime in 1983 or 1984, David Rosenbloom received a letter from a search committee of members of the American Society for Public Administration (ASPA), which publishes PAR, asking him to apply to be editor-in-chief of *Public Administration Review*. At the time, the *Review* had a circulation of about eighteen thousand and was considered the preeminent journal in the field of American public administration. Subsequently, its circulation declined to about fifteen thousand, but its status has remained the same or even increased somewhat. PAR is one of the few public administration journals that enjoys a high ranking among political scientists in the United States and abroad.[1] In response to the search committee's invitation, Rosenbloom drafted a letter of application. It emphasized the desirability of using the editor's gatekeeping role to lend coherence to an otherwise fragmented field—one that is fractured along many lines, including marked differences between academics and practitioners in cognitive styles and intellectual interests. He also stressed the need to upgrade the intellectual quality of materials published in PAR and to maintain greater consistency of quality. At the time, Rosenbloom had no prior experience in editing a journal. Not surprisingly, the position went to someone else.

At about the same time that his application for the editorship of PAR was under consideration, Rosenbloom was asked by Stuart Nagel of the Policy Studies Organization (PSO) if he would like to edit or coedit the *Policy Studies Journal*. In order to do so, institutional backing from the Maxwell School of Syracuse University would be necessary. After gaining assurances from Maxwell dean Guthrie Birkhead that the school would provide the necessary $3,500 annual subvention and sufficient telephone, copying, graduate assistant, and secretarial support, Rosenbloom agreed to take on the PSJ editorship.

Confusion set in at the outset. The Policy Studies Organization's financial situation required twice the subvention agreed to by the Maxwell School. After a number of discussions, Melvin Dubnick, who was in the Department of Public Administration at the University of Kansas, was brought in as coeditor. He had been literature review editor for PSJ and the *Policy Studies Review* (another PSO journal). Dubnick and Rosenbloom proved intellectually and temperamentally compatible. A mutually satisfactory and durable working relationship (and friendship) was forged.

In 1990, the *Public Administration Review* editorship opened up again. Having taken on the coeditorship of PSJ in part to obtain experience necessary to become a stronger candidate for the editorship of PAR, Rosenbloom again applied. PAR had traditionally used an editor-in-chief and managing editor organizational format. Dubnick, who had moved to Baruch College of the City University of New York in 1988, agreed to join the application as Managing Editor. (In 1992, he moved to Rutgers–Newark.)

As in the case of the Policy Studies Organization, ASPA was very concerned about finances and support. Applicants were required to supply a statement pledging institutional backing, which could take many forms including subsidies and funding for postage, telephone, copyediting, copying, and so forth. Personnel support could include a reduction in teaching load for the editors, graduate assistance with the *Review*, and secretarial help. The total value of institutional support was expected to be in the range of $50,000 to $70,000, much of which would be "in kind" commitment of faculty and staff hours to editing and production. Our joint application was complicated by Rosenbloom's concurrent opportunity to leave his distinguished professorship at the Maxwell School for a similar position at The American University's School of Public Affairs. He agreed to switch positions, and the School of Public Affairs offered to match the institutional backing pledged to ASPA by Syracuse University.

Four pairs of editor-in-chief/managing editor partnerships made ASPA's short list. Each pair was interviewed by the ASPA president, Bill Collins; the president elect, Enid Beaumont; the executive director, Shirley Wester; and ASPA publications staff. Rosenbloom and Dubnick told the selection committee that their objectives would be to:

1. Increase the level of interest in PAR by broadening its focus, which they thought had been overemphasizing narrow concerns with public management technologies, such as computerization and information systems, and underemphasizing such areas as human services, bureaucratic politics, and administrative law. As a field, public administration was enjoying a resurgence among political scientists, but their work was infrequently appearing in PAR. In consequence, PAR was drifting toward being categorized by academics as a nonacademic journal, that is, one devoted to practice only. (Practitioners nevertheless continued to view it as "too academic.") It also seemed to publish a lot of material by a relatively small number of authors who were generally identified as solid citizens of the public administration community.

2. Upgrade and update the methodologies presented in PAR. Although public administration is eclectic in its logics of inquiry, PAR tended not to include articles employing statistical techniques common to contemporary social science, such as regression and time series analysis. Its methodology was lagging, in part, because complicated statistical techniques tended to deter practitioners from reading PAR. Dubnick developed the idea of setting off descriptions of methodology in self-contained shaded boxes within the articles. These "grey boxes" would force authors to be very explicit about their methods and yet allow readers who were uninterested in methodology to skip over them conveniently without losing the logical flow of the article.

3. Include a "Research Notes" section to permit the efficient

transmission of new findings, especially in areas that were well developed theoretically and did not require lengthy introductory reviews of the pertinent literature.

4. Continue to present materials on public administration's intellectual history and core concepts and ideas.

5. Make every effort to enhance the *Review's* appeal to practitioners and to obtain publishable manuscripts from them.

6. Maintain a smooth and quick double-blind submission review system.

When we were selected for an initial three-year term (1991–1993), extendable to five years (1995), we immediately sought to achieve these objectives.

Transitions

The transitions at both journals were very difficult. At PSJ, we had to set up a new peer review system, develop a strong list of reviewers, and design reviewer forms. We inherited only a few articles that had been accepted for publication. The files on submissions in process were adequate, but some materials were unaccounted for. We were unaware of any computerized manuscript tracking system used by the previous editors. At an early date, Rosenbloom brought a hefty suitcase full of PSJ materials to Dubnick at the University of Kansas in order to put the editing on track.

In all respects but one, the transition at PAR was smoother. We had a longer lead time between becoming editors and the publication of our first issue (from July 1990 to January 1991). Managing Editor Dubnick met extensively with the departing editor, Chester Newland, at the University of Southern California in Sacramento. Newland had a computerized review system in operation that tracked each manuscript, and this made the transition orderly.

The only difficulty, and it was a major one, was that only fifteen of the ninety-six pages for our first issue had been accepted. Other materials were in the pipeline, but we did not know if they would arrive on time or be publishable. Newland preferred to edit without a substantial backlog in order to publish accepted articles quickly. His editing was something of a high-wire act, which he executed with near perfection. We preferred more flexibility and less tension in making each issue's page count. Because we did not want our first issue to appear thin on substance, we spent a lot of time obtaining reviews, making revisions, and copyediting the accepted articles. It was not until the summer of 1991 that we were able to develop a comfortable backlog.

Expectations

Gatekeeping

In seeking to be editors of PSJ and PAR, we were predominantly driven by the prospect of having an impact on the direction of the policy and public administration fields. Journal editing is a form of gatekeeping. Our key expectation was that as editors we would be able to steer the policy and public administration fields. Steering has had several main dimensions. First, we have sought to publish articles that promote coherence in these fragmented fields. This effort, in turn, breaks down into three major components:

1. Friendliness toward articles about the fields as a whole. For example, we have welcomed meta-analyses, descriptive, and theoretical discussions about the study of public policy and public administration. At PAR, in particular, this approach has been so common that some believe we are spending too much time studying ourselves.

2. Articles that offer, enhance, or seek to build conceptual frameworks for these fields have also been sought. For instance, in the public policy field, the policy cycle framework shows great potential as a conceptual device for integrating and ordering much extant research. Where authors were able to conveniently locate their work in the policy cycle, as agenda setting, policy formulation, policy design, policy analysis or evaluation, or policy revision, we encouraged them to do so. In our view, this prods contributors to think in terms of the field as a whole.

3. We have also been favorable to the publication of articles dealing with the intellectual history of these fields and their core concepts and ideas. At PAR we actively solicit articles on intellectual leaders in the field, and expect to have published several by the end of our initial three-year term. In 1992, we began publishing some articles in Retrospect. These are authors' current reflections on classic articles of high impact that they wrote a decade or more ago.

A second aspect of steering regards quality. Neither the policy studies nor public administration fields have a single methodology, or set of methodologies, that can be considered dominant. Efforts to generate knowledge take many paths. We have been dogmatic in one respect only—the logic of inquiry must be clear, correct, and efficient. In an editorial in PAR, Rosenbloom posed the question "How do we know what we know?"[2] Asking authors and members of the public administration community to give serious thought to the logic of inquiry and cognition had an almost immediate salutary effect. Several subsequent submissions dealt directly with the "how do we know" theme and many others mentioned it in conjunction with their methodological approaches. In our view, PAR should publish case studies, articles testing hypotheses with aggregate data, experiments, theoretical discussions, and even descriptive reports on interesting administrative processes. Flawed inquiry, however, must be corrected or rejected.

Third, steering often involves a somewhat tedious effort to encourage authors to revise their manuscripts. Virtually no manuscripts go through our review process at PAR without suggestions for revision. In some cases, these are straightforward—the submissions are too long, they fail to cite an important work, another statistical technique should be tried, they need to be expanded, and so forth. In about 10 percent of the cases, though, the author has an important finding to report or a theoretical statement to make, but fails to convey it effectively. In such instances, the editor-in-chief tries to give very explicit advice on how substantive revisions should be made. The managing editor works closely with authors on questions of methodology. In one case, our recommendations ran to about six single-spaced pages of closely packed text; in others, we successfully urged authors to add material about an important area that was neglected in the original draft. In many instances, the editor-in-chief urges authors of manuscripts with useful findings, but cluttered with already well-worn literature reviews, to recast their work as research notes.

Successfully working with authors toward improvement of their analyses requires a breadth of knowledge about the field. Both editors are authors of successful textbooks in public administration.[3] Although this is hardly a prerequisite to editing a major journal, it is a useful indicator of substantial familiarity with all major aspects of a discipline or field.

Fourth, we have been self-conscious in seeking to bring new ideas into the journals. Unconventional studies and theoretical statements have been welcomed at PSJ and PAR during our editorship. In some cases, this involves taking a risk that what we consider offbeat will be viewed as off-the-wall by others. So far, we have been more successful than not with unconventional material in the sense that it has stimulated interest and, sometimes, even debate.

Finally, at PAR, our steering involves a concerted effort to publish articles and research notes about public administration in other nations. We view the field of American public administration as seriously limited by failing to learn much from or about experiences in other political systems. In Rosenbloom's view, a tremendous amount of American public administrative thought and practice is culture bound. Such core areas as organization, personnel, budgeting, ethics, and administrative law are often treated as though they do not have counterparts in foreign systems. Comparative studies should help overcome this tendency and offer insights into American practices and options.

Dealing with Sponsoring Organizations, Authors, and Reviewers

In our experience, a large part of journal editing involves dealing with the sponsoring organizations, authors, and reviewers. At PSJ we did not anticipate how difficult dealing with the Policy Studies Organization would be. Editing *Policy Studies Journal* was complicated by the fact that each issue contained a symposium over which we had little control. Symposia were commissioned by the PSO and took up approximately 96 of the 220 pages in a typical issue. The symposia were not consistently refereed and varied wildly in quality. Many times—probably most—they were late or required substantial copyediting for such basics as consistent referencing and footnoting. Few issues came out in our five years at PSJ that did not involve long difficulties with PSO and symposium editors and authors.

By contrast, relationships with the American Society for Public Administration have been smooth and efficient. PAR is typeset by the staff at ASPA headquarters and most of our interaction with the organization has been in that context. We also spend considerable time in selecting members for our editorial board. The board consists of approximately forty-five members. Appointments are for one year, with the expectation that members will serve three consecutive terms. One-third of the board rotates off each year. Selections are made with reference to individuals' status in and contributions to the public administration community. Balance is sought with regard to academics and practitioners, region, area of specialized expertise, and a number of social factors, including gender, age, race, and ethnicity. We also try to ensure that all the top academic public administration programs have at least one faculty member on the board. It is the prerogative of the editor-in-chief to select board members, in consultation with the president of ASPA.

Dealing with authors and reviewers has consistently taken more time than we anticipated. Several authors have called to protest some aspect of our treatment of their work. Either we have held it too long, asked for revisions that they deem inappropriate, or rejected it on insufficiently explicit or reasonable grounds. Although we try to be clear and polite in our rejections, some authors of rejected papers call to let off steam. Many authors are under intense pressure to publish. Some view a close editorial call for rejection as essentially negotiable. Sometimes, the tenure pressures faced by academics lead them to oppose recasting their analyses as research notes. Apparently these are considered less valuable in some institutions (wrongly in our view). From an editorial vantage point, the academic personnel systems that count titles and pages, rather than the impact of ideas and findings, are a tragic perversion and waste of intellectual talent. From time to time, reviewers also have peculiar requests. For instance, they would like to know who wrote a manuscript so that they can get in touch or they would like to phone in their evaluations and discuss them with one of the editors.

In short, our experience suggests that one who harbors the expectation that a journal editor can pore over manuscripts and think through the gatekeeping process, while avoiding the human interface, is off the mark. Editing turns out to be relatively low tech and high touch. The "people process" is extensive.

Processing Submissions

At both PSJ and PAR, Managing Editor Dubnick took charge of the mechanics of the manuscript review process. For articles and research notes, both journals use an anonymous referee process. Guest editorials are not refereed. Communications may not be, depending on their substance. As mentioned earlier, symposia were not consistently refereed at PSJ, though they are at PAR. PAR has a section called TOPs (Those Other Publications) that reviews government reports and documents. Review essays in this section are currently refereed. Both the book review section and TOPs are independently edited, with little direction from Rosenbloom and Dubnick. Currently, Irene Rubin of Northern Illinois University edits the book review section. Beverly Cigler of Penn State–Harrisburg is the TOPs editor. Jerry Mitchell, now at Baruch College, was our book review editor at PSJ.

The basics of the review process have been similar at both journals. Authors are required to submit several copies (currently four) of the manuscript to the managing editor and one to the editor-in-chief. Upon receipt by Dubnick, the manuscript is logged in and assigned a journal item number. At least twice a week, editors discuss the submissions and to whom they ought to be sent for review. At PAR, reviewers are given a two-page form on which to respond. One page is for the editors only. It asks the reviewer to rate the manuscript on a number of criteria. The other page is for comments and recommendations to the author. Reviewers are asked to respond within six weeks. Generally, three or four reviewers are selected for each manuscript. In a substantial number of cases, one of the editors also acts as a reviewer. Members of the Board of Editors do a substantial number of reviews, but nonmembers are used as well. During our first year at PAR, we received about four hundred manuscripts and contacted several hundred referees.

Dubnick has adapted a journal-management software package for tracking submissions. Data regarding the author(s), title, and date of arrival of manuscripts are logged in along with information regarding the referees and eventual disposition. These computerized files also contain information on the nature of referee responses and the eventual disposition of the manuscript. They alert us to reviews that are overdue and automatically rate referees on timeliness. By the end of our first year, we were aware that some reviewers were always chronically late and we began bypassing them.

The reviewers' evaluations are sent back to Editor-in-chief Rosenbloom, who makes a copy for Managing Editor Dubnick. Rosenbloom studies the evaluations, reads the manuscripts thoroughly, and decides whether to reject, ask for revisions, or publish as is (the latter is an empty set). He feels free to augment and/or override the reviewers, if he views their points as inadequate. It is easier to do so where the reviewers urge rejection, because authors are apt to complain, perhaps rightly, about getting positive reviews along with a rejection letter. In most cases, however, the reviewers are either divided, uniform in urging rejection, or only moderately positive. It is interesting that our reviewers have a greater consensus on what should not be published than on what should be. Rejections are often on the grounds that a manuscript would be of little interest to our readers and therefore PAR is not an appropriate forum for it.

A great deal of time is spent drafting letters urging authors to revise and resubmit their manuscripts to us. This is where an editor can have a great impact on what appears in the literature. Rosenbloom often urges authors to reconfigure their manuscripts, to cite additional works, to be more explicit about their logic of inquiry, and to discuss the implications of their findings or theoretical observations more explicitly.

Many rejection letters are pro forma, but some take a good deal of time as well. The previous editor of PAR viewed the review process as a "floating seminar." Serious authors are entitled to serious discussion and criticism of their work, even if the piece is so flawed as to be irretrievable. Rosenbloom tries to synthesize the points made by the reviewers and his own observations into a clear statement of why we are declining to publish a manuscript. Every effort is made to avoid excessive or harsh criticism, and to encourage authors to submit their future work to PAR. Sometimes we suggest that a manuscript is more appropriate for another journal.

Rosenbloom has been surprised by some authors' reactions to rejections. One author apparently sends almost all his work to PAR first, in hope of gaining acceptance or good advice on how to improve it. He uses us as a review service and views acceptance as an added, but unnecessary, benefit. Another author said she was glad her piece was rejected because she was fed up with her coauthor, who in her view ruined it!

The review process, including thoroughly reading the manuscripts, is very time-consuming. Some weeks it entails a commitment of thirty or more hours.

At PAR, the editors are also responsible for annual awards for the best lead article, general article, article by a practitioner, TOPs essay, and book review. They appoint committees from among the Board of Editors for each award. Awards are presented at the ASPA annual meeting.

Getting to Print

The publication processes at PSJ and PAR differ in several respects. Initially, in 1985, PSJ was put into camera-ready form by the editors at their respective universities. Each editor was responsible for two issues a year. Later, the journal was typeset by a word-processing service. In the early years, articles had to be retyped or word processed. Later, we began to receive materials on disks. Once the issue was set and corrected, it was sent to PSO headquarters, where materials pertaining to PSO activities, cartoons, and advertisements were added (without our knowledge of their content). It was then sent to a printer in Ann Arbor, Michigan, for printing and binding. Subsequently, it was returned to the University of Illinois for labeling and mailing. This convoluted printing arrangement and the difficulties we had in obtaining symposia on a timely basis contributed to PSJ's tendency to run three to six months late.

By contrast, PAR is typeset and composed currently by John Larkin at the ASPA headquarters. We require all authors to send us hard copies and disks. All articles, research notes, and commentaries are professionally copyedited. Copyediting changes are made on the disks by the staff at The American University or sent back to the authors, who then make the changes. Dubnick works closely with Larkin in writing executive summaries for these materials and in pulling out the methodological discussions to create "grey boxes." They also identify passages that will be displayed as "read outs" within the text. Page proofs are sent to the authors for corrections. These are returned to Larkin, who sets up the entire issue for a final round of proofreading. The editors, copy editor, and a graduate assistant[4] proofread the final copy. Rosenbloom creates a master copy for correction and sends it to Larkin, who completes the publication process. Printing is done by a press in the Washington, D.C., area.

PAR runs on a tight schedule. It is sometimes a few days early in arriving in subscribers' hands, but it has never been late. Proofreading is intensive. Despite the number of eyes that proofread it, typographical errors are apparently an inevitability—and one to which we are alerted by our readers. The editors believe most errors are a result of the authors' inattention to the page proofs.

One of our surprises was that PAR's cover—more specifically, its wrapper—seemed to attract as much attention as its contents. Those concerned about the environment strongly urged us to get rid of the plastic wrapper. Beginning in our second year, we successfully experimented with mailing the *Review* "naked."

There is no doubt that the details of production are very time-consuming. Proofreading, grey boxing, and indexing each volume at the end of the year come in addition to other activities and responsibilities. At times, it is simply impossible to stay abreast of the review and production processes simultaneously. Nevertheless, we have found that careful attention to details and appearance counts. Dubnick changed the look of both PSJ and PAR, which in both cases generated more interest in their contents.

Lows and Highs

Editing academic journals is an important, but sometimes frustrating, activity. As described earlier, gatekeeping at a leading journal can potentially have a significant impact on an entire field. Faith in human progress demands that we expect our knowledge to appear limited or even primitive to people of the future. Nevertheless, whatever advances we can help make are clearly worthwhile. At times, though, the lows are substantial.

The low point for both editors was at *Policy Studies Journal*. Rosenbloom's was in the production of early issues, which were typeset on an IBM typewriter with proportional spacing. Corrections were difficult and page numbers were typed separately on small labels, which were affixed when the final copy was ready. The process was very labor intensive and the secretarial staff was overloaded. Dubnick, who took the lead in dealing with the Policy Studies Organization, was constantly annoyed by difficulties in obtaining symposia on a timely basis, their poor quality, and the cartoons placed in PSJ without our knowledge. The major lesson here is that frustration is inevitable if the editors do not fully control the content of each issue and if production technology and staff are unequal to the task.

Although not really a low, at PAR we are under constant pressure to "do something for the practitioners." We were warned by previous editors that PAR is largely produced by academics and consumed by practitioners. The articles' authors and readers are frequently somewhat mismatched. We work hard to connect the two groups. For instance, we urge academics to explain the relevance of their findings or observations for practice. We ask practitioners to be broadly reflective about their practices. However, the gap has been evident for several decades and is likely to continue. Public administration is an applied field—at best a design science like engineering. Practice and theory are bound together, but not smoothly.

The highs come from learning. We read many manuscripts that are on the cutting edge of their fields and subfields. We help shape their final content. Improving a really important manuscript with our review process, our own input, and final editing is clearly an important intellectual contribution. It is all the better when feedback from our authors and readers is favorable. At PAR, in particular, we have been able to broaden the range of topics analyzed and bring in authors who might otherwise have bypassed the journal. Although we may be naive or pretentious, we genuinely hope to advance the field of public administration through our editing. We are not creating new knowledge, but we believe we can expand the knowledge base of public administration through judicious gatekeeping and by obtaining the revisions we desire from authors. Our hope is that when our term as editors expires we will have played an important role in the field's intellectual development.

A Concluding Word

Editing an academic journal is a time-consuming, difficult endeavor. In our experience, it cannot be viewed as an essentially clerical task. We take an active role in determining what should be published and how it should be revised, in the appearance of final copy, and in obtaining thoughtful reviews. The opportunity costs are high: each of us has been unable to write articles and books that we would liked to have seen in print by now. But the opportunity is also great. In sum, editors make a difference!

Notes

1. Ivor Crew and Pippa Norris, "British and American Journal Evaluation," *PS: Political Science and Politics* 24 (September 1991): 524–531.

2. David H. Rosenbloom, "How Do We Know What We Know and How Can We Extend What We Know?" *Public Administration Review* 5 (March/April 1991): 95– .

3. David H. Rosenbloom, *Public Administration: Understanding Management, Politics, and Law in the Public Sector*, 3rd ed. (New York: Random House/McGraw Hill, 1991). Melvin J. Dubnick and Barbara S. Romzek, *American Public Administration: Politics and the Management of Expectations* (New York: Macmillan, 1991).

4. Rosenbloom has been very fortunate in having the highly competent and dedicated assistance of two MPA students, Dianne Shaughnessey and Beth Cooper.

5

Cops and Robbers in Academe:
Editing *Justice Quarterly*

*

James J. Fyfe

Some History

In 1989, I began a three-year term as editor of *Justice Quarterly*, the journal of the Academy of Criminal Justice Sciences (ACJS).[1] JQ reaches about 3,000 subscribers, approximately 2,400 of whom receive it as a benefit of their ACJS memberships.

ACJS was established during the 1960s by a group of academicians and practitioners who wished to reverse what they saw as the American Society of Criminology's emphasis on theory over criminal justice policy and practice. ACJS's first official periodical was *Journal of Criminal Justice*, a proprietary quarterly with which the academy maintained a relationship for several years. In time, however, strains developed between Kent Joscelyn, JCJ's owner-editor-publisher, and the academy over editorial direction and policy. Hence, in the early 1980s, ACJS's Board of Directors began studying the feasibility of an academy-owned periodical that, like other membership journals, would be edited on a rotating basis by members.[2]

For a short period, Jack Greene of Temple University served as acting editor for the fledgling, and as yet unpublished, journal. Then, after a search, Rita J. Simon, at the time my dean at The American University's School of Justice, was chosen as founding editor. Rita was responsible for assembling an editorial board of three deputy editors, twenty-four associate editors, and one book review editor. She asked me to serve as her resident deputy editor and I accepted. With our AU colleague Richard R. Bennett as resident associate editor and Georgetown University law student Gloria Danziger as copy/managing editor, we published JQ's first issue in March 1984.[3]

This first turn at JQ ended for me two years later, when I resigned at the beginning of my sabbatical leave. In 1986, ACJS asked for proposals to replace Rita's successor, and Frank Cullen of the University of Cincinnati was selected. I applied for and won a term as editor from September 1989 to September 1992.

Current State of the Journal

Earlier experience had taught me that solid in-house editorial assistance would be necessary to keep the journal's wheels turning. I assured that by coercing James Lynch and Richard Bennett to serve as my in-house deputy and associate editor,[4] respectively. Our managing editor was Heide Shintani, a doctoral student at AU who, at first, did this work as her graduate fellowship assignment. Shintani, who automated our record-keeping system,[5] was assisted on sort of a catch-as-catch-can basis by Lisa Blank, a master's student. The remarkably competent, final two members of JQ's in-house editorial staff were copyeditor Karen Feinberg and proofreader Polly Campbell. Both Feinberg and Campbell are based in Cincinnati, where their services originally were secured by Frank Cullen. By this coup alone, Cullen has earned a place in the ACJS Hall of Fame.

Publishing Policy and Priorities

During my editorship, JQ received approximately 125 manuscripts a year. Since the journal represents the Academy of Criminal Justice Sciences, I attempted to encourage articles that were closely identified with the issues of crime, crime control, and criminal justice policy and operations. To some degree, this policy narrowed the precedent set by Simon who, as a legal sociologist, encouraged writings on a broader range of topics. Substantively, the balance of our articles were tipped slightly toward system issues, police, courts, legal procedure, and corrections, and away from sociological or psychological theory. This distribution was driven more by the content of submissions than by conscious editorial policy, and I like to think that it represented ACJS's mandate for the journal. By my interpretation, this mandate was to fill a clearly identifiable niche among a pool of crime and criminal justice related journals that include *Criminology* (the American Society of Criminology's journal), *Journal of Criminal Justice, Journal of Criminal Law and Criminology,* and *Journal of Research in Crime and Delinquency.*[6] A slight preponderance of the articles published were characterized by some variety of quantitative analysis, although we welcomed other methods.[7]

When Simon edited JQ, she commissioned one or more prominent authors to write "opinion and debate" articles for each issue. In JQ's early days, I was enthusiastic about this method of enlivening, and filling the journal, but my ardor quickly waned as I saw how difficult it was to hold busy volunteer authors to our tight publishing schedule. Thus, I was gratified to see that Cullen had dropped these articles when he assumed the editorship. Instead, Cullen commissioned a "review essay" on a critical criminal topic for each journal issue. I liked these essays very much,[8] and believed that they served a valid purpose of summarizing the state of particular arts in ways that would be useful to scholars and students for years to come. Although I have never asked Cullen, I also suspected that authors' delays in meeting essay deadlines accounted in no small measure for JQ's chronic lateness. Unwilling to contribute any more than necessary to this tardiness, I decided to drop the journal's commitment to these essays. Instead, I solicited and made commitments to publish them as page space allowed.[9]

The Editorial Process

Our editorial policy required exclusive submission to us, and urged that manuscript submissions not exceed thirty pages. Although this limit was a suggestion rather than a mandate, I declined to send out for review a few articles that substantially exceeded this limit.[10] I also rejected out-of-hand a small number of essays submitted by people who obviously had never seen the journal or its editorial policy and who, I assume, learned of *JQ* from a guide to criminal justice periodicals. I returned these submissions with polite notes that their topics (on the order of "How to Justify Polygraph Use in Court," "Building Humane Quarters for Officers' Canine Partners," "Correction Officers: Government's Unsung Heroes")[11] might find more receptive readerships in practitioner magazines than in an academic journal.

It was my practice to send to referees everything that survived these tests of length and scholarship. Consequently, referees occasionally received manuscripts that, in my view, were destined to be recommended for rejection. In addition to such recommendations, I have drawn some fiery criticisms in the portion of our review form called "Comments for the Editor (not to be shared with author)":

This was a shameful abuse of the review process.

Fyfe—what's wrong with you? This is not even a C undergraduate paper! You owe me one for forcing me to read it!

My cavalier answer to referees I know well is *better you than me*. My more serious reasoning was based on experience and equity. Early in Simon's editorship, I occasionally was asked to conduct prereview readings of manuscripts that she felt were so bad that the review process would waste referees' time and cost us goodwill. When the in-house staff (and/or the journal's two other deputy editors)[12] agreed with Simon's assessments, these articles were returned to authors with notes to the effect that the editorial board had deemed them not suitable for JQ. A few authors responded to this notice vehemently and with logic that had unfortunately been lacking in their scholarly work.

How dare you, they asked, summarily reject work that academy members have prepared and submitted to the publication that their dues support? In my view, and, I think, in Simon's present view, they are right. However slight its chances of surviving review, scholarly work submitted to a membership organization's journal should be peer reviewed unless it obviously flunks the length and scholarship criteria. I am not sure that I would apply this rebuttable right of authors to reviews were I editing a proprietary journal or nonmembership publication. But I believe that this presumption should be operative in a dues-supported membership organization's journal. Thus, like the prosecutor who would rather bring bad cases to a jury than be accused of playing favorites or otherwise shortcircuiting justice, I tried to leave most judgments to authors' peers.

Each jury we selected included three anonymous referees. Our associate editors, all excellent scholars who were chosen for philosophical, geographic, substantive, and methodological diversity, did the lion's share of our reviews. But had I asked them to review all our papers, I would have quickly exhausted their patience. Consequently, we drew reviews from a large pool of individuals who answered our *calls for referees*, as well as from others that I pressed into service on an ad hoc basis because of their expertise in specific topics or methodologies, regardless of whether they were ACJS members.

Like jury selection, the choice of referees is very sensitive. The good editor should identify individuals who know the subject area well, but should avoid selecting people whose work has been ignored or savaged, or praised, by the author whose work is in hand. In trying to assure that referees base their evaluations on the merits of work under consideration rather than on what authors say about the referees themselves, or how many times they say it, I applied a *one citation rule*: if a name that popped into my head when I thought about the topic addressed in a manuscript did not appear in the paper at least once, I tried to find other referees; if the name of the suspect appeared substantially more than once, I also looked for other referees.

In addition, and almost without regard to subject matter, I tried to pick referees on the basis of methodological expertise. I maintained an informal short list of *quantoids*, who reviewed a substantial number of papers that employed time series analysis, PROBIT, LOGIT, rotated varimax factor analysis, and other techniques that make many referees' heads spin.[13] In relying on these individuals, I also found myself fighting the constant temptation to overload the most prompt, thorough, and expert referees. They know who they are and when I took advantage of them, I received comments such as: "HEY . . . GIVE ME A BREAK! DON'T YOU THINK I'VE GOT ANYTHING TO DO BUT THIS?" Subtle cues that I should give them brief respites.

This process, combining the one citation rule, obtaining appropriate methodological counsel, and trying not to overload the readily cooperative, generally worked well. One cause of vexation was the occasional paper on an arcane subject that nobody seemed anxious or able to review. In one case, I corresponded with seven referees before I was successful in obtaining three reviews. Even then, the referees were all over the lot: one "great, get it into print right away"; a second, "competent, but I am not sure that anybody cares about this"; a third recommended that the author send the work to a comic book. At that point, the obvious choice, rejection, was no longer easy.

It is unpleasant to say no to an author who has been kept in suspense for an inordinately long period of time, during which a paper has been withheld from publications for which it may have been better suited. Still, problems in even identifying referees for a manuscript speak eloquently about its appropriateness for a journal. A paper for which appropriate referees cannot be found is unlikely to find interested readers. The moral is that, when controlling for the objective quality of an article, subject matter obscurity necessarily works against publication.

A more vexing problem is the reluctance of some of the best-known and most prolific scholars to review the work of others. On occasion, unread manuscripts with scrawled notes "I have no time for this now" were returned by the same people who were quick to call when it took longer than we all would have liked to secure reviews of their own work. Worse, some referees promised "it's in the mail"; but somehow we never received it. One editor whose opinion I value suggested in a conversation that some academic *superstars* do not truly believe in the peer review process because they do not believe that they have peers. This insight had led my fellow editor to rely heavily on referees at the associate professor level. Associate professors, this editor reasoned, had achieved some professional status and security, but were not so self-involved that they could not make time to participate in meaningful professional dialogue. Fortunately, my discipline is full of excellent associate professors, and volunteers at all other levels, so that it became increasingly easy to avoid sending manuscripts to *superstars* who prefer one-way involvement in the publishing process.

A more frequent editorial dilemma is the question of how closely editors should adhere to referees' recommendations, especially when referees' opinions are divided. With at least one of the in-house staff (Lynch and/or Bennett), I read each article and its reviews carefully, which makes it clear that division among referees sometimes is a matter of perspective or philosophy that can be resolved satisfactorily. Just as there are good and bad manuscripts, however, there are good and bad reviews. When bad reviews miss major weaknesses in authors' arguments, logic, or analyses, and also end with enthusiastic recommendations for publication, they make the editor's job very difficult. Consequently, most editors probably would prefer referees to omit in comments to authors any conclusions on the *ultimate issue*: to publish or not to publish? JQ referees were specifically asked not to include conclusions in comments to authors but, occasionally, some do (e.g., "This is excellent work and will make a great contribution to the literature. I recommend PUBLISH"; or "This is naive and unsophisticated work that is far below JQ's usual standards"). In such cases, I had no compunctions about cutting and pasting in order to bring reviews into conformity with editorial policy, and/or to avoid unnecessarily hurting authors' feelings or pride.

Editorial Decisions

JQ's requests for reviews asked referees to complete their work within three weeks, so that authors could be advised of initial editorial decisions within twelve weeks. On average, we adhered to these parameters but, especially when manuscripts were received in academic down times (summer, end of year recess), some manuscripts are not turned around so quickly.

Depending on article length, about thirty manuscripts make it to print in JQ each year,[14] but acceptances on the first round are a real rarity. During my interrupted five-year association with JQ, I can recall only one article that was scheduled for publication without at least some changes. Only 4 or 5 percent were accepted conditional on minor changes after the first round. On the grounds of length or inappropriateness described above, I rejected out of hand about 5 percent of the manuscripts we received. Another 45 percent were rejected on the first round of reviews.[15] Thus, 40–45 percent of the submissions were returned to authors with recommendations to "revise and resubmit." Some of these *R and R*s included suggestions for change so great that authors eventually dropped their projects or, at least, chose not to revise them for JQ. Others come back for a second (and, on rare occasion, even a third) round of reviews, those manuscripts had about a 50 percent chance of acceptance. The bottom line is that slightly less than a quarter of the manuscripts submitted to JQ eventually found their way into our publishing queue.

When I assumed the editorship, I was surprised to see the detail with which Frank Cullen critiqued authors' submissions in his letters to them. Cullen typically summarized reviewers' suggestions and objections, and made very specific suggestions to improve papers. I was a bit reluctant to go into such detail, not only because of the great work involved, but also because I was anxious to avoid implying that authors' work would be published if the revisions suggested in such editorial feedback were met. Sometimes, for example, revisions made in response to referees' methodological suggestions merely confirm the referees' suspicion that the authors' original findings were the spurious results of inappropriate data analysis or, worse, that the data themselves contained some fatal flaw. Hence, I typically attempted to identify the commonalities that ran through referees' comments and, where appropriate, suggested ways in which they might be addressed. A stock phrase, altered as appropriate, proved to be extremely useful:

I have enclosed the referees' comments to you, so that you may consider them and decide whether you wish to revise and resubmit the paper. The referees' criticisms generally speak for themselves, so I will not repeat them here. I will, however, emphasize some themes that run through all the reviews. Please take them into account in deciding upon your next course of action. First. . . .

. . . If you decide to resubmit the paper, I request that you include with the second iteration four copies of a memo explaining your responses to (or rejections of) the referees' criticisms and suggestions.

To this, I sometimes added an encouraging statement, such as:

Although substantial, I do not believe that the flaws pointed out by the referees are fatal. Indeed, I believe they can be addressed with a minimum of effort, and I encourage you to do so.

Or, less positively:

I feel obliged to point out that I agree with the criticisms of the referees, and that the revisions they suggest amount to a major overhaul of your work.

Although JQ does not solicit *research notes*, referees' comments occasionally led me to suggest that manuscripts be revised and shortened for reconsideration in that abbreviated format. In all cases, referees were sent packets containing copies of all reviews and my decision letters to authors. This process of providing referees with feedback on their efforts is time-consuming but proved to be extremely popular. I have been told at professional meetings that being able to compare one's own review against anothers increased referees' interest and, presumably, acuity.

Advice to Potential Editors

Shortly before he died, Malcolm Forbes spoke at an American University commencement. He told his audience that the best advice he could give any young man or woman, was to be born to a father who owned many businesses, and to be on good terms with him when he died. My best advice to anyone considering a journal editorship is even more terse: *Get a good support staff and stay on good terms with them.*

Table 1
Typical Written Correspondence
for a *Justice Quarterly* Manuscript

Nature of correspondence	Items received	Items sent
Receipt of manuscript	1	
Acknowledgment of receipt		1
Request for reviews		3
Return reviews	3	
Notification to author and request for decision of whether manuscript will be revised		1
Notifications to referees, with copies of all reviews		3
Receipt of author's decision to revise	1	
Acknowledgment of author's revision notice		1
Receipt of revised manuscript	1	
Acknowledgment of receipt		1
Request for second reviews		3
Receipt of second reviews	3	
Notification to author of acceptance and request for third iteration for copyediting, etc.		1
Notification to referees, with copies of all reviews		3
Receipt of third iteration	1	
Acknowledgement of receipt		1
Third iteration to copyeditor		1
Receipt of copyedited third iteration	1	
Copyedited third iteration to author		1
Receipt of copyedited third iteration from author	1	
Copyedited third iteration to publisher		1
Receipt of acknowledgment from publisher	1	
Receipt of first proofs from publisher	1	
First proofs to author		1
Receipt of first proofs from author	1	
First proofs to publisher		1
Receipt of acknowledgment from publisher	1	
Receipt of second proofs from publisher	1	
Second proofs to author		1
Receipt of second proofs from author	1	
Second proofs to proofreader		1
Acknowledgment from publisher that proofreader has forwarded second proofs	1	
Receipt of book proofs from publisher	1	
Book proofs returned to publisher		1
Receipt of acknowledgment from publisher	1	
Totals	21	26

The volume of correspondence and production work involved in publishing a peer-reviewed journal is prodigious. Consider Table 1's description of the mailings involved in a single *R and R*. The modal paper that made its way promptly and without such glitches as tardy reviews or reluctant referees through two rounds of reviews required us to handle at least forty-seven pieces of incoming and outgoing correspondence. Multiply this figure by the thirty or so manuscripts that JQ published each year, add to it the paper involved in our other ninety-five manuscript submissions; correspondence with authors, deputy and associate editors, and ACJS staff; requests for reprints; reprint permissions; responses to inquiries; reminders to tardy referees, and the like, and the result is a large number of envelopes to be stuffed. Thus, prospective editors should make certain that their universities or other institutions understand and are committed to providing the support staff necessary to accomplish this. Without adequate staff assistance, editing a journal can be extremely tedious and unrewarding.

Advice to Authors

Because other contributors to this volume make important points for prospective authors, I would like to devote my remaining pages to some less-obvious observations. First, some of the most contentious correspondence in my editorial experience involved work, parts but not all of which, had previously appeared in other publications. Most frequently, this phenomenon involved authors who used large sections of lengthy research documents (often their dissertations) as *boilerplate* in several article-length manuscripts. On some occasions, this involved repeated use of single and lengthy "methodology" or "data sources" sections. In one such case, a referee was in the midst of reviewing the literature on a topic at precisely the time I asked him to review a paper on the same subject. A few days after providing a lukewarm review (to the effect that the work really was "nothing new"), the referee called to say that he had come to see why he had not regarded the paper as new information. After reviewing the manuscript, he had come across several prior publications with which the article under consideration shared large (one- to three-page) passages. These, by and large, explained data and methods and did not pass off the same research results more than once. Still, I felt obliged to reject the paper. With my letter to the author, I enclosed photocopies of the prior work (some of which had been coauthored) with what I thought was a very politic suggestion that less duplication would enhance the probability of publication elsewhere. In return, I got an angry letter that my accusations of plagiarism and multiple submissions were baseless and libelous. I had not made either accusation. I regret that the whole episode could have been avoided had the author not relied so often on his word processor's MOVE BLOCK feature.

Another author made imaginative use of a word processor by developing the skeleton of an analysis of a large data set and subsequently prepared several manuscripts that varied only in the single independent variable plugged into the text. Assume that the data set involved reported robberies and, one at a time, plug into the following fictional, but illustrative, discussion such victim characteristics as age, sex, race, social class, and degree of intoxication:

> The data set provided an excellent opportunity to identify the degree to which victim [*insert independent variable*] was associated with robbery victimization. This relationship has both theoretical and operational significance.
>
> [*Insert discussion of a popular theory related to independent variable. What is operational significance? Figure this out, and briefly discuss it, too*].
>
> [*Dichotomize independent variable, run two-by-two tables, and insert appropriate figures*].
>
> . . . In conclusion, this analysis shows [*no; a weak; a moderate; a strong*] association between victim [*insert independent variable*] and the likelihood that individuals will suffer robbery victimization. More specifically, the analysis demonstrates that [*insert one value of independent variable*] are [*no more; slightly; somewhat more; considerably more*] likely to be victimized than [*insert alternative value of independent variable*]. These findings must be considered only tentative, of course, because they do not take into account the extent to which robbery victimization also may be affected by such important characteristics as [*insert all independent variables not used in this analysis*]. Such questions are beyond the scope of the present study and will be examined in future research.

As my teenage daughter would say, "Nice work—NOT!" *Authors should carefully cull boilerplate from their work and should never submit anything that gives even the appearance of duplication.*

Another tip of special relevance to social scientists who conduct program or policy analysis is this: *Know the difference between an agency-sponsored research report and a publishable scholarly article.* Especially at the state and local level, government agencies that sponsor research and evaluations are interested, first and foremost, in determining how well they are doing. Understandably, they are concerned only secondarily, if at all, with the implications of their work for people and places not included on their own tax rolls. Scholarly social science articles, by contrast, should be grounded in theory and should present and interpret analyses and results in manners that are broadly generalizable. To whatever extent possible, scholarship also should contribute to development and understanding of theory. These differences are so fundamental that program evaluations rarely can be turned into publishable articles without substantial revision.

Proper planning, however, can help to reconcile these differences and ease the metamorphosis of agency research into scholarship. In the design of any such research, scholars should anticipate these differences and build into the work allowances to capture and analyze data in ways that may be applied beyond the specific phenomenon and setting under analysis. It is my experience that this usually can be accomplished at minimal cost. Further, despite their justifiably local concerns, most administrators and research sponsors can readily be convinced of the value of serving as a site for scholarly research. On ego alone, virtually all administrators welcome the opportunity to see their innovations serve as *national models* in widely reported research. I see no ethical problems in advancing the state of knowledge in this way.

A Final Note on Patience

Finally, I remind authors that *patience is a virtue.* Except for some proprietary periodicals, academic journals typically are run by volunteers who squeeze in their work among their other responsibilities. Referees, in particular, must be granted some flexibility. Although they usually have volunteered to review papers *generally,* they receive individual manuscripts without prior notice and, often, at inopportune times. They are chosen as referees because they are themselves productive and well-known scholars. Thus, in order to review other peoples' writing thoroughly and objectively, they must set aside their own work, as well as their own biases. Authors should understand and expect that referees may not always manage to do this in a manner that suits the schedules of the people who have asked for this service.

Notes

1. JQ has recently been joined among ACJS publications by *Journal of Criminal Justice Education*, a semiannual currently edited by Dean Tim Flanagan of Sam Houston State University in Huntsville, Texas.

2. This divorce apparently was a good thing for everybody. Joscelyn still publishes *Journal of Criminal Justice*, which maintains a high level of quality despite loss of ACJS sponsorship.

3. The journal is printed by the Joe Christensen firm in Lincoln, Nebraska. Christensen is a widely respected and highly professional journal and law review printing house. I have the highest regard for its staff and its product.

4. Julius Debro of the University of Washington and Jill Rosenbaum of California State University–Fullerton accepted my invitations to fill JQ's two additional deputy editorships. I have also nominated eight new associate editors to three-year terms each year, so that the entire editorial board will have been replaced when my editorship expires.

5. JQ uses the PC-based PARADOX system, which has proven excellent for our purposes.

6. Other, more specialized, or regional, journals include *American Journal of Criminal Justice*, *American Journal of Police*, *Criminal Justice and Behavior*, *The Justice Professional*, and *Police Studies*. In addition, the National Council on Crime and Delinquency publishes *Crime and Delinquency*, a prestigious but, as I understand it, nonrefereed journal.

7. My conversations with other social science editors lead me to conclude that accusations of bias toward quantitative research are an occupational hazard. Ironically, some of the self-proclaimed *qualitative types* who make this criticism themselves frequently trash nonquantitative scholarship when they are asked to review it. After providing peers reviews that use such pejoratives as "anecdotal," "nonscientific," "impressionistic," "simple assertion," and "fancy journalism"to characterize such work, they bemoan its absence from the literature.

8. At Cullen's request, I even wrote one. See James J. Fyfe, "Police Use of Deadly Force: Research and Reform," *Justice Quarterly* 5 (June 1988): 165–205.

9. Despite this commitment to timeliness, unanticipated glitches invariably have kept me from substantially improving JQ's on-time record. It was four months behind schedule when I assumed editorship and is now two months behind.

10. One manuscript more than twice the suggested length was submitted with a letter that said, in effect, "we realize that this paper is substantially longer than your policy requests. If, after the paper has been reviewed, you feel that it should be shortened, please advise us and we will do so." I returned the manuscript to the authors with a suggestion that they revise it to comply with the policy before they asked referees to wade through it. I have not yet heard back from them.

11. These titles are composites meant to illustrate the types of papers rejected in this way, and do not reflect specific submissions.

12. Michael Gottfredson of the University of Arizona and Marvin Zalman of Wayne State University.

13. In-house, and after referees have finished their work, I have relied very heavily on Dick Bennett and Jim Lynch for such counsel.

14. We have also published 8–12 book reviews annually.

15. By December 31, 1991, 47 of the 126 papers received during 1991 had been rejected. By extrapolation, we will have rejected 55–60 (43–48 percent) on the first round by the time all 126 have been reviewed. This is consistent with prior years.

6

Explorations in Economic History

*

Larry Neal

Background

Explorations in Economic History is a "niche" journal, one of several published by Academic Press to serve various fields within economics. It receives a little over one hundred manuscripts in a year and publishes twenty to twenty-four of them over the course of the next year or two. The journal appears quarterly and averages about five hundred pages per annual volume. Under my editorship, which now spans over a decade, it has tried to serve two functions: (1) to bring the lessons of economic history for the study of the modern economy to the attention of the economics profession in the United States; and (2) to bring the results of research performed by economist historians outside the United States to the attention of the international scholarly community.

The journal is directed to a readership of trained economists, whose research may be focused on either contemporary problems in applied economics or on historical issues, and who are willing to take as instructive examples results derived from the study of any time period in any place. While informally associated now with the Cliometrics Society, formed in 1985, *Explorations* began life in 1948 at the Harvard Graduate School of Business Administration as the journal of the Harvard University Research Center in Entrepreneurial History. This center was established by the distinguished economic historian, Arthur H. Cole, who was its director from 1948 until his retirement in 1958.

The journal was then called *Explorations in Entrepreneurial History.* Early issues included some classic pieces, often the first publications of Harvard graduate students or visitors to the research center who were destined to become leaders in the field of economic history. Bernard Bailyn, Alexander Gerschenkron, and Fritz Redlich as well as Cole himself contributed articles, but also Alfred Chandler, David Landes, Douglass North, Henry Rosovsky (who was editor of the journal for a short period) from the United States and from overseas H. J. Habukkuk and Peter Mathias (Great Britain), Herman Kellenbenz (Germany), Noel Butlin (Australia), and Michael Flinn (Scotland) were represented. These are all names immediately recognizable to economic historians, and most have distinguished themselves since, outside the field of economic history.

Upon Cole's retirement in 1958, the journal lapsed. It was reborn in 1962 as *Explorations in Entrepreneurial History, Second Series*, under the aegis of the graduate program in economic history at the University of Wisconsin. Ralph Andreano and his colleagues at Wisconsin saw that it was the natural outlet for pieces then emerging by economists writing on topics in economic history. They were finding that their work was being systematically excluded from publication in the official journal of the Economic History Association, the *Journal of Economic History*. The economists' work was too arcane for the historians who were the dominant readership of the journal. It was based on new economic theory that had to be explained from first principles, and too often it used statistical techniques that were coming into fashion among economists, but were not yet part of the training of historians.

Finding their work rejected by historians on grounds of the techniques used, the new generation of economist–historians turned to economics journals. There, they commonly found their work rejected on grounds that the point was more interesting to historians than to economists concerned with contemporary policy issues. In short, work that was interesting for the understanding of important historical issues and was technically competent from the viewpoint of professional economists was being rejected by journals directed toward historians and by journals directed toward economists.

The revived journal from the Harvard Business School was the natural outlet. Many of these early authors were either students of Cole directly while at Harvard or, if they were from other major graduate programs in economics, they were very much under the influence of the ideas of Joseph Schumpeter and therefore familiar with the original *Explorations in Entrepreneurial History*. In volume 7, published in fall–winter 1969, the editor and editorial board recognized the emerging market for its services as the journal for the new economic history and changed its name formally to *Explorations in Economic History*. It became the outlet for cliometric work (cliometrics: the application of formal statistical techniques and explicit theory to historical issues) being produced in increasing volume by the new generation of economic historians receiving their training in economics departments.

A change of venue occurred in 1974 when Gary Walton, one of the new economic historians then at Indiana University, assumed the editorship. Under his aggressive leadership, publication of the journal, until then done by university presses, first at Antioch and then at Kent State, was turned over to Academic Press in 1975, which began publishing it as part of their large list of scholarly journals.

The format of the journal was changed to conform with the standards used in the other economics journals already published by Academic Press and the journal's circulation was immediately enlarged to the libraries overseas already subscribing to many of Academic Press's scholarly periodicals. In 1982, I became the editor when Gary Walton found the pressures of academic administration as dean of several business schools in succession were preventing him from continuing the policies that had made his editorship a success. (The primary policy was devoting a lot of his time to attending economic history conferences and conversing personally with potential authors.)

I have tried to imitate this strategy by actively cultivating the current generation of economic historians to consider *Explorations* as the natural outlet for their work. One of the truisms that any editor quickly learns is that your power is strictly limited in one respect—you cannot publish articles in the areas desired if you do not receive manuscripts in the first place. An editor of a freestanding journal such as *Explorations* must recruit manuscripts actively, especially in the areas he/she regards as deficient. This requires attending in person most of the academic conferences where potential authors congregate. In the case of economic history this means the annual meetings of the Economic History Association, the Cliometrics Conference, the Social Science History Association meetings, the Business History Conference, the Allied Social Sciences Association meetings, and the British cliometrics conference, as well as the Canadian cliometrics meetings every eighteen months, and the International Economic History Association meetings quadrennially.

In addition, I use travel funds provided by Academic Press to help finance a weekly workshop at the University of Illinois in economic history. Members of the editorial board and recent or potential authors are invited to present working papers on the verge of submission to a journal. Based on the reaction of myself, Illinois colleagues, and graduate students to the paper, the author may decide to submit it to the tender graces of the journal or submit it elsewhere. I always feel a bit ambivalent about receiving offprints of papers later published in other journals, with acknowledging footnotes expressing gratitude for the helpful comments received at Illinois. Over the years, in fact, it appears to me that more and more of the papers presented at the Illinois workshop in economic history are ending up in the main economics journals or in the official journal of the Economic History Association!

I like to attribute this not so much to the offensive nature of the treatment we give visitors but to the maturing of the academic subdiscipline of cliometrics. Work in this field may now be considered interesting and insightful by the broader economics profession, in which case it will be published in the main, broad-coverage journals. Or it may be considered accessible as well to the vast majority of the current generation of economic historians and so be publishable in the *Journal of Economic History,* which has a substantially larger circulation and a longer history of publication. So the niche filled by *Explorations* has changed necessarily as the field of cliometrics has evolved.

Currently, it seems devoted more to work produced by economic historians abroad. By the mid-1980s, for example, *Explorations* was the main outlet for cliometric publications in British economic history, whether produced by American, Canadian, Australian, or British authors, far surpassing the number published in the official journal of the British economic historians, the *Economic History Review.* As that journal has accepted more work with statistics and economic theory, however, and the mainline British journals have become increasingly receptive to publishing historical work, *Explorations* has received more and more work from continental Europe. We have published articles by Scandinavian, Dutch, German, Spanish, Italian, and French authors. On occasion, an issue will appear with no article on either an American or British topic. As the geographical frontier for the new economic history moves outward, so the niche for *Explorations* becomes increasingly international.

Within the economics profession, major research topics that bring in historical issues naturally—role of women in the labor force, economic–demographic relationships, financial innovations, monetary regimes, market integration, technical change—may generate a large volume of research papers, only a few of which are deemed publishable in the broad-coverage journals. *Explorations* often finds itself the recipient of the excess supply of these papers and in the position of alerting policy economists to the stricter scholarly standards of the economic history profession, which require fresh insights into historical issues, not mere validation of a new statistical technique enjoying its debut in the economics literature.

In an effort to elicit more promising papers in deficit areas, I initiated a series of survey articles entitled "Essays in Exploration." These are intended to alert economic historians to the potential in a new area of research, surveying the recent literature, and then identifying the issues that seem most promising for economic historians to pursue. Initially, these were invited, actually dragooned, but now appear fairly naturally in the course of normal manuscript flow. Authors may be concerned that their piece will be discounted as a nonrefereed article, but I do subject these manuscripts to refereeing as well and make them the lead article in the journal when they appear. It is not clear how effective these have been in generating a flow of manuscripts in the desired area— the payoff in these efforts is necessarily long-term and uncertain— but they certainly increase the visibility of the journal, as the survey article will become a standard citation in the future.

The outcome of these efforts has been gratifying. The manuscript flow continues to be healthy, even if from ever more distant ports of entry. The backlog of manuscripts is sufficiently large that the publishing deadlines for the editor are no longer a problem, but an author's manuscript will appear in print within a year or less of final acceptance. The quality of the final pieces has improved markedly, due to an ability to require one or more rounds of revisions from the authors.

And every once in a while, actually only once in a blue moon, the editor receives a gratuitous compliment for his efforts. A 1992 review article of periodical literature published in the British journal *Business History* included this unexpected encomium: "Were there an Oscar-style award for journal of the year my nomination for 1991 would be *Explorations in Economic History*. Its issues consistently covered both a wide subject area and a long time-period with a sense of intellectual excitement and informed risk-taking which was sometimes lacking in other journals." Needless to say, I have circulated photocopies of this far and wide.

Moreover, the journal continues to be commercially viable, thanks to an aggressive pricing policy directed at academic libraries and an international marketing organization built on the basis of Academic Press's scientific journals. The circulation is modest, but growing slowly over the years. The authorship has become increasingly international and the size of the journal has increased from four hundred to five hundred pages per year. It is abstracted in the *Journal of Economic Literature* as well as *Historical Abstracts* and various other abstracting services.

Policies

In common with most other economics journals, whether they are niche or broad-coverage publications, *Explorations* is a double-blind refereed journal—the author is not identified to the referees and the referees are not identified to the author, at least in principle. This means that after the editor has chosen two qualified referees for each manuscript submitted, he or she must remove any obvious features from the manuscript that might identify the author or authors to the referees. Further, the editor must pass on each referee's comments to the author in a neutral format which will conceal the referee's identity. Supposedly, this enables the referees to make objective, professional assessments of the manuscript without their personal opinions of the author influencing their recommendations one way or the other. It provides, ideally, a level playing field for junior scholars, perhaps submitting their first attempt at a journal publication from their dissertation, with senior scholars, perhaps producing yet another nearly identical product off the assembly line of their well-funded research projects. For the author, the referee reports can be taken as dispassionate appraisals and responded to in a similarly dispassionate, professional way, recognizing that misunderstandings that have arisen may be due to deficiencies in the presentation, if not in the research itself, and corrected by careful rewriting or by improved research methodology.

In fact, the system is as open to abuse as a hands-on, buddy system would be. It is difficult for authors to conceal their identities, even if they wished to do so, and most want to make as many self-references as possible so that even the most attentive editor cannot remove all clues to the author's identity. Further, most referees take it as an intellectual challenge to deduce the identity of the author, some finding it impossible, apparently, to make an appraisal of the manuscript without making simultaneously an appraisal of the author. Then, to compound the difficulty, some referees under the cloak of presumed anonymity will indulge in scathing remarks, intended to impress the editor by their erudite ridicule of the paper that he or she should never publish anything by the benighted, incompetent, nearly illiterate author. The editor may be impressed, but wonders how to relay these comments, typically from relatively junior members of the profession, to the author, who more than likely is a senior member of the profession with a lifetime's worth of accumulated academic enemies, or is the senior member's current star graduate student. Authors, in turn, may take offense at the apparent insensitivity of even well-meaning referees to their importance or their past record of accomplishment, and let the editor know about the incompetence of the referees—and the editor for selecting them in the first place.

The problem is compounded by the nature of the field of economic history, which requires minimum levels of competency in both economic analysis and historical inquiry. Consequently, most manuscripts need appraisals of both the economic content and the historical material. There is usually one hard-working economic historian capable of appraising the manuscript in both dimensions, but I have imposed the requirement of two referee's reports. So the second referee is typically chosen to compensate for the relative weakness of the first referee, whether it is with respect to the historical material or to the economic content. Moreover, as the journal's intended audience is the economics profession, an attempt is usually made to use an economist who has done recent research in the particular economic problem as one of the referees. So the problem of unwarranted contempt, encouraged in its expression by lack of familiarity with the author, or the referee, seems compounded in our case.

I have tried to deal with this in several ways. The most useful, in my opinion, has been to adapt a standard refereeing form used by the biochemistry journal published by Academic Press, and provide this to each referee along with the apparently anonymously authored manuscript. The form provides concise instructions for the standards of appraisal to be used, space for substantive comments to be provided, check boxes to give summary recommendations, and then a short space where confidential comments to the editor can be provided. In this way, referees can decide personally which of their comments they wish to make directly to the author and which they feel are best interceded through the editor. As editor, I can then act as an intermediary. It is then clear to the authors that they are dealing through me with two referees representing the potential professional audience for the paper, and not just with me as an arbitrary gatekeeper deciding on the basis of passing whims how far to open or close the gate. I can also interject my own weighting of the importance of comments from the historian referee or the economist referee. These may be nit-picking and just require more careful references or precautionary footnotes, or they may be quite basic and require complete reworking of the manuscript. Ultimately, I try to give the author a sense of how strongly I weigh the criticisms and suggestions made by each of the referees. Confining the referees' latitude in their evaluatory comments to the limits of a preprinted form may seem anti-intellectual, but I have found that it works effectively to maintain a professional demeanor in the dialogue that must take place between them and the author. In turn, this increases the effectiveness of the revisions made by the author in response.

A further problem arises in the case of non-Anglo-American authors, whom we are trying to encourage. They are often used to a different academic culture, one that partakes more of a patron–client relationship than of a competitive marketplace of ideas. Encouraging a potential author from this culture to submit work to the journal is typically taken as a guarantee of publication. Confronted with withering criticisms from the referees and a rejection letter from the editor, a European or Asian scholar may feel quite abused, as would an American or British academic receiving the same treatment. But instead of responding by revising the paper constructively and appealing to the good graces of the editor to reconsider, as might an Anglo-American author, he or she may just publish it elsewhere and warn colleagues to avoid the journal in the future. Compensation has to be made, therefore, in my decision letter, which will typically be one or two paragraphs longer for a foreign author, especially one whose native tongue is not English, than for one who may be judged acculturated to the sometimes harsh nature of refereed journals.

Similar care has to be taken with junior authors, who are submitting their first professional papers for peer review, either with or without the approval of their faculty advisors. Indeed, I try to read over the first-time submission papers more carefully than usual before selecting the referees. Referees are not paid for their services to this journal and they should not be asked to do the work of the graduate student's faculty advisor in addition to evaluating the merit of recent research in their field. If the work seems poorly presented or ill conceived, I will either send it back to the young scholar without refereeing it, explaining why it is not presentable in its present form, or send it to one of the two associate editors of the journal, Stanley Engerman at Rochester or Gavin Wright at Stanford. Both are senior scholars, well known for their careful work with their own students and for making constructive suggestions to colleagues who send them their working papers. This is a service to young scholars that they probably do not appreciate sufficiently, not realizing that once a referee has a bad impression of a piece of work, she or he is very unlikely to change the fundamental evaluation of its merit even after two or more revisions. The more polished the presentation and persuasive the argument and logic on the first draft, the more likely acceptance will come on first or second revisions of the paper.

Procedures

To help authors understand the importance of a professional presentation of their work in order to get it accepted for publication, it may be useful to describe the working procedures this editor uses in evaluating a manuscript. The first step is to identify the author: senior citizen to be treated deferentially, junior apprentice with a particular master craftsman in economic history, one of the master craftsmen in person, an economist trying to cross over to the economic history audience, an historian trying to communicate, or simply a seriously misguided individual. The next step is to identify the contribution of the paper: Is it another variant on a theme that has been played repeatedly and perhaps once too often in the journal, is it a completely novel contribution in terms of time period, geographic area, or economic problem, an attack on a previous article, or, usually, a minor but useful contribution to a topic area in which the journal has been establishing itself as one of the forums for presentation of results from major, ongoing research projects?

Once the identity of the author and topic is understood, then it is usually clear what kind of expertise I need in the referees. Usually one of the referees will be a match for the paper—same kind of author who has written on similar topics. More often than not, if the author is competent in his or her command of the literature, this referee will be cited in the list of references. But to maintain the continuity and identity of the journal, the other referee has to be one of the master craftsmen or an accomplished artisan. Usually this referee is drawn from the current membership of the editorial board. If the topic is just too novel, then the referee will end up being drawn from the past membership of the editorial board, or one of the associate editors, or, in truly desperate cases when time is running out, myself.

After the referees are chosen, the manuscript is stripped of obvious self-references by the author to conceal his or her identity and sent to the referees with the standard referee form and the standard cover letter. I have deliberately made this as neutral in tone as possible, making no appeal to the referee's sense of noblesse oblige or professional pride, and, as mentioned earlier, no pecuniary incentive is offered either. Instead, they are asked to review it within the next six weeks if they are able, or to return it if they are not, perhaps suggesting alternative referees.

It has been a source of amazement and much comfort to me that very few individuals refuse to respond positively at least to some degree to my requests. The cover letter with the accompanying manuscript is, after all, nothing more than an onerous overture. I suspect the blind refereeing ploy is a large part of the reason for the favorable response rate. Most academics cannot resist trying to figure out what the paper is about or who the author is, so they will almost always take a look at the paper. Having done that, they will be drawn in to read the entire paper if I have guessed correctly that it is on a topic interesting to them. Once a referee has read a paper, the bulk of the work has been done and it is usually an easy matter to write up the referee report, following the form prescribed—at least it will be after a reminder letter arrives from me in six to eight weeks. The task of the referees is made easier by the fact that their identities are withheld from the author and that I deliberately provide space for them to convey confidential remarks to me that are not to be passed on to the author.

But even this does not explain why economic historians in general, in contrast to the typical economist, take such pains to write detailed, constructive comments and often return their copy of the paper with marginal comments and copyediting remarks intended to aid the author in presenting the material more effectively. After a decade of observing this commitment to excellence and improvement among my colleagues in economic history, I am forced to conclude it is in the nature of the field. As one of the members of the editorial board remarked to me years ago, economic history is a field populated by a few individuals who are very bright, well informed with broad interests, very productive, and who are not in it for money. That does not make it an attractive field for graduate students in economics—the point he was making at the time—but it does make the life of an editor of a journal in the field much easier. Perhaps editors in other fields find comparable experiences—I certainly hope so.

When the referee reports are back, either from the original referees or substitutes, I have to make a decision. This can be to accept the article as is, which is very rare—less than once a year, perhaps only once a decade; accept, subject to only minor revisions, usually in presentation without further substantive research— also rare except after one or more revisions already made; accept, subject to major revisions requiring new research work and subsequent rewriting of the paper with perhaps reorganization as well; reject in its present form but encourage revision and resubmission if the author finds the referee comments constructive and feasible; reject but allow the possibility of looking at a completely redone paper on the same topic once the author has digested the harsh comments of the referees; reject outright; reject and actively discourage any further submissions on this topic—usually after two or more failed attempts to revise in response to the referees.

It is intriguing then to discover the varied responses of authors. There are some files still awaiting a promised revision after years have gone by. There are revisions received in response to what I had thought were the firmest of rejection letters. There are, I blush to admit, puzzled responses about receiving the wrong referee reports or, on one occasion, the wrong decision letter. But, just when I think I have made every conceivable mistake an editor could make, I am encouraged to carry on by the discovery that I have just made a new one.

7

Gatekeeping among the Demographers

✳

Avery M. Guest

I served as editor of *Demography,* the journal of the Population Association of America (PAA), from 1991 to 1993. I was elected to the position by the PAA Board of Directors, who were, in turn, elected by the members.

The job was virtually full-time and involved many pressures, especially related to decisions on manuscripts. Some 200–250 manuscripts were submitted each year. From these, my journal published four issues and roughly forty research articles per year. Over four thousand copies of each issue were printed, and most major academic libraries subscribed.

I came to the position with at least moderately high hopes about personally affecting the discipline through my editorial decisions, perhaps as an outgrowth of my observations about other editors from the somewhat distant vantage point of author. But, in fact, I had a fairly minor (but still real) effect on the discipline.

This essay is primarily about the constraints that severely limited (although not eliminated) my power as editor. My central point is that the history and organization of the demographic profession created an intellectual and social community that exerted tremendous influence over my actions. The key factors that constrained my behavior were (1) the high consensus within the discipline on important substantive issues and methods and (2) the dense social networks or ties among demographic scholars. These constraints led to a moral contract between me as the editor and the demographic profession that was implicit but nevertheless very real.

By the end of my editorship, I felt great personal satisfaction, but not in the ways that I had originally envisioned. In particular,

I became more consciously proud of demography as an academic discipline; and increasingly I experienced pleasure in working with authors to produce high-quality manuscripts. In addition, I learned a tremendous amount about the field of demography. I became a mini-expert in numerous areas, and developed a sense of personal efficacy that flows from mastery of something.

The rest of this essay is really an elaboration of these points. To understand me as "gatekeeper," I must first discuss the community that influenced my actions, including (1) the nature of demography as a scholarly field, (2) the history of *Demography* as a journal, and (3) my selection as editor. I shall then show how, as editor, I behaved within the implicit moral contract (what might be called "wheeling and dealing"). There are really three types of dealings that need to be emphasized—with goals, with reviewers, and with authors.

Demography as Discipline

Academic disciplines may be categorized along a number of dimensions, but a key one is the degree of consensus on substantive issues and research approaches (Hargens, 1975, 1988). The field of demographic studies would definitely score high on the consensus end, especially among the social science disciplines. As editor, I had few degrees of freedom to change the journal subject matter/orientation, even if I had wanted to.

There are several definitions of demography as a field. The most common one, by Hauser and Duncan (1959, pp. 29–45), argues that demography is the study of the size, territorial distribution, and composition of populations, and how these change over time. The major components of change are fertility, mortality, and migration (or social mobility). Population studies, often considered the study of the relationships of the demographic variables to larger social and economic variables, turn the demographer into a social scientist. In practice, demographers have most often focused on the social causes of variations in fertility, mortality, migration rates, and population distribution patterns. As Preston (1993) points out, demographic research has been unusually responsive (relative to other social sciences) to demand factors such as short-term patterns of world population growth, changes in fertility and mortality, and the evolving nature of the family.

Historically, social science demography developed with three different (and not always compatible) constituencies—university academics, bureaucratic scholars, and family planners.

Academic demography is typically housed in sociology departments, often the most prestigious ones. While most sociologists share little consensus on methods, theories, and topics, the demographic model of research has been closer to that of many natural and biological sciences. Usually, the demographic shops have had a star researcher who sets the tone for research and training. Faculty and students have frequently collaborated on research topics, with many resulting coauthored papers. Many newly minted Ph.D.s from these programs have been traded with other shops, either as faculty members or post-docs, and many of the Ph.D.s have been sent out to other sociology departments (the "provinces") to serve as their token demographers.

The various demographic shops do differ in their orientations, with some clear implications for the types of manuscripts reviewed by the journal. Yet, to the outsider, academic demography probably seems like a monolithic discipline.

Most demographers, especially male, are "super straight." They were the nerds in high school—the kids who liked algebra and trigonometry and were great at memorizing the dates of rule for various British monarchs. Due to their relatively conventional personalities, demographers tend not to be troublemakers. They are largely accepting of conventional issues, including research topics and approaches. As a result, they feel most comfortable writing quantitative papers that make incremental contributions to previous literature. It is my observation that, in contrast, many academic sociology departments are filled with "deviant" personalities, often attracted to the study of society by a preoccupation with their alienation from it.

Demography also has other "practical" constituencies (beyond the academics) that have developed as a result of two factors. One is the worldwide interest in the high rates of population growth by historical standards. The other is the rise of state planning, with an associated need to measure and analyze broad social trends on such topics as the family, population distribution, and the labor force.

One practical demographer is the researcher hired by many bureaucracies, such as governments and foundations, to understand the underlying social causes of demographic phenomena. Most of these bureaucratic demographers serve applied goals, but they share the scientific model (and personal style) of the academic researcher.

Another practical demographer is the family planning expert, often hired to help in the development and implementation of contraceptive programs around the world, to reduce fertility rates. While these demographers typically have a scientific orientation, they are much more politicized in their outlooks. Fundamentally, they see family planning as the way to reduce population growth, and they tend to view scholarship as closely melded with political action.

Demographers have struggled with each other and their consciences for years over the question of whether the discipline should be scientific (try to understand the problems) as opposed to applied (solve the problems). The scientists have maintained clear dominance in the PAA, and, except for a brief time, there has never been much doubt that *Demography* should reflect this orientation.

In recent years, the subject matter in the field has broadened to encompass "family demography," involving such topics as marriage, divorce, parent–child interactions, child care, and female roles as housewives versus wage workers (Teachman, Paasch, & Carver, 1993). This has brought many female scholars into the discipline, but may have also resulted from the unusual historical prominence of women in the field. In addition, there have been numerous statistical advances in analyzing categorical data that have opened topics that were previously difficult to study (Allison, 1984). Family demography has especially benefited from these advances because many of the major events (marrying, divorcing, having a spouse die, bearing a child) are categorical.

The growth of interest in family demography has also made the field more interdisciplinary. In particular, many economists have become interested in theories of family behavior; those with an orientation toward empirical analysis have particularly been attracted to demography. In addition, researchers from fields such as anthropology, geography, and public health have shown a growing interest in demographic studies.

In many respects, demography as a discipline has what sociologists might describe as a gemeinschaft (folk) quality (Lyon, 1987, pp. 3–16). The annual meeting draws about 1,200 individuals; many participants know each other, and there is an easy camaraderie. It is like a big family reunion, with the different major demographic centers being various wings of the family, and most participants claiming some relationship to the major demographic centers.

Because of the often strong interpersonal bonds, scholarly critiques at paper sessions tend to be gentle. There are as many bad as good papers presented, but an outsider would often not realize this from the nature of the discussion. Participants in the paper sessions rarely receive enough help to turn weak papers into publishable ones. This occurs even though the discussants at most of the sessions are competent to make searching critiques; yet, it would seem unfriendly and anticommunal to do so.

The editor, elected by the PAA board and a committee on publications, is generally known personally by the selectors before being picked for the office. Specific candidates for editor will only be selected if they view demography as fundamentally a scientific profession (and reject political activism in their professional roles), have published on mainline demographic topics, believe in the prevailing positivist methodologies of the field, and have been associated with some leading figures in the field. The editor does not have to be a distinguished scholar, but distinguished scholars must vouch for him or her.

Demography as a Journal

The journal was established in 1964, largely through the efforts of Donald J. Bogue, an energetic demographic entrepreneur. In his personal interests, he bridged the scientific and family planning wings of the discipline. Bogue had to sell the idea of the journal to the PAA leaders; some thought *Demography* would fail because there were other scholarly outlets that existed for demographic research, including sociology and other population journals (Bogue, 1983). But Bogue persisted, served as editor for five years, and established the journal as a leading social science publication.

Bogue's best-known act was running a special issue on family planning as his last edition of the journal (Vol. 5, No. 2). While the articles had some scholarly pretense, a number (especially the summary pieces) were clearly directed to the notion that demographers should be solving the population problem by distributing contraceptives. The reaction from the dominant scientific wing of the discipline was severe. The scientists solidified their hold on the PAA Board of Directors and exerted careful subsequent control over the selection of the editor, so that only other "scientists" were seriously considered.

After Bogue's tenure, the journal's editor was selected for a three-year term, with the general implicit notion that the editorial offices would be moved among the major demographic scientific centers. Except for minor deviations, this policy has been followed for over twenty-five years. No center has had the editorship more than once, and almost every major center has had a turn.

While the editor can control the competence and political orientation of the articles, there is little ability to control the topics or approaches. The well-defined nature of the field and the orientation to scientific analysis of quantitative data greatly constrains the submitted articles. In addition, the trend toward family demography, using categorical statistical techniques, has had a major effect on the types of submissions.

While the contract of the PAA with its editor has never been written down, the whole history of the organization has created a strong moral understanding. Fundamentally, the PAA views the editor as having an obligation to uphold universalistic norms of a scientific community, although implicit ideologies may affect the articles published (Watkins, 1993). In addition, there is a belief that the editor must behave in terms of the social obligations of a gemeinschaft community. The terms of the implicit moral contract include the following:

1. You are part of a larger intellectual community, and you are in this position of power only because of its grace; being arbitrary or cranky will not be tolerated.

2. Each demographic center is important, and just because you have the editorship, you should not assume you are morally or intellectually superior.

3. In three years (when your term ends), Center X will have the right to judge your work, and thus be careful in your judgment of scholars from Center X.

4. You have the obligation to treat your peers with understanding and respect.

5. You have an obligation to communicate reasoned, somewhat detailed rationales for editorial decisions. This last point is especially crucial, for the PAA membership would never be comfortable with the form rejection letters that are sent out by many journal editors in other disciplines.

While the quality of the post-Bogue editors has varied greatly, I know of none who has violated the implicit contract. Indeed, as each successive editor behaves according to expectations, the implicit contract has become more sharply drawn, making rule violation more difficult.

Becoming Editor

Becoming a demographer was for me something of an accident, but it must have been preordained. As a child, I always had a great interest in two seemingly unrelated things: (1) the nature of social behavior, and (2) counting things. I was an avid newspaper reader, and I loved books about history and biography. I was also an obsessive counter—the kid who kept track of all the baseball player batting averages. I always loved math, but knew that I did not want to be a mathematician.

After devoting myself to journalism throughout school and my early postgraduate years, I decided to get a master's degree in sociology at the University of Wisconsin (Madison). There, I had a course in urbanism and urbanization, from Leo Schnore. It was a great course for me, because Schnore was interested in social theory and analysis, moving beyond simple description. Importantly, he also seemed to love counting as much as I did. I was hooked, and in 1970 obtained a Ph.D. in sociology at Madison with a focus on demography.

I have never been considered a star in sociology or demography, but I do not look back with regret. I have published many articles on many subjects (demographic and nondemographic). Almost all have involved counting, although I have published a few qualitative articles. It has been a great feast for me.

In 1989, I decided that I wanted to do something in my career besides pure research and teaching undergraduate courses (which was largely my lot at the University of Washington). Being a somewhat rambunctious personality, I surmised that I would never be selected as an administrative leader in the Sociology Department or university. Thus, I decided to apply for the editorship of *Demography,* which became open, as the previous editor finished a three-year term in May 1990.

I believe that, as is true of many things, I became a gatekeeper somewhat by accident. At first, the selection committee tried to recruit the greats and near-greats to the editorship, and some were interested. But most of the true-greats were too great to do this kind of grunt work, and so they fell by the wayside.

In the end, the contest was largely between a better-known demographer at one of the leading centers and me. This seems to be a common example from the history of *Demography* editor selections; only a very small number of candidates ever apply. Fortunately for me, the other candidate came from a center that already had a leading social science journal, and another demographer there previously had held the editorship of *Demography.* I received the appointment because it did not seem fair (in the egalitarian, gemeinschaft style of the PAA) to give it to him.

Appointments to positions, certainly in the PAA, are also a

reflection of social networks. I was helped because one of the original members of the selection committee was a close colleague at Washington. While he immediately withdrew from the selection process when I became a candidate, his charismatic personality undoubtedly generated pressure to pick me. In addition, another member of the selection committee was a colleague of a distinguished academic friend of mine.

Other factors in my selection were probably the diversity of topics in my research and my ambiguous identification with the various demography shops around the country. Consistent with the selection of other leaders, editors are often picked because they will not offend anyone too much, or at least they will offend equally. I am a person who offends equally, and this undoubtedly helped.

As editor, I spent most of my time reading manuscripts, assigning reviewers, writing letters to authors, and handling angry complaints from authors. It is a fascinating job, but one should do it for only a few years. There are so many moral choices to make; even the most pure of us cannot make the right choice 100 percent of the time. At the end of my term, I was not quite sure whether to declare myself emperor for life or to confess all my sins to the nearest parish priest.

Wheeling and Dealing

Dealing with Goals

Upon becoming editor, I struggled with the formulation of editorial goals. What type of journal should be produced in terms of topics, methods, and approaches? Obviously, we wanted to publish the best articles available. But this idea carried few specific implications.

Given the constraints of previous editors, it was clear that there were some political things I had to do. I knew (1) that the journal had to be scientific, rather than family-planning oriented; (2) that a broad definition of demographic subject matter had to be tolerated, consistent with directions of the field, and (3) that different demographic shops and topics needed to appear.

After becoming editor, I received remarkably few suggestions from other demographers or official directives from the PAA Board. The board did decide, after I served one year, that the range of papers in the journal was "too narrow in scope." But multiple members of the board apologized to me for this position.

Superficially, it was like I had been appointed absolute monarch for three years. Indeed, given the lack of demand for the editor's job, the PAA would have a severe problem in replacing me if I "got out of hand." But, in reality, I knew that I had implicitly agreed on a contract with the PAA membership. They needed to warn me of that only if I violated the agreement. In addition, I knew that highly personalistic decisions on my part would lead to a "trashy" reputation for the journal, bringing shame to the profession and me.

I had a wonderful deputy editor, Diane Lye, who was an untenured assistant professor at Washington. Since Lye did not have tenure, it was clear that her actual work on the journal would have to be minimized in the interest of producing published research of her own. Yet, Lye was an indispensable sounding board; she was most helpful in talking about each manuscript with me. Lye and I mostly agreed, but I always depended on her to tell me "the right thing to do." Even though a relatively young person, she had extensive experience with the culture of demographers and the PAA. She knew the implicit contract, too, and she had a terrific ability to remind me of it, when I deviated.

In terms of personal goals, I had been impressed by my conversations with the previous editor, Gordon De Jong of Penn State. His primary criterion of publishing competently executed articles was the degree to which they advanced research and theorizing in demography. In other words, De Jong asked whether the implications of the paper were general, both in affecting other research on this topic and research on all topics in demography. Lye and I called this the "so what?" question.

While this criterion may seem superficially trivial, I think it is very important. During my editorship, I repeatedly asked the implications question about the research, particularly in marginal or ambiguous cases. To satisfy the "so what?" question, authors did not have to produce papers of high theoretical importance, but they did have to convince me that the findings clearly advanced demography as a research field. Of course, one may miss the implications of a paper or not completely understand them, but I was amazed at how often I agreed with other readers of papers on this issue. This consensus on evaluation primarily reflected a high consensus among demographers on the primary substantive issues and means to address them.

I also had an interest in trying to increase the number of papers that had a "macro" orientation to demographic phenomena. Much demographic research during the years preceding my editorship had been based on surveys that collected the responses of individuals, typically in the United States. This survey approach to demography has been especially facilitated by the development of several national data files that either collected extensive cross-sectional information or followed individuals over several time points. While surveys are important, it seemed to me that demography needed to consider how broader social structure (such as urbanization and industrialization) related to demographic patterns such as fertility rates. This, of course, also meant more cross-cultural research.

A final goal involved minimizing the number of published papers that were essentially self-contained statistical exercises. Fortunately, many had come to the field (as I did) because they liked to count. Unfortunately, a number had a preoccupation with the counting or manipulation of equations but could not explain to anyone why it was interesting. While I was not especially successful with many of my goals, I did follow through on this one, often to the anger of authors who felt that the elegance of their statistics could overcome any lack of implications for the social world around us. Apparently, the word got out on my policy, because the number of self-contained statistical exercises decreased over my editorship.

Having submitted lots of papers to journals (with mixed success), I assumed that the editor would actually have a great deal of influence over the contents of the journal. I also thought that I was uniquely qualified to spot some underrated papers that would be brought to the attention of the readers.

What I actually discovered was:

1. A large proportion of submitted papers have some really serious methodological or theoretical flaws that make them unlikely to ever be publishable, in my journal or others. Given the agreement on issues and approaches in the field, it was usually easy to identify serious problems with manuscripts.

Given the consensus in the field, why were so many flawed manuscripts submitted? One factor was the origin of many manuscripts from scholars outside the major center network. These scholars were often uninformed about the latest issues and techniques. Many flawed manuscripts also came from recent Ph.D.s (typically from the major centers) who were trying to publish the results of their dissertation research. In most of the demographic centers, there is only half-hearted supervision of work by graduate students, and, as a result, they are improperly socialized in how to write a journal article.

But established scholars from major demographic centers were also often adept at sending bad manuscripts (some were very good too). In many cases, the bad papers seemed to have been written by committee with no one taking responsibility to integrate the material in a central coherent statement. In other cases, I think that these submissions stemmed from the hurried pace of much demographic research. Major demographic entrepreneurs maintain their reputations and centers by juggling large sums of money over several grants. Too often, little time is available to devote to specific reports.

2. Most manuscripts are not especially good or bad. They are just OK. The distribution of paper quality follows a fairly normal distribution, with the mean somewhere between fair and good. One rarely has the opportunity to chose whether to publish one good manuscript as opposed to another. The issue is usually whether the manuscript at hand is good enough to publish.

Before becoming editor, I had surmised (mainly from conversations with colleagues) that there were a lot of brilliant, but erratic papers out there. In other words, fellow demographers were producing papers with numerous insights but only weak or controversial documentation. It simply was not true. Most demographers are really just fairly ordinary above-average people. In addition, the operational style of most centers and the personal styles of most scholars within them encourage numerous incremental contributions rather than selected "break through" reports.

3. People usually submit to the journal what they want to submit, and they tend to ignore any priorities that the editor sets. Research topics in demography seem to be influenced primarily by funding trends and by the general directions of previous research. Some researchers will strike off in new directions, if a particularly innovative article or idea appears. However, most follow-ups of innovative work are not very innovative.

Consistent with my hope for a more macro orientation, I tried to organize a special issue on the study of longitudinal fertility declines across societies. I wrote letters to several individuals and requested their participation. After receiving hardly any submissions, I canceled the special issue.

4. Regardless of specific methods, theories, or findings, most papers are poorly written—even those that are potentially publishable. You almost always have to make authors rewrite or reorganize their papers in order to get them published.

Some of the problems with writing are understandable. Many authors try to "sell" their papers in fairly general terms or as making general contributions to the literature, but do not tell the readers very clearly in the initial stages what they actually plan to do in the paper. This is understandable because the author wants to convince the reader and the editor that the work is really very important, even though it is probably not.

Many other authors heavily overwrite their papers, making them much longer and detailed than they need to be. Since the papers are overwritten, it is often difficult to distinguish the important points. This is understandable because the author does not want to be rejected for leaving something out of the article.

5. Reviewer comments really constrain the editor in what can be published. Given the consensus on methods and issues in demography, most reviewer recommendations are quite similar. As editor, I generally faced a common front from my reviewers on the issue of whether the paper was satisfactory or not.

Since authors receive the reviewer comments, they have some sense of whether they have been had by the editor. In other words, they can tell (to some degree) whether the reviewer likes their paper. Woe to the editor who rejects a paper that the reviewers like. Yet, few papers receive really positive reviews, and thus some of the burden of rejection by the editor can be transferred to the anonymous reviewers.

6. A number of articles are published as a consequence of bureaucratic inertia. Very few papers were ready for publication on first submission. In order to fill the journal, I handed out a large number of invitations to revise and resubmit. It was difficult to tell how good the paper might become with additional work, but one had to send the invitations. In some cases, authors of potentially very good papers never bothered to revise them. In other cases, authors revised but essentially ignored all the major suggestions; there was no choice but to reject what might have been a very good paper. In still other instances, authors revised papers according to the suggestions, but the paper was still blah. However, it was necessary to publish the paper because the author had followed the directions.

Yet, while these observations minimize the importance of editor as gatekeeper, I did have some real impact in deciding which papers were published. Because extremely few papers receive rave reviews, the editor must "save" some papers in order to fill the journal.

In retrospect, my decisions on which papers to save were quite mysterious. While giving little conscious thought to the choices at the time, I probably acted heavily from some sense of distributive justice. Given the strong social solidarity of the field, it was important to make sure that all the major population centers and substantive topics were represented in our pages. In addition, it was important to keep open lines to new emerging topics, such as family demography, and to academics (particularly economists) from other disciplines who were dancing at the margins of the demographic field.

I also probably had some tendency to save papers on topics that I knew something about. As a specialist in urban population spatial distributions, I found that I could easily identify the problems with and solutions to the research in this area. In contrast, I often felt hopelessly lost when trying to advise authors on how to understand the correlates of child care choice or how to improve stable population theory. Some may think that I actually favored publishing an unusual number of papers in my specialty area, but I think not. The results might seem to support a Machiavellian view of what gets published, but I decided the process was more fumbling and not especially rationalistic.

Dealing with Reviewers

Most papers submitted to the journal are deemed worthy of outside review by experts in the substantive area. *Demography* generally sought three reviews of each submitted manuscript, although often had to accept two to complete the review process within a reasonable period of two to three months.

Reviewers are crucial gatekeepers since they are generally experts on the research topic of the paper, and they provide an overall thumbs up or thumbs down recommendation. Given the traditions of the demographic profession, it would have been unthinkable for me to ignore reviewer input for competent submissions.

Editors need to obtain high-quality reviews (to make a scholarly judgment), and they need to obtain them quickly (so that authors do not become irked at the time length of manuscript consideration). In addition, I needed to obtain lots of reviews; remember we had over two hundred submissions per year.

For most scholars, the tangible benefits of reviewing manuscripts are low. They can keep up with research trends in their field by reviewing, but a high proportion of manuscripts is not very good. In addition, they can claim general recognition on their vita by listing their reviewer status for various journals, but the importance of this honor quickly wears off once a few papers have been reviewed.

Mostly, scholars review because they feel it is an obligation to the community. It is a symbol of social solidarity with the profession, in this case, demography. Due to the strong social integration of the demographic field, most invited persons cooperate. Some scholars, especially young ones, help as reviewers because they feel honored to be asked.

My greatest gold mine of reviewers was Australia, where a small but strong colony of academic demographers survives. I can recall only one Australian demographer turning me down for a review. One colleague explained that the Australians are hungry for intellectual contact with the rest of the world.

While always amazed at how many individuals would do reviews, I was often frustrated, too, by the high proportions (at least one-third) of invited reviewers who would not serve. Much of my time as editor was spent trying to find suitable reviewers of papers. In many circumstances, I was gasping to find any reviewers for a manuscript, much less a highly qualified expert.

Unfortunately, those who are too busy to do reviews are a specific subsection of the discipline. They are drawn disproportionately from older, established scholars who should be the most informed readers. These scholars have little personal incentive to do reviews, and they are also besieged by many outlets for their opinions and their time. The direction of *Demography* was heavily influenced by young scholars, who were often conscientious but disproportionately lacked experience in judging the overall value of research. In particular, younger scholars emphasized methodological skills in their evaluations, rather than the "so what?" question.

I also found that those with peripheral intellectual involvement or training in demography were often unwilling to review. While I wanted to expand the number of articles by economists, I was often frustrated in finding reviewers in that field; many economists apparently feel their time (the opportunity cost) is too valuable to spend in reviewing papers.

High proportions of reviewers hold manuscripts for relatively long time periods (about two months), even though a review may typically be done in one or two hours, at most. I am convinced that holding manuscripts is a form of communication from reviewer to editor. While the reviewer is willing to review, he or she is also signaling his or her status relative to editor and author by deferring the review. In addition, the reviewer is symbolizing the degree to which the field exerts social control over the editor.

We sent stamped, self-addressed postcards to our reviewers with the manuscripts so they could indicate whether they would help. Even if high-status colleagues eventually do reviews, they tend not to return the postcards before sending in the review. Again, this mainly symbolizes the power and status of the reviewer relative to the editor.

Since I was not well informed about many research areas in demography, I had a somewhat haphazard approach to selecting reviewers. The following were some of my sources:

1. A list of reviewers with their areas of expertise was provided by the previous editor.

2. The annual programs of the PAA yielded the names of papers and authors, and one could look for scholars on topics similar to the manuscript at hand.

3. Reference lists in submitted papers provided a ready-made directory of potential experts in that paper's subject.

I also frequently used authors of papers under submission as reviewers for other papers on similar topics. This was a trick that frequently worked, as most such authors were willing to help out. However, even some of those authors refused to review the manuscripts of others.

In the best of all worlds, I should obtain the most competent reviewers for each paper. This was unlikely, however, given my limited knowledge of many research areas and the reluctance of many individuals to review. In addition, so many manuscripts were submitted on specific topics that I could not repeatedly ask the most competent people to review.

Yet, in my view, the reviews were amazingly helpful. I had anticipated that the reviewers would frequently disagree and that the similarity of reviewer–author intellectual perspective would be crucial in the tone of the reviews. I actually found very high agreement on manuscript quality among reviewers, especially on major points of concern. This pattern was quite different from that reported for the more general social science journal, *The American Sociological Review* (Marwell, 1992). In addition, the reviewer's intellectual perspective seemed to have little influence on evaluation.

Clearly, the consensus among reviewers was related to the high integration of the demographic profession. The reviewers shared an agreement on the major topics and methods, but more generally they held to a notion of scientific objectivity. The facts could speak for themselves, or at least the facts as viewed from the prevailing intellectual perspectives.

The major problem for reviewers (and, in turn, for the editor) is what to recommend as the fate of each submitted article when reporting to the editor. Reviewers are trapped in a situation in which they do not know the evaluations of the other reviewers. As a consequence, they are extremely reluctant to go out on a limb with either a very strongly positive or negative recommendation on a paper. Most reviewers suggest that papers should be revised, even if they have fairly serious problems. They also have some tendency to find fault with very good papers, even though they are quite deserving of publication. As I have suggested above, the editor is often forced to be more positive about some papers to save them for publication.

I really believe that the reviewers ran *Demography*, which was consistent with the democratic spirit of the PAA. Most of my contributions involved saving manuscripts in marginal cases and getting authors to rewrite their papers so that they were economical and clear in presentation.

Due to the gemeinschaft nature of demography, I had to provide some exchange for my reviewers. For many years, the journal has published annually a list of reviewers. We also sent form thank-you letters to each reviewer, and I usually tried to insert a brief handwritten note to indicate my appreciation. Copies of all the reviews and my letter to the author (with all name identification removed) were enclosed with the thank-you letter. These tactics may have ingratiated me to some, but, in the end, I think that most people reviewed because they felt a loyalty to the demographic profession.

Dealing with Authors

As editor, I rejected at least 75 percent of the manuscripts, but experienced little guilt about the vast majority of the specific decisions. After reading the reviews, perusing the paper myself, and talking with my deputy editor, I rarely had serious doubts on the strengths or weaknesses of a paper, or on what should be done with it. But rejecting papers is a very difficult task, not only because one leaves a trail of disappointed colleagues but also because the means of communicating the decision may have important influences on the social solidarity of the discipline.

As I have indicated above, reviewers for *Demography* rarely indicate that papers should be rejected, even when they identify critical problems. I do not know whether this is true of other journals, but, in the case of *Demography*, it stems at least partially from the gemeinschaft nature of the profession.

The buck stops with the editor. I had to identify the potentially publishable papers, and I had to do it decisively. Of course, one reason is that there is only so much space to publish articles. But more importantly, in the long run, the profession would not tolerate a journal filled with shoddy papers. In addition, I had to reject decisively a high proportion of the submissions because we could not feasibly consider repeated revisions. No matter how kind in their recommendations, most reviewers would not read manuscripts repeatedly, and I could never find enough bodies to do all the reviewing.

As true of many roles, the editor skirts a thin line between being authentic and being a good politician in dealing with authors. In being authentic, one wants to communicate a reasoned, specific judgment on why the paper failed. In an intellectual community, authors need to know where they went wrong. This helps in their personal education, but it is also important to emphasize the principle of constructive criticism in our academic relationships with each other.

In being a politician, the editor simply wants to avoid the interpersonal antagonisms that almost always result from criticizing the work of others. Furthermore, criticism of individuals has broader group implications because most studies arose out of shops or traditions in the profession that have long, eminent histories. By being critical of individual work, one almost always runs the danger of saying that certain streams of work are not valid.

While the editor acts as politician to protect himself or herself, there is also a need in an organization such as the PAA for the editor to act politically to preserve the broader integrity of the profession. Through communication with authors, the editor wants to emphasize the continued importance of the enterprise—doing high-quality demographic research.

Many editors of social science journals handle the struggles between politician and authenticity by emphasizing the former. Typically in cases of rejection, form letters are sent to each author, usually indicating that the journal received many good submissions but cannot publish them all due to a shortage of space. Given my nature, I probably erred on the side of authenticity. I typically wrote one- to two-page letters in which I explained specifically why the paper was being rejected.

While still being critical, editors can deal with authors in ways that minimize conflict and maintain the "integrity of the profession." Some of my tactics are listed below.

1. Emphasize as much as possible the similarity of evaluation

among the reviewers and the editors. Always emphasize the judgment of the profession as opposed to individuals.

2. Emphasize the importance of the De Jong goal of "contribution to the profession," and the specific ways that the paper at hand contributes or fails to contribute.

3. Emphasize your inherent interest in the topic they are writing about. This was generally easy for me, as I did find most of the topics to be interesting.

4. Emphasize that problems with the paper relate more to specific issues of logic and technique rather than to fundamental approach or intellectual perspective. Nothing seems to anger authors as much as being attacked for their theology of how to study demographic issues. Indeed, we have so few accepted answers to questions in the social sciences that most such attacks on theology are unwarranted.

5. Emphasize the specific ways in which papers may be improved. Always provide hope to the author that there is a potential publication somewhere down the road.

6. Emphasize the certainty of your judgment but the possible unreliability of it. Reviewing papers is really an art rather than a science, and just about everyone realizes it. One does not want to communicate indecision to the author, for one will be clearly branded as a wavering fool. At the same time, one does not want to come on as a zealot of the truth either, because just about all demographers realize (if only deep in their hearts) that the one way to truth has not arrived.

The other major problem of the editor–author relationship is how to deal with revisions. Just as reviewers emphasize their status relative to editors by delaying the return of reviews, many editors emphasize their status relative to authors by handling requests for revision in protracted and relatively arbitrary ways. In addition, editors indicate their disdain for the authors by investing little time in the evaluation of their work.

In sociology, editors usually request revisions by writing letters to the authors that put the invitation in quite vague terms. Generally, the authors are told to respond to the reviewers' comments, which are almost always all over the map. Some of the criticisms are very good, but others are just foolish. When the author responds, the editor sends the paper back to a set of reviewers for another few months. Then, a decision is made, but it often seems arbitrary to the author because no clear rules for the revision were established by the editor.

In the more gemeinschaft community of demography, I decided

that the editor owed the authors a better deal. Indeed, I doubt that the demographic profession would have tolerated well the typical procedure for handling revisions. As a result, I took quite seriously every potential invitation for revision. First, I indicated to each author whether the manuscript could be published with only minor revision or required more fundamental reworking (a long-shot). Then, I listed the specific things in the paper that needed to be corrected, and how this might be done. Finally, I told the author that publication would be forthcoming if the contract were met. Generally, I made decisions on revisions a few days after receiving them. I read them, determined whether the contract had been followed, and then made a decision.

While others might disagree with my procedures for dealing with authors, I felt that they were crucial for the social solidarity of the discipline. I took a lot of hits for being an icky editor, but I think that few saw this as part of a larger plot to sabotage or push one view of demography. I feel that my dealings with the authors maintained the profession, which was really the key issue.

Did my dealings with authors affect the number/quality of the manuscripts submitted to the journal? I doubt it. Over my three years as editor, I noticed little overall trend in number of submissions, quality of submissions, or the subject matter of the submissions.

Conclusion

As I write this, *Demography* is in transition to a new editor. While we are very different individuals in many respects, I am amazed at our similarity in many characteristics that are crucial to the operation of the journal. We are positivists, users of survey and census data, enthusiastic about demographic research and the profession, committed to generally sociological interpretations of demographic phenomena, published in the same journals, and oriented to eclectic theoretical and methodological perspectives. The name on the masthead will change but the gatekeepers will not. My guess is that future editors will be very similar to us.

I have talked only very briefly with the new editor, but I am struck by the degree to which she shares my view of demography as a community of scholars (rather than just a group of scholars). In addition, the notion of the implicit moral contract also seems very important. In our discussions, it is clear that she will act not only in terms of what she wants but also in response to what she views as the expectations of the PAA membership.

The future content of *Demography* will be heavily driven by what I call the technology or "the means of production" of scholarly research. New techniques of data analysis will develop, making outmoded some of our current knowledge, although not necessarily the major substantive topics (for a further discussion, see Preston, 1993). The field of demography has seen a perpetual methods revolution in the past two decades, and there is no reason to believe it has ended. To get published, one will have to know the new techniques and use them well.

Another key factor in the gatekeeping future of *Demography* will be trends in population growth and composition. Yet, since demographic patterns are not abruptly shifting, the journal's tone will probably change little. On the international front, we still face high rates of population growth (by historical standards), and much of the variation across countries reflects differences in fertility levels. As long as this pattern continues, research will emphasize studies of fertility and the family. On the U.S. domestic front, increasing rates of in-migration from abroad, along with festering racial inequalities, have led to high interest in the composition of the U.S. population. Undoubtedly, many future accepted articles will include variables that measure ethnic and racial differences, either as causes or consequences of social behavior. In addition, the aging of the U.S. population, due to low fertility and declining mortality at older ages, will be a prime stimulus for *Demography* papers.

The general continuity of the journal will also probably be facilitated by continued concentration of most research in a few scholarly centers. Funded by relatively large sums of federal and foundation moneys, these centers will move in the direction of new research topics but will try to maintain their traditional interests. The articles that receive positive readings from outside reviewers will primarily come from these centers, and few others will have a realistic chance of publishing in the journal.

At the end of their three-year terms, future *Demography* editors will feel as I do. They will conclude that being editor was a fascinating experience, but, occupying the job probably had little significant independent impact on other individuals or on the direction of demographic scholarship.

References

Allison, Paul D. 1984. *Event History Analysis: Regression for Longitudinal Event Data*. Beverly Hills: SAGE Publications.

Bogue, Donald J. 1983. "How Demography Was Born." *PAA Affairs* 16: 2.

Hargens, Lowell L. 1975. *Patterns of Scientific Research: A Comparative Analysis of Research in Three Scientific Fields.* Washington, DC: American Sociological Association.

———. 1988. "Scholarly Consensus and Journal Rejection Rates." *American Sociological Review* 53: 139–151.

Hauser, Philip M., & Otis Dudley Duncan. 1959. "The Nature of Demography." Pp. 29–45 in *The Study of Population: An Inventory and Appraisal,* edited by Hauser and Duncan. Chicago: University of Chicago Press.

Lyon, Larry. 1987. *The Community in Urban Sociology.* Chicago: Dorsey Press.

Marwell, Gerald. 1992. "Let's Train Reviewers." *American Sociological Review* 57: iii–iv.

Preston, Samuel H. 1993. "The Contours of Demography: Estimates and Projections." *Demography* 30.

Teachman, Jay D., Kathleen Paasch, & Karen Price Carver. 1993. "Thirty Years of Demography." *Demography* 30.

Watkins, Susan C. 1993. "If All We Knew About Women Were What We Read in Demography, What Would We Know?" *Demography* 30.

8

A Quest for Interdisciplinary Scholarship

❋

Charles M. Bonjean

Interdisciplinary scholarship is encouraged by many social scientists, but practiced by relatively few. This is hardly surprising given the formal and informal organization of academe and the criteria used for evaluating and rewarding its members. Disciplinary boundaries are reinforced by the norms and values of national and regional professional associations, the key decision-making role of departments in colleges and universities, and the prestige accorded to mainstream disciplinary journals, especially those sponsored by national associations. Moreover, increasing specialization and fragmentation within each of the social sciences have stimulated the development of informal networks of scholars who are likely to identify more closely with their own specialized research and teaching areas than with their larger disciplines. Smelser (1991, p. 525) notes that "(w)hen some new and conspicuous kind of phenomenon appears on the social horizon such as mental illness there tends simultaneously to develop a psychology of it, an economics of it, a sociology of it, perhaps a comparative study of it in anthropology, and certainly a history of it." It is within this fragmented academic context that a few journals, including *Social Science Quarterly*, attempt to promote interdisciplinary awareness and collaboration.

This essay examines the problems and opportunities faced by one interdisciplinary journal over its seventy-three-year history and attempts to relate them to their immediate organizational context as well as to some of the broader academic and social contexts in which they took place. It is a story based on a combination of some speculation and many documented facts.[1] It also attempts to illus-

trate "the emerging opportunity . . . for historical analyses of social science and for the analysis of social history through the documentary record [provided by] . . . the aging academic journals"
(Walton, 1981, p. 2). Finally, readers will be offered a glimpse of
the usually interesting and occasionally nasty "backstage" events
that influence the editorial policies of journals and the behavior
of their editors.

From Political to Social Science, 1920–1930

In December 1919,[2] two members of The University of Texas
Department of Government took the first steps toward founding
the oldest of the regional social science organizations, the Southwestern Political Science Association.[3] Their distance from the annual
meetings of the American Political Science Association (rarely held
within a thousand miles of the geographical center of the Southwest) and the absence of articles in national journals dealing with
topics of local and sectional interest were the major stimuli for
their actions. Four months later, at the new association's first meeting,
arrangements were finalized for the publication of the first regional
social science journal. The first issue of the *Southwestern Political
Science Quarterly* appeared only two months later, in June 1920.
Perhaps not coincidentally, early regional journals in other social
science disciplines were also established in southern states—
Social Forces (North Carolina, 1922), *Southern Economics Journal* (North
Carolina, 1933), and *Journal of Politics* (North Carolina, 1939).

The *Quarterly* differed from the later regional journals by adopt-
ing an interdisciplinary (or perhaps imperialistic?) orientation at
the outset:

> It is the intention of the editors that "political science" shall be
> understood as comprising the fields now commonly designated
> in higher institutions as political science, economics, and soci-
> ology, in so far as these subjects relate to and bear upon gov-
> ernment, public administration, and the problems connected
> therewith. (Haines, 1920, p. 1)

The rationale for this orientation probably had several sources.
First, it reflected the interdisciplinary tradition of political science
at that time. Indeed, the first American center in political science,
founded at Columbia University in 1880, had a similarly encom-
passing scope (Somit & Tanenhaus, 1967, p. 18). Still, the vast
majority of articles in the early volumes were by political scien-

tists. Economic necessity was a second and possibly stronger reason. In September 1921, the sponsoring association's bank balance reached a precariously low fifteen cents.[4] Thus, while the initial courtship with other disciplines may have been motivated by the assumption that an interdisciplinary orientation was essential to understanding political phenomena, it was more likely the response to a poor income/expenditures ratio (Ewing, 1950, p. 39). Indeed, after association members discussed various means to raise funds, they invited historians to membership. The historians refused to enter unless their "disciplinary integrity" was maintained (Ewing, 1950, p. 41) and, apparently, unless the name of the association was changed to "The Southwestern Political and Social Science Association." In June 1923, the journal became *The Southwestern Political and Social Science Quarterly*.

Though perhaps forced to the interdisciplinary pattern by necessity, the association's move was consistent with academic structure at the time. Nationally, many social science departments were combined: economics and sociology, political science and history, or sometimes three or all four of the disciplines.

In 1926, the journal became more explicitly interdisciplinary with the introduction of a trio of coeditors—a political scientist, an economist, and an economist/sociologist. Their efforts brought about what could be regarded as the journal's golden years. In one three-year period (1929–1931), articles were published by five economists who were to become presidents of the American Economic Association (as did one of the editors), three sociologists who would later head the American Sociological Association, and three scholars who were to become American Political Science Association Presidents. In these years

> the Quarterly was probably the most authoritative source of scholarly opinion on an important, if limited, number of topics. The most outstanding areas of its expertise included Mexican immigration to the United States and the broader diplomatic relations between the two countries, public policy in general and its particular workings in Texas, Latin American political development, [and] race and ethnicity in the regional context. (Walton, 1981, p. 2)

From Interdisciplinary to Multidisciplinary, 1931–1940

At the same time the *Quarterly* was achieving national recognition and demonstrating the promise of an interdisciplinary orientation, its sponsoring association was rife with conflict. The concern for "disciplinary integrity" first manifested by historians in 1923 accelerated to the point that groups of specialists within disciplines demanded separate status and recognition. Agricultural economists and business administration scholars insisted on seceding from the parent economics group. By 1930, the association was divided into six sections with each group holding separate meetings and electing its own officers (Ewing, 1950, p. 41). Thus, the organization became a multidisciplinary confederation rather than an interdisciplinary organization. This was reflected in its journal, which became cross-disciplinary rather than interdisciplinary.[5] These changes created additional problems that have plagued the Southwestern Social Science Association and threatened its journal from that time to the present.

Association members representing disciplines other than political science complained about the disproportionate number of political science articles in the *Quarterly* and moved that "representation be given to each section of the association in the editorial management of the Quarterly."[6] After a spirited discussion the motion passed and a board of associate editors was established with two representatives elected or appointed by each section, no matter what its size.

Agitation continued for changing the name of the association and its journal. The motion was made to drop "Political and" from both titles because "(w)ith the present name a writer in the field of economics or sociology or any of the other groups, except political science, will not turn to this publication because it is addressed more particularly to the political scientists. . . ."[7] After a heated debate and attempt to table the motion, the social scientists won. The resulting bitterness is evidenced by many documents in the journal's files. One of the association's founders complained that "the name 'social science' in ordinary use would tend to connote sociology. God forbid that the association should degenerate into a gathering of sociologists!"[8] Another letter insisted that "Department of Government" be removed from *Quarterly* letterhead (even though the editorial office remained there).

In June 1931, the journal displayed its more interdisciplinary title, *Southwestern Social Science Quarterly*, but its golden years were waning. A combination of organizational, academic, and societal phenomena led to a decline in the journal's quality and stature.

Aside from pride of discipline (or academic ethnocentrism?), the social sciences had entered a more separatist era, each developing its own characteristic research style, which further distanced the disciplines from one another. These segmentation trends were exacerbated by the journal's new associate editor structure described above. An examination of editorial records from the early 1930s indicates that (with a few exceptions) advisory editors recommended publication of almost every manuscript submitted from their own discipline. Thus final decisions were left up to the general editors after all. Yet working with advisory editors who were neither appointed nor approved by the editor(s), and in the context of the disciplinary rivalry and conflict rampant in the association, it is not surprising that editorial turnover peaked between 1931 and 1956. During its seventy-three-year history, the *Quarterly* has had only fifteen editors, but eleven of them resigned or retired from the position during this twenty-five-year period. These editors, as well as another who served from 1956 to 1966, faced formal and informal pressures much more intense than those experienced by editors of other journals or by today's editors. Several somewhat threatening internal memos from advisory editors to the general editors (one as recent as 1964) support this assertion. It is not unlikely that still other inflammatory documents were destroyed; and it does not seem unreasonable to infer that there were many similar personal conversations and telephone calls, which, of course, are not a part of the journal's archives. Internal squabbling and demands made by the various sections at least required considerable attention, time, and effort on the part of the journal's editors and, at worst, interfered with rational decision making.

In summary, the decentralized and segmented formal structure of the sponsoring association and the type of editorial board imposed on its journal contributed to neither the *Quarterly's* interdisciplinary mission nor its quality. In all fairness, however, these features reflected the centrifugal processes characterizing the various social science disciplines at the same time.

These same centrifugal processes also contributed to the establishment of new disciplinary and subdisciplinary journals, which increased competition for both manuscripts and subscribers. The proliferation of social science journals started in the 1930s and accelerated rapidly during the following three decades. In 1929, for example, only a few journals offered space for articles by sociologists—the flagship was the *American Journal of Sociology* (1895)—and *Social Forces, Sociology and Social Research* (1921) and the *Quarterly* were the only alternatives. The 1930s saw the founding of a new national journal, *The American Sociological Review* (1935), a number of specialized journals including *Rural Sociology* (1936) and *Public Opinion Quarterly* (1936), and some of the strongest regional journals, including the *Southern Economics Journal* (1933) and *Journal of Politics* (1939). Aspiring authors had more options, but fewer depression dollars to spend on subscriptions.

The depression dealt some crippling blows to the *Quarterly*. Faculty salaries were cut severely, and the journal's sponsoring association received letters similar to the following: "A reduction of 55% in my income makes it impossible for me to keep my membership in any club or association. Kindly accept my resignation as a member of the Southwestern Social Science Association."[9]

The financial picture was so bleak that the association secretary-treasurer suggested the inadvisability of sending out definite notices as to dates of publication of articles until there was greater assurance regarding the future of the *Quarterly*. The Committee on Research in the Social Sciences at The University of Texas came to the rescue by appropriating five hundred dollars for the publication of research articles on southwestern subjects. As a result, the journal's national orientation (and, no doubt, reputation) was diminished by a new editorial policy announced in 1933: "additional emphasis is to be given to southwestern articles either as to subject matter or as to authorship."[10] Indeed, throughout the thirties, regional topics and regional authors dominated the journal's contents. At the same time, however, the dominance of political science diminished somewhat and the *Quarterly*, with more contributions by economists and sociologists, became more cross-disciplinary, although not really interdisciplinary.

Cross-disciplinary or Interdisciplinary? 1940–1965

Two events of the 1940s, an academic conflict and a world conflict, signaled the *Quarterly*'s interdisciplinary potential. The June 1940 issue displayed Clarence Ayres's bold title, "The Wealth of Nations," as its lead article. Ayres was known not only as a brilliant scholar, but also as the acknowledged leader of a group of dissident economists who were critical of their discipline's classical perspective and who were usually denied space in its most prestigious journals. Thus, institutional economics and its interdisciplinary origins and orientation found a forum and became one of the journal's strongest hallmarks for almost three decades.

During the World War II years, however, the war itself was the distinguishing feature of the *Quarterly*. Articles published by scholars in almost every social science discipline dealt with war-related issues ranging from the wartime adjustment of "Negro" families to international alliances. The focus on war issues by a broad range of social science scholars suggests (at least in retrospect) a potentially important ingredient for creating a market for interdisciplinary journals—a focus on issues or problems of significant national or international concern, topics transcending the scope of a single discipline. Yet, four months after the war ended, the journal reaffirmed its commitment to publish articles on southwestern subjects by southwestern authors (Allen, 1946, p. 134).

A change of editors brought a new perspective in the early 1950s and the *Quarterly* published its first topical or thematic issue. "How Vulnerable is Communism?" was published in 1952, with two articles by political scientists, and one each by an economist, a sociologist, and an historian. Other thematic issues—"Foreign Policy in Review" and "The Roots of Power"—followed. The stimulus for these experiments was the successful use of this format by another interdisciplinary journal, the *Annals of the American Academy of Political and Social Science* (Benson, 1948). A fourteen-year hiatus of planned topical issues followed, although "An Unpremeditated Symposium on the Economic Theory of Clarence Ayres" appeared in 1960.

By the 1960s, the focus of the journal was somewhat less regional than during most of the previous three decades, but the fragmented and regional character of the "elected" editorial board created in 1930 persisted. Each of the parent association's twelve sections (accounting, business communications, business law, business management, economics, finance, geography, government, history, marketing, quantitative methods, and sociology) continued to elect or appoint its own associate editor, many (if not most) of whom were primarily concerned with publishing papers by authors in their own discipline. Correspondence between the editor and his or her advisory editors also revealed continued pressure for giving preference to southwestern authors. One editor, after reviewing a manuscript which he knew was by a distinguished scholar from another region noted: "I believe authors who make their livelihood here in the Southwest should have prior claim to space in the Quarterly." [11]

During the same period, the region served by the journal became much smaller. The *Midwest Journal of Political Science* (now the *American Journal of Political Science*) was established in 1957 and the *Sociological Quarterly* was founded two years later. The net effect was a decline in *Southwestern Social Science Quarterly* circulation and manuscript submissions. In the early 1960s, the journal had only 750 subscribers (including libraries) and received only seventy to eighty manuscripts a year for publication consideration. Its acceptance rate was about 33 percent. None of these factors stimulated financial support for the journal and the editor's job was not an easy one. He had no regularly employed clerical assistance and was

> forced to spend three to four hours per day on routine clerical tasks which could be done better by a clerical worker . . . [including] the typing of correspondence, collecting and shipping back numbers ordered, keeping records on the manuscripts . . . , handling funds received for subscriptions, advertising or from the sale of back issues, handling orders for reprints and advertising, and all of the details of publishing a journal of this sort.[12]

In the mid-1960s, the *Southwestern Social Science Quarterly* was a respectable, cross-disciplinary, regional journal with a political science bias (Walton, 1981: 3). Most of its advisory editors (84 percent), authors (75 percent), and individual subscribers (89 percent) were from academic institutions in Texas, Oklahoma, Arkansas, Louisiana, and New Mexico.

National and Interdisciplinary Aspirations: 1966–1980

The unexpected death of *Quarterly* editor Harry Estill Moore in 1966 left the journal without an editor for three months. A new editor was appointed on September 1, 1966.

> At the time, the appointment must have appeared a gamble. Despite a precocious record of publication in the area of political sociology, Bonjean's youth, nonsouthwestern (a native of Pekin, Illinois) and nonpolitical science origins departed from tradition—although his immediate predecessor was a sociologist from the same university. (Walton, 1981, p. 3)

It was a gamble for me as well. I was advised by several colleagues and my department chair not to accept the editorship since it would take time away from research and writing and because the position itself would not advance my career. I did not take their advice for several reasons: (1) my background in journalism (a B.A. and M.A.) stimulated editorial interests and predispositions that I wanted to express; (2) as an author, I frequently waited many months for editorial decisions and thought that journals could and should be better organized and more responsive to authors; and (3) probably because of my own interdisciplinary training in journalism (communications), the interdisciplinary nature of my areas of specialization within sociology (political sociology and formal organizations), and Ph.D. minors in both communications and economics, I thought there was a need for an explicitly interdisciplinary journal and that the *Quarterly* had the potential to fill this important niche.

Some of the same colleagues whose advice I failed to take were among the first to offer their support as referees, authors, and advisors. Indeed, one submitted a path-breaking (and at the time controversial) article, "Crime, Punishment, and Deterrence" (Gibbs, 1968), which was widely cited and brought national attention to the *Quarterly*. Their contributions and encouragement fueled my aspirations for the journal—to move it from regional to national stature and to emphasize an interdisciplinary, as opposed to cross-disciplinary, orientation. From the outset, I knew that this dream could not be achieved without the collaboration of many colleagues from both within and beyond the Southwestern region.

The 1960s was an opportune time to assume the editorship of a journal with interdisciplinary aspirations. The responses to Sputnik and Soviet technological advances were in full force. Federal agencies were pumping new funds into higher education and the numbers of graduate students, graduate programs, and graduate degrees were increasing rapidly. Moreover, policymakers were generous in funding social science research concerned with major domestic problems such as "poverty, urban problems, educational reform, racial discrimination, and inequalities of opportunity" (Turner & Turner, 1990, Chap. 4). Sociologists, economists, and political scientists devoted increasing attention to these issues and often worked together in new interdisciplinary research organizations, such as Wisconsin's Institute for Research on Poverty and Northwestern's Center for Urban Affairs and Policy Research.

As was the case elsewhere in the United States, social science departments, and especially graduate programs, were growing rapidly in the Southwest. Southwestern governors and state legislatures gave higher education and academic research a new priority, which, in turn, attracted federal funding and created new faculty positions, which were increasingly likely to be filled by scholars from beyond the region. The Southwestern Social Science Association was also growing and changing. It seemed to be the right time to make some changes in the journal's policy and procedures and to suggest others that would require the approval of its executive council and general membership.

At the March 1967 meeting of the Southwestern Social Science Association's executive council, I reviewed several modifications in policy introduced during the first four months of my editorship:

1. Sending each manuscript deemed worthy of refereeing to two or more external reviewers.

Past practice was to ask only the elected associate editor to review each manuscript submitted by scholars in his or her discipline. The editor served as the second referee. Given the journal's scope (at the time, twelve disciplines) and the manner in which associate editors were selected, the rationale for this change was, of course, to assure more rational editorial decision making. A few years later, the number of referees was increased to three—usually two from the same discipline as the author(s) and one with similar substantive interests, but representing a different discipline.

2. Increasing the number of topical issues. One such issue, "Rural America," appeared the month before these meetings because four articles on this topic had already been accepted and two more by nationally recognized scholars were invited. Such issues seemed to be a promising means to improve the quality of submissions, gain greater national attention, and promote interdisciplinary scholarship. Another topical issue, "Community Politics," was already in process and still others were being planned on youth and adolescence, Black America, and planned social intervention.

3. The adoption of standardized manuscript evaluation forms.

These forms included two scales—one rating general evaluation ranging from (1) a major contribution to (5) insufficiently sound or important to warrant publication; the other rating the manuscript's potential interdisciplinary appeal, ranging from (1) of interest to social scientists in general to (4) too narrow in scope to warrant publication in an interdisciplinary journal. At the time, few social science journals used such forms, and it was often difficult for the editor to infer from reviewers' comments whether they supported or opposed a request for revision or their degree of enthusiasm in regard to publication. The second scale was included to emphasize the journal's interdisciplinary orientation to both referees and authors and to guard against poor judgment or any biases in this regard on the part of the editor.

A fourth change required approval of the association's editorial policy committee and its executive council before it could be implemented:

4. Adding a board of advisory editors who would be appointed by the editor.

My intent, of course, was to dilute the influence of the existing board of associate editors and their control of the journal's contents. The manner in which they were elected or appointed by the dozen association sections yielded an incredibly uneven array of talent, objectivity, punctuality, and interest. I was aware of the burden and constraints that this aspect of the journal's structure placed on previous editors and was determined to change it. Yet I also knew how difficult it was to achieve organizational change—especially in the context of long-standing traditions. Thus, my plan was to be cautious and to gradually increase the size and influence of the advisory board and at some later time (perhaps in two or three years) to recommend doing away with the associate board. There were several associate editors who were thorough, fair, and punctual and who offered important and creative suggestions in regard to journal policies and content. I hoped they would be reelected and intended to move them to the advisory board if they were not.

My scheming underestimated the flexibility, intelligence, and goodwill of the members of the association's editorial policy committee. Not only did its members unanimously approve the addition of an advisory board, but they also felt the editor "must have the necessary authority commensurate with responsibility"[13] and thus suggested that the associate editors be appointed by the editor! Their recommendations were, in turn, presented to the association's executive council, which, after some discussion and debate, approved both—even though the latter required an amendment to the association's constitution and could not go into effect until the following year. The support of the association was a pleasant surprise and commenced what has been, with few exceptions (discussed below), an exciting, pleasant, and mutually supportive relationship.

The following year, association officers and members were asked to consider another major change, an explicit move to deemphasize the regional nature of the journal and to stress its interdisciplinary orientation. Both the executive council and the general membership responded favorably, voting unanimously in April 1968 to change the name of the journal to *Social Science Quarterly*. Two months later the *Quarterly* became SSQ:

With this issue we drop our "Southwestern" and become the Social Science Quarterly. . . . Recent volumes . . . show no special regional orientation in regard to content and . . . only a

slight over-representation of Southwestern authors. Our editorial boards now include scholars from other regions, and our
circulation has more than doubled over the last five years. During
the same period manuscript traffic has increased by almost 400%.
We believe all of these trends are indicators of the need for a
national publication of general appeal to social scientists, and
our aspirations are to meet this need.[14]

By 1970, the changes in organization and policy were fully
implemented and, for the most part, were succeeding in giving
the journal more national exposure and increasing its interdisciplinary orientation. Its fifty-one associate and advisory editors
included well-known scholars from thirty-six universities in eighteen states. No single factor has contributed more to SSQ's quest
for national stature and an interdisciplinary orientation than the
contributions made by editorial board members during the past
quarter of a century. From the outset, they were asked to do more
than evaluate manuscripts. Annual reports are sent to each urging
suggestions for topical issues, symposia, and changes or modifications in journal policies. Their collective suggestions for topical
issues and symposia are then collected and sent to all board members who, in turn, are asked to prioritize them. Using this procedure to select topics for special issues and symposia assures
interdisciplinary appeal as well as the interest and expertise needed
to plan and produce a successful product. Those board members
suggesting the topics are then asked to co-edit the issues or symposia selected by the board.

The journal's paid employees (usually graduate students) were
also asked for suggestions and advice. During most of my tenure
as editor, SSQ has had only one paid employee at a time—an assistant or associate editor whose work would be better described
by the title "managing editor." Each worked more than the 20–30
hours a week for which she was paid, and each offered important
suggestions leading to changes and/or innovations in journal procedures and content. Among the most significant were initiating
nonsexist writing and editing (before it was adopted by most other
journals) and encouraging the editor to be more proactive in soliciting and publishing articles on gender. One managing editor
may have been a little too enterprising in this regard when she
edited the concluding sentence of an author's article, changing it
from "benefits to mankind" to "benefits to mankind and woman-
kind." The editor was not aware of this change until the paper
was published and the author complained.

Topical Issues

From 1967 through 1980, SSQ published sixteen topical issues (most of double length). The vast majority reflected the concerns of academic social scientists and the social issues, problems, and policies of the time. "Black America" (coedited with Norval D. Glenn) appeared only a year after the summer 1967 riots in Newark, Detroit, and other cities, and only months after the publication of the Report of the National Advisory Commission on Civil Disorders. The report was reviewed and its implications were examined by eminent black and Anglo historians, political scientists, economists, and historians. Twenty-three additional articles explored a wide spectrum of topics dealing with blacks in the United States and race relations in the late 1960s. Another 350-page special issue reflected the growing reliance of government on social science research, and anticipated the increasing interest of social scientists in applied research and policy studies. Coedited by Louis A. Zurcher, "Planned Social Intervention" included articles by Peter Rossi, Joseph J. Spengler, Ralph K. Huitt, Mayer Zald, Walter Gove, Herbert Costner, Amitai Etzioni, and many other well-known scholars. An early indicator that SSQ was achieving national stature was a telephone call from the White House requesting a dozen copies of this issue.

Other extralength special issues were entitled "Urban Problems and Policies," "Education: Problems and Policies," "Youth and Society," "Political Attitudes" (the cover of which displayed both the American flag and the peace symbol). Other topics were suggested by editorial board members. Seven of them (most solicited by publishers) were revised, reorganized, and supplemented with additional text and other materials and were subsequently published as anthologies. Royalties were returned to the journal to underwrite future topical issues.

Yet it was another topical issue that brought the greatest amount of scholarly attention to SSQ and set all records for the journal's circulation to date. In 1973, an issue titled "The Chicano Experience in the United States" (suggested by and coedited with Rodolfo Alvarez) explored in depth (290 pages) a topic that had been largely ignored by the major disciplinary journals—America's second largest minority. Interest in the issue was keen before it was published and, after much pleading and persuasion, the usually fiscally conservative University of Texas Press reluctantly agreed to an overrun of one thousand copies. Multiple-copy orders for library and classroom use were astonishing and, within months, a second printing was necessary. No small number of Chicano scholars let us know that Grebler, Moore, and Guzman's 1970 landmark publication and this SSQ special issue helped to elevate the previously regional academic and public policy concern with Latinos to a national level.

The issues and topics suggested by editorial board members for these early topical issues and symposia enhanced SSQ's reputation among scholars in several substantive areas—race and ethnicity, gender, American politics, environmental social science, public policy, and, to a slightly lesser extent, social, economic, and political theory. Since then, many of the most innovative and important manuscripts submitted to the journal have continued to focus on these substantive areas of concern to both social scientists and society at large.

Encouraging Academic Debate

The journal's interdisciplinary thrust, its review policy (two referees representing the author's discipline and another from a different one), a public policy orientation, and the substantive areas appearing with greatest frequency in its pages often led to academic disagreements. More often than not, these were quite productive. It was not unusual, for example, for a reviewer representing a discipline other than that of the author's to suggest a different theoretical perspective or a body of relevant literature that an author had overlooked (probably because he or she was not aware of it). Sometimes, however, the outside reviewer recommended rejection of a manuscript for these same reasons—even when the author's disciplinary colleagues urged publication. Much of this type of disagreement was only in-house knowledge until 1969, when economist Gordon Tullock submitted "An Economic Approach to Crime" and sociologist Walter Firey took issue with his concept of "utility" in a review that, itself, was a nicely written essay. With Tullock's permission, Firey was asked to expand his review. The essays by Tullock (1969) and Firey (1969) were published in the same issue. This initiated a policy of publishing Position Papers on a more-or-less regular basis. Some of these were conceived in the same manner as the Tullock and Firey disagreement. Others were suggested by reviewers who recommended papers for publication, but suggested the need for balance in orientation, interpretation or policy recommendations—and they were given the opportunity to express their views in print.[15]

The positive response to position papers stimulated a keen

appreciation for those especially creative contributions made by editorial board members and occasional reviewers. Thus, a policy was adopted of accepting some papers either on the basis of a positive response to a reviewer's recommendations or upon the author's agreeing to the publication of the article along with the review in question (revised for publication purposes) and, of course, a reply. Publishing a paper, a critical comment, and a reply in the same issue seemed to be more efficient, more instructive, and much more interesting than publishing comments and replies in later issues, for which a new section of the journal, called "Forum," had been initiated in 1968. The emphasis on scholarly disagreement and debate in the pages of SSQ proved to be another way to emphasize the value of an interdisciplinary orientation. In some cases (including one discussed below), it also brought national attention to the journal and to informed disagreements on important social issues.

Professional Dissent

SSQ's new emphasis on social issues did not have equal appeal to all Southwestern Social Science Association disciplines and members. By 1973, only 41 of the 477 manuscripts submitted were by business scholars and only 3 of those were accepted for publication. The association's rapid growth was also uneven, resulting in proportionately more political scientists, sociologists, and economists and proportionately fewer business scholars. Thus, few were surprised at the association's 1973 annual meetings when the seven business disciplines announced their intent to disassociate in order to form a "smaller more cohesive organization that accordingly can satisfy the scholarly professional needs of [their] membership."[16]

The business–social science divorce turned out to be a mixed blessing for the journal and its sponsoring association. In the short run, a significant decrease in the number of subscribers and the parent association's decision to distribute a pro rata amount of its assets to the newly organized Southwestern Association of Financial and Administrative Disciplines placed financial constraints on SSQ, which had to curtail its previously successful policy of publishing at least one double-length topical issue each year. In the long run, however, it resulted in a more cohesive social science association that, with one possible exception (discussed below), was more compatible with its journal's editorial policies, contents, and successes.

The SSQ submissions, however, did not decrease and thus leaner issues required a higher rejection rate and the publication of only the very best manuscripts. This, of course, resulted in elevating the quality of articles, which led to an even greater emphasis on the topics listed above. These emphases seemed to serve the needs of most members of the remaining disciplines, except history.

In 1974, the editor was invited to attend the business meeting of the Southwestern Historical Association where he was called on the carpet by its president and many of its members. In spite of the fact that historians submitted fewer manuscripts than members of all but one of the other social science disciplines (geography), historians had the highest acceptance rate of any social science discipline (because the editor, striving for a better interdisciplinary balance, accepted papers by historians even if it meant relaxing the criterion of two "enthusiastic" endorsements). Also, at the time, historians constituted the second smallest number of association members and SSQ subscribers. The editor encouraged historians to submit to SSQ, wrote dozens of letters to historians who presented papers at the association's annual meetings encouraging their consideration of SSQ, and successfully solicited papers from several outstanding historians.

The result, however, was disappointing. Submissions by historians did not increase and they became even more dissatisfied, insisting that the association adopt a dual dues structure for their members—one with a journal subscription and one without. The association executive committee accepted their demands and SSQ's budget suffered another blow. The editor continued to solicit submissions from historians, but with little success. An exception was an article by Pulitzer Prize winner William Goetzmann (1976), which was widely recognized and applauded by social scientists other than historians (most of whom were no longer SSQ subscribers).

The steady decline in manuscript submissions by historians since the mid-1960s could have been related to a mainly post–World War II trend in the other social sciences. The quantitative revolution first in economics, then in sociology, and later in political science no doubt further distanced historians from their colleagues in these disciplines and, in fact, led many of them to (incorrectly) assume that SSQ was not receptive to papers without tables and numbers.

My greatest regret and disappointment during my term as editor has been my inability to secure the participation and support for the journal by most southwestern historians. Their relative absence in SSQ's pages has been our loss as well as theirs.

Progress and Problems, 1980–1992—Déjà Vu?

By 1980, SSQ had developed a reputation for giving authors punctual decisions and for publishing quality papers in those areas originally emphasized by the early topical issues—race, ethnicity, gender, inequality, environment, American politics, and public policy. John Walton, in an article surreptitiously commissioned by Southwestern Social Science Association officers, SSQ board members, and University of Texas Press staff members (and published without the editor's knowledge), brought coherence to these seemingly diverse topics and their importance to the academy and society:

> Collectively, these themes indicate a timely sense of major issues that have concerned the academy and the polity during the last 15 years. Through their selection the Quarterly has demonstrated a commitment to the scholarly and human values of social equity and civic ethics. These two banners are hoisted over recurrent issues and symposia that treat racial problems, sexism and women's rights, political power, the hidden injustices of electoral mechanisms or the impact of sanctions on deviant behavior—all areas in which SSQ has published major contributions. (Walton, 1981, p. 4)

Walton's surprise essay was intended to acknowledge this editor's contributions to SSQ's successes. It touched me deeply. In fact, however, it acknowledges the success not of an individual, but of an editorial style that actively seeks intense and broad-based participation in the development of journal policies and the shaping of its contents by hundreds, if not thousands, of others—occasional reviewers, editorial board members, deputy editors, managing or associate editors, and authors. This policy was both reflected and amplified in 1982 when the idea of appointing a deputy editor for each of the five social science disciplines became a reality. These deputy editors would work especially closely with the editor by recommending referees and editorial board members and helping to solicit manuscripts with interdisciplinary appeal from authors in their disciplines. This change in editorial structure was not intended to dilute the participation by others, but rather to supplement it and to make explicit the editor's desire to represent all social science disciplines in the journal's pages. It was also a deliberate effort to "stimulate and encourage the submission of more articles from the disciplines of history and geography" (Graves, 1982, p. 791).

By no stretch of the imagination could I be regarded as a "strong" editor, as the term is commonly used. I decentralized as much decision making as possible (short of anarchy) and, in turn, SSQ was rewarded with many more good ideas than it could implement in a little over a quarter of a century. Some of these reached audiences far beyond SSQ's academic subscribers and other readers, which suggests that the journal is achieving its goal to be a nationally known interdisciplinary publication.

Some Recent Indicators of Success

Most of SSQ's major successes over the past decade built upon the format and content emphases suggested by editorial board members during the late 1960s and early 1970s. A few of the most significant ones are described in this section.

In 1980, editorial board member and Southwestern Social Science Association president Donald Vermeer suggested a written symposium, "Environmental Disruption and the Social Sciences." He had invited biologist Paul Ehrlich to give the plenary address at the 1980 Southwestern Social Science Association meetings and recommended its publication (in revised form) in SSQ as part of a written symposium. Comments were solicited from other scholars, including economist Julian Simon, who strongly disagreed with Ehrlich's perspective and predictions and concluded his essay with "a public offer to stake $10,000 in separate transactions of $1000 or $100 each, on my belief that the cost of non-government controlled raw materials (including grain and oil) will not rise in the long run (Simon, 1981, p. 39).

Ehrlich (1981, p. 46) called Simon "an economist in Wonderland" and decided to accept his "astonishing offer before other greedy people jump in." The winner would be decided by the costs of chromium, copper, nickel, tin, and tungsten on September 29, 1990.

The symposium and especially the bet captured the attention of many and was reported in *The Chronicle of Higher Education*. The wager's outcome and the bases for it were given even broader public exposure a decade later in a *New York Times Magazine* article, "Betting on the Planet," by John Tierney (1990). The article outlined Ehrlich and Simon's diverse perspectives, reviewed the details of the wager, and announced the winner—Simon. It was exciting to see a review and update of a scholarly debate originally published by SSQ in one of the nation's most highly regarded popular publications (even though SSQ was not mentioned in the article).

An article that reached an even larger audience than the Ehrlich/ Simon debate examined the effect of socioeconomic status on the segregation of blacks, Hispanics, and Asians in sixty U.S. metropolitan areas. The authors found that while Hispanics and Asians moved easily into the U.S. mainstream as their occupational, educational, and income status improved, "blacks are still unable to translate their socioeconomic achievements into greater [residential] integration within mainstream society" (Denton & Massey, 1988, p. 814). Thanks to the University of Chicago Press, which summarized the article in a press release sent to newspapers in the sixty metropolitan areas studied, most (if not all) of the large metropolitan dailies gave the study's findings prominent placement and considerable space. All cited its source, and several (including the *San Francisco Chronicle*, *Chicago Sun-Times*, and *St. Louis Post-Dispatch*) stressed its news value by reporting that it was published in "today's edition" of SSQ.

SSQ's dominant role among academic social science journals in publishing research findings on race, ethnicity, and gender was documented in a study comparing the number of articles on these topics published between 1964 and 1988 in "what are generally recognized as the most prestigious mainstream journals in the disciplines of political science and sociology and one interdisciplinary social science journal" (Avalos, 1991, p. 242). Of the eight journals studied (*American Journal of Political Science*, *American Journal of Sociology*, *American Political Science Review*, *American Sociological Review*, *Journal of Politics*, *Social Forces*, *Social Science Quarterly*, and *Western Political Quarterly*), "SSQ has the best overall publication record of articles on Latinos and Blacks" (Avalos, 1991, p. 242). Moreover, 31 percent of all articles on race, ethnicity, and gender published in these journals during this twenty-five-year period appeared in SSQ. Avalos (1991, p. 246) did not include research notes in his analysis "since some of the journals . . . did not use this format and in some cases the use of research notes was intermittent." Because SSQ publishes more research notes (including forty-one on race, ethnicity, and gender during the period studied) than any of the other journals included in the study, his findings and discussion underrepresent SSQ's relative contributions to these substantive areas and their priority among academics.

SSQ has nurtured and been receptive to submissions in these substantive areas not only because of their social significance and probably the value placed on social equity by many of its editorial board members, but also because of the interdisciplinary appeal of race, ethnicity, and gender. Indeed, the authors of the numerous articles and research notes on each of these topics are members of all of the social science disciplines the journal has represented over the last twenty-five years political science, sociology, economics, history, and geography.

During the last decade, SSQ has published fewer topical issues than in the previous fifteen years. There are several reasons for this. First, the earlier topical issues were more successful in achieving their intended results than we had expected. They stimulated manuscript submissions on topics that had appeal across the social science disciplines and also reflected major social issues and problems. Second, they enhanced SSQ's reputation in the academy and beyond in several substantive areas. Third, manuscript submissions increased in both quantity and quality to the point where frequent topical issues would interfere with our goal to give authors prompt responses and a short lead time between acceptance and publication. Indeed, many authors (especially those not yet tenured) have told us that our median review time of seven weeks and (until recently) our relatively short lead time of six to eight months compared favorably with other journals and were significant factors in their decision to submit to SSQ. Finally, the increased publication costs of the late 1970s and early 1980s made extralength topical issues a luxury that we could no longer afford.

Only three topical issues have been published during the last decade. One (coedited with Thomas R. Dye, William Serow, David F. Sly, and Wilbur Zelinsky) dealt with the striking changes in the spatial distribution of people and social and economic activities in the United States. Several of the articles in this issue were especially innovative, widely cited, and reprinted elsewhere. Another (coedited with Curtis L. Gilroy, Peter D. Karsten, Aline Quester, David R. Segal, and James A. Thomas) entitled, "The Military and American Society," was published in 1992.

The other, published in 1984, focused on the topic that, more than any other, put SSQ on the academic map and made the journal an undisputed leader in that substantive area. Indeed, by this time the editor had been given an ID bracelet by a board member, which was inscribed "Carlos Bueno Juan." "The Mexican Origin Experience in the United States" was coedited by Rodolfo Alvarez, Frank Bean, Rodolfo de la Garza, and Ricardo Romo. Subsidies from The University of Texas Center for Mexican American Studies and the Hogg Foundation for Mental Health assured a double-length issue. Yet we did not anticipate the tremendous response in terms of the number of manuscripts submitted or their theoretical and methodological sophistication and range of topics. More than two hundred manuscripts were submitted for consideration and not all of those that referees recommended for publication could be included in the space made available by the subsidies for the double-length issue. Thus, some were scheduled for future issues. This largest special issue published by SSQ (439 pages) included thirty-five articles by sixty-two authors representing eight disciplines.

After a press overrun sold out, its editors wrote introductions to various subtopics and new papers (with other coauthors), asked some authors to rewrite their articles for student use, and commissioned two additional articles for an anthology published by the University of Texas Press in 1984 (de la Garza et al., 1985). To give the anthology the scope and depth its editors intended, only one previously published article was reprinted in the anthology. This singular exception was from the SSQ 1973 special issue on the same topic (Alvarez, 1973).

There can be no doubt that SSQ is the leading social science journal on a topic that will become even more important in future decades. Perhaps it is ironic that, seemingly contrary to the editor's original goals of moving the journal from regional to national stature, a topic that academics once regarded as only of regional importance became SSQ's major claim to national recognition.

Recurring Problems

The problems faced by SSQ during the last decade have been variations on those experienced by the journal throughout its history—fiscal constraints, satisfying the various components of its sponsoring association, and difficulties associated with the continued quest for a truly interdisciplinary orientation.

In the late 1980s, increased manuscript submissions and a higher proportion of favorable reviews resulted in larger issues at the same time that production costs, such as composition, copy editing, and paper also increased. In July 1988, the University of Texas Press journals manager offered a gloomy financial forecast that required emergency action, including a decision to reduce SSQ issue size and to raise subscription rates (indeed, they had not been increased for about a decade). The Southwestern Social Science Association also created a long-range financial planning committee.

Issue size was reduced by 20 percent immediately and some articles scheduled for issues in press were postponed to later issues, with a domino effect that increased our lead time to more than a year. These shorter issues came at a time when the journal was receiving more and better manuscripts and thus resulted in a severe space crisis and the highest rejection rate (87 percent) in more than a decade.

One of the new long-range financial planning committee's first actions was a recommendation that journal pages be restored as soon as the increased subscription rates showed a favorable balance between income and expenses. As has always been the case, the association's executive council reaffirmed its support of the journal by approving this recommendation. Thus, a year later issue length was increased by about 10 percent. But the space crisis continues. As this essay is being written, SSQ treats most of its authors well in terms of the time needed to obtain reviews and make an editorial decision. In 1990 the journal's median review time was 6.0 weeks, while the mean review time was 6.7 weeks. Yet, if a paper is accepted, most authors must wait 10 to 12 months before it is published rather than the 6 to 9 months that had been the norm for several decades.

Disciplinary integrity also continues to be a problem. At the 1991 annual meetings of the Southwestern Social Science Association, historians again registered a strong complaint to the editorial policy committee in regard to their representation in SSQ's pages. One of them suggested changing the journal's orientation from "interdisciplinary to cross-disciplinary." As in 1974, I noted that, in spite of written requests to historians presenting papers at the Southwestern and other meetings, very few papers were submitted by historians—about 3 percent of all manuscripts received in 1990.

I also indicated that a major motivation for deciding to publish the topical issue "The Military in American Society" was the expectation that it would increase the number of submissions by historians. The results were disappointing. Only seven historians submitted papers for consideration in this issue. One was accepted after revision and another was returned for revisions but they were not made.

Immediately after the annual meeting, I (as usual) studied the program of the Southwestern Historical Association and wrote letters to the authors of thirty-five papers, indicating their topic seemed to have interdisciplinary appeal and inviting them to submit the paper for SSQ's consideration. While the number of responses (five) was disappointing, their quality was not. One paper was accepted subject to moderate revision, and the authors of two papers were encouraged to revise and resubmit.

The small number of papers by historians in SSQ is a problem in itself, but it is symptomatic of an even larger difficulty—attempting to achieve interdisciplinary balance in the journal. Throughout the 1980s, about 90 percent of all manuscripts submitted were by political scientists, sociologists, and economists, and the balance among these disciplines improved throughout the decade. The journal was no longer dominated by political scientists or any other discipline. In 1990, however, submissions by political scientists and sociologists increased sharply. In 1991 and 1992, these increases continued to the point where 40 percent of all submissions were by political scientists and 36 percent were from sociologists.

The only way to correct this imbalance will be to work more closely with the deputy editors representing these underrepresented disciplines to actively seek more submissions from their colleagues. Means that we have used in the past will be tried again: placing notices and (exchange) advertisements in their disciplinary journals, perusing the programs of various meetings to solicit papers for consideration, and planning topical issues likely to have special appeal to members of these disciplines.

Conclusions

The quest for interdisciplinary scholarship runs counter to traditional and contemporary trends in academia. Knowledge can be described as "a great mass into which each discipline has sunk a narrow shaft in which each of us digs and mines and where . . . we have walled ourselves off from other diggers into the mass" (Graves, 1982, p. 791). Indeed, even narrower shafts are being sunk within those segments of the mass identified with specific disciplines. Carving "horizontal interdisciplinary tunnels through the mass of knowledge" is the difficult task of interdisciplinary journals and interdisciplinary scholarly associations.

SSQ has helped to carve some of these tunnels throughout its seventy-three-year history. Some of the tools used in this endeavor were discovered by accident, as during World War II when the journal published thematic issues without explicitly planning them. Others, such as the topical issues of the late 1960s and 1970s, were deliberate responses to the concerns of society and social scientists. Still others, such as the techniques adopted to emphasize academic disagreements and debate, were proactive efforts to demonstrate the value and unique contributions of an interdisciplinary perspective for scholarship and/or public policy.

These policies not only carved interdisciplinary tunnels, they also built bridges between the academy and the public. A continuing series of articles on the representation of minority groups in at-large versus district elections were cited in court decisions and, on several occasions, two or more SSQ authors were called to provide expert testimony on different sides of the issue. Several of these articles were also cited in a U.S. Supreme Court decision (*City of Mobile v. Bolden*). On another occasion, SSQ itself narrowly avoided being taken to court. An article that criticized the notion of "defensible space" led to a threatened lawsuit against the authors and SSQ for $5 million in damages.[17] On many occasions (as noted above), SSQ articles have been featured or cited by national media.

Yet the journal's interdisciplinary success has waxed and waned and, at best, has been limited. At times, the sponsoring association rolled boulders into the interdisciplinary tunnels by modifying its constitution and imposing editorial policies that strengthened the walls surrounding disciplinary shafts. Disciplinary integrity has remained a strong orientation not only among historians, but among other social scientists as well. Thus, much of the work published in SSQ today and in the past is by no means interdisciplinary in content or approach. In order to fill our issues and achieve some degree of disciplinary balance, the interdisciplinary criterion discussed above is relaxed for research notes and short articles.

The quest for interdisciplinary scholarship in SSQ has involved cooperation, collaboration, conflict, and compromise. At first glance, it appears that this goal has been variably stressed or ignored by those fifteen individuals who have served as the journal's editors over the last seventy-three years. But there should be little doubt that the societal, economic, academic, and immediate organizational milieux concurrent with their terms were the most important forces shaping both the opportunities and constraints of these editors and their journal.

Notes

1. In addition to a full run (seventy-one volumes) of SSQ, sources include a nearly complete file of editorial correspondence, financial records, minutes of meetings of the Southwestern Social Science Association, and correspondence and discussions with three previous edi-

tors (two of whom are now deceased). These are cited and fully documented in notes only when directly quoted. Published reports are also included in the notes, unless an author is explicitly designated, in which case citations are included in the text and complete bibliographical information is included in the references.

2. Much of the material in this and the following two sections is abridged and adapted from Benson and Bonjean (1970).

3. State historical societies are possible exceptions to this generalization if one classifies history as a social science (rather than among the humanities) and if one does not require the concept of region to include more than a single state.

4. Austin National Bank check stub, September 26, 1921.

5. Throughout the journal's history, there have been tension, debate, and sometimes conflict over whether its primary mission was to publish a collection of papers, each of which would appeal primarily to members of a single social science discipline (i.e., a cross- or multi-disciplinary orientation) or papers that, in themselves (because of their scope of their topic or perspective) would be of interest to members of more than one discipline (i.e., interdisciplinary).

6. "Eleventh Annual Meeting of the Southwestern Political and Social Science Association," *Southwestern Political and Social Science Quarterly* 11 (1930): 92.

7. William C. Smith to the Southwestern Political and Social Science Association Executive Committee, November 17, 1930.

8. Herman James to Charles A. Timm, February 26, 1931.

9. Subscriber's letter to J. L. Meecham, October 6, 1933.

10. "Thirteenth Annual Meeting of the Southwestern Social Science Association," *Southwestern Social Science Quarterly* 13 (1933): 75.

11. Editorial board member's note to Harry E. Moore, May 12, 1960.

12. Harry E. Moore and Leonard Broom to John Alton Burdine, December 12, 1960.

13. "Minutes of the Executive Council of the Southwestern Social Association," *Southwestern Social Science Quarterly* 48 (1967): 119.

14. "In This Issue of the Quarterly," *Social Science Quarterly* 49 (1968): 5.

15. See, for example, the position papers on the status of black women by political scientist King (1975) and sociologist Almquist (1975). Both authors told me later that they received more requests for reprints of these papers than any others they had published.

16. "Minutes of the Southwestern Social Science Association General Business Meeting," *Social Science Quarterly* 54 (1973): 228.

17. For a detailed account of this adventure, see *Social Science Quarterly* 61: 322–332.

References

Allen, Ruth A. 1946. "Report on the Quarterly." *Southwestern Social Science Quarterly* 27: 134.

Almquist, Elizabeth. 1975. "Untangling the Effects of Race and Sex: The Disadvantaged Status of Black Women." *Social Science Quarterly* 56: 129–142.

Alvarez, Rodolfo. 1973. "The Psycho-Historical and Socio-demographic Development of the Chicano Community in the United States." *Social Science Quarterly* 53:920–942.

Avalos, Manuel. 1991. "The Status of Latinos in the Profession: Problems in Recruitment and Retention." *P.S.*, 24: 241–246.

Benson, Oliver. 1948. "Report on the Quarterly." *Southwestern Social Science Quarterly* 29: 102.

Benson, Oliver, & Charles M. Bonjean. 1970. "The Social Science Quarterly, 1920–1970: A Case History in Organizational Growth." *Social Science Quarterly* 50: 806–825.

de la Garza, Rodolfo O., Frank D. Bean, Charles M. Bonjean, Ricardo Romo, & Rodolfo Alvarez (eds.). 1985. *The Mexican American Experience: An Interdisciplinary Anthology.* Austin: University of Texas Press.

Denton, Nancy A., & Douglas S. Massey. 1988. "Residential Segregation of Blacks, Hispanics, and Asians by Socioeconomic Status and Generation." *Social Science Quarterly* 69: 797–817.

Ehrlich, Paul R. 1981. "An Economist in Wonderland." *Social Science Quarterly* 62: 44–49.

Ewing, Cortez A. M. 1950. "History of the Southwestern Social Science Association." *Southwestern Social Science Quarterly* 31: 39–48.

Firey, Walter. 1969. "Limits to Economy in Crime and Punishment." *Social Science Quarterly* 50: 72–77.

Gibbs, Jack P. 1968. "Crime, Punishment, and Deterrence." *Southwestern Social Science Quarterly* 48: 515–530.

Goetzmann, William. 1976. "Time's American Adventures: American Historians and Their Writing Since 1776." *Social Science Quarterly* 57: 3–48.

Graves, Lawrence L. 1982. "A Message from the President of the Southwestern Social Science Association." *Social Science Quarterly* 63: 790–792.

Grebler, Leo, Joan W. Moore, & Ralph C. Guzman. 1970. *The Mexican-American People.* New York: The Free Press.

Haines, C. G. 1920. "Editor's Foreword." *Southwestern Political Science Quarterly* 1: 1.

King, Mae C. 1975. "Oppression and Power: The Unique Status of the Black Woman in the American Political System." *Social Science Quarterly* 56: 116–128.

Simon, Julian. 1981. "Environmental Disruption or Environmental Repair." *Social Science Quarterly* 62: 30–43.

Smelser, Neil J. 1991. "The Social Sciences in a Changing World Society." *American Behavioral Scientist* 34: 518–529.

Somit, Albert, & Joseph Tanenhaus. 1967. *The Development of American Political Science: From Burgess to Behavioralism.* Boston: Allyn and Bacon.

Tierney, John. 1990. "Betting on the Planet." *New York Times Magazine*, December 2, pp. 52–81.

Tullock, Gordon. 1969. "An Economic Approach to Crime." *Social Science Quarterly* 50: 59–71.

Turner, Stephen Park, & Jonathan H. Turner. 1990. *The Impossible Science: An Institutional Analysis of American Sociology.* Newbury Park, CA: Sage.

Walton, John. 1981. "Social Science Quarterly: Two Histories of Tradition and Renovation." *Social Science Quarterly* 62: 1–6.

Part II

Series, Commercial, and Monograph Editors

9

Publishing in a Proprietary Law Journal

﹡

Fred Cohen

I have been editor-in-chief of the *Criminal Law Bulletin* (CLB) for more years than I wish to remember—actually for some twenty years. When I was appointed editor, Warren, Gorham & Lamont (WG & L), the publisher, worked from a suite of about four offices in a New York City hotel and had a modest business office in Boston.

WG & L, now a major figure in the law book and periodical publishing world, and especially strong in the areas of banking, tax, and commerce, purchased the CLB in the late 1960s from two young lawyers and brought me in as their first editor with a mandate to reshape the *Bulletin*.

Displaying all of the certainty of (relative) youth, I had insisted that I would brook no interference with my editorial work; that I wanted to take all of the credit for any success and would accept the full blame for any failure. This display of bravado must have impressed the then vice-president of WG & L since I was retained almost immediately. I then had to figure out just what an editor did to warrant the power I had just insisted on.

When I inherited the CLB, it was essentially a reprint journal. The lawyer-editors would select law journal articles of interest, obtain permission, and simply reprint them. When I began my work I had no manuscripts, no in-house writers, no network of potential contributors, and a mandate to put together twelve issues a year. Looking back, I am not certain how I met those deadlines and continued to teach and write on my own. But, I did.

I do not mean these introductory remarks to sound particularly heroic or self-promotive. My experience in editing what many consider to be one of the leading journals in the area of criminal law seems unique among my eminent, fellow contributors to this volume. Within broad limits, I have had the opportunity to actually create and shape a journal and move it from the mechanics of reprinting to publishing original work and, with some regularity, publishing the work of outstanding practitioners and academics.

Indeed, while most of our authors are lawyers, many are not. James Fyfe, for example, whose work appears in this book; Larry Sherman, a highly regarded political scientist; and B. F. Skinner all have published in the CLB.

The CLB is a proprietary journal lacking the army of free "worker bees" attached to every law school review and lacking also the membership base for the relatively inexpensive and widely distributed, member-affiliated journals. The *Bulletin*, then, must initially develop and retain a readership able and willing to pay $105 for our current six issues a year, averaging about ninety-six pages per issue. Where the scholarly journals need be concerned only with quality, a proprietary journal must be concerned with a profit-and-loss statement. If we are not-for-profit, it is an unhappy accident that will not long be tolerated.

Incidentally, in the proprietary world of law journal publishing, renewal rates are viewed as a more accurate indicator of success—whatever that ultimately may mean. Indeed, not until the second renewal can you be relatively certain that you have sold the subscription. The CLB has a renewal rate of over 80 percent, which is considered very good and especially so during the current recession in which periodical subscriptions are highly vulnerable to cost-conscious managers.

The characteristics of our readership base are the most important element in understanding the factors that enter into the decision concerning what and whom to publish. While I have an all-star editorial advisory board composed of academics and staff practitioners,[1] and while there is some input from WG & L staff, the decision to publish, and in what sequence, is essentially mine. I will return to the philosophy and mechanics of this decision shortly, but for now I simply want to develop the relationship between those who subscribe and, presumably, read the *Bulletin* and its contents.

From the beginning of my editorship perhaps the most basic problem that I have had in selecting manuscripts is the tightrope I walk between articles that are scholarly and aimed at an academic audience and those that are less scholarly and aimed at the legal practitioner. I understand all too well that the dichotomy between "scholarly" and "practical" is in some ways misleading and artificial. On the other hand, like the late Justice Potter Stewart's problems with obscenity, I tend to know one from the other when I see it.

Scholarly work tends toward the systematic and original research of a significant legal problem; it may make a theoretical contribution; it may advance our understanding of significant legal doctrine. Most important, in my view, are the objectives of the author. On the one hand, is the author providing practical tips on jury selection, a list of questions to pursue, and characteristics to observe? Is he or she writing about the jury as an endangered, democratic institution in need of resuscitation; as a last bastion for populism in government? Is he or she studying small-group decision making as a function of jury size?[2]

Obviously the first type of article described above has a how-to-do-it objective while the second type is more attuned to law reform and policy matters. The *Bulletin* has published variations on both types of articles and therein is a dilemma. Our readership is heavily weighted toward the legal practitioner: prosecutors, defense attorneys, judges, and law enforcement agencies. We are, of course, found in all the major law libraries and referenced in the *Index to Legal Periodicals*, thereby making the CLB accessible to a wider audience than those readers with individual or, more likely, institutional subscriptions.

Is it possible, then, to satisfy a subscriber list that is heavily practitioner and at the same time provide the kind of ideas and advancement of law-type articles that are more academic or scholarly? Clearly, I am not the best person to answer that question since that has been the tightrope I have attempted to negotiate over this twenty years of editorship.

In my biased view, we do accomplish a satisfactory balance, not in every issue and perhaps not in every volume, but over time I think that we do. How? First, I totally avoid the checklist–handy diagram "practical" article. We simply do not publish an article with which the reader may feel an urge to reach for the crayons. This is not to say that material of this type may not be useful on occasion to the practitioner. It is only to say that we do not (consciously) publish anything quite like it.

Second, I try to avoid the extraordinarily long article, weighted down with footnotes exceeding the length of the text, which either examines a sliver of a legal problem in exquisite detail or examines a legal-philosophical question of such magnitude or of such global significance that it is best published elsewhere.

The ideal lead article for publication in the *Bulletin* is one that prints out to somewhere between fifteen and twenty pages and that examines a legal issue in a way that there may be some immediate applicability while at the same time there is attention to history, to implications beyond the present, perhaps a critique and a call for reform. Most important, there is analysis and not simply a case-by-case reportorial approach.

Articles that do not appear to have immediate utility may, indeed, prove to be very practical. For example, an article that traces recent developments in, let us say, the good faith exception to the exclusionary rule may land on the desk of a judge or a practitioner faced with just such an issue. Even without how-to-do-it steps, the analysis we provide may serve as the springboard for legal advice or the fashioning of a judicial opinion.

Again, I realize I am on thin ice setting out our ideal characteristics for an article knowing full well that the nature of the topic is likely to suggest other criteria; that some articles may be quite valuable if they simply provide an accurate overview of a topic; and that I am attempting to objectify what is primarily—but not exclusively—an intuitive approach honed by experience.

Some further examples may provide a better insight into this dilemma and how we work at resolving it. The *Bulletin* is simply not the place to try to publish one's exegesis on the overall failures of the criminal justice system in the twentieth century; a Marxist perspective on American criminal procedure; or a one-hundred-page exploration of the relationship between a "good faith belief" and a statutory requirement of "willfulness."[3]

Manuscripts reach me in a variety of ways. Many, perhaps most, are invited. I realize, of course, that this feature alone distinguishes the CLB from the other publications represented in this book. When a criminal law procedure topic is "hot" due to legislative developments (sentencing guidelines, e.g.) or because of important judicial developments (restriction on appeals from death row, e.g.) then I will search my inventory of potential authors and invite an article on a proposed topic.

Indeed, over the years we have published some symposium issues—an earlier one on the death penalty, more recently on federal sentencing guidelines—and these issues are all invited papers. Parenthetically, symposium issues, in my mind, are quite valuable but they also require an enormous amount of work. Working with very limited staff assistance, I am unable to take on such issues with any regularity.

Other manuscripts are received unsolicited. Sometimes that

manuscript is from someone we previously have published and, at other times, it is from someone either unknown to me or simply unpublished by us.

Whether solicited or not, every manuscript I receive is read by me. I serve as a gatekeeper for any further review and for the unsolicited work, I apply a kind of "probable cause" standard to the issue of publishability. That is, is there more reason than not to characterize this manuscript as publishable or unpublishable?

Some manuscripts are rejected simply because the topic is not suitable for our journal or, while it may be suitable, it is in an area where the CLB already has published material, or has in the pipeline, similar material. When that occurs, the manuscript is given only cursory review by me; and a personal, individualized letter is prepared and sent to the author.

Of course, other unsolicited material is so clearly not well done— poorly written, little evidence of requisite research, poorly analyzed, and the like—that I will reject if after a first reading. I am not obliged by contract or practice to submit such a manuscript for some type of external or peer review. Any doubts that I may have about publishability are resolved in favor of further review, a process I will turn to shortly.

Incidentally, I have made it a practice not to adopt form letters and while the length of my rejection letter may vary, it is always individualized. I make every effort to provide substantive commentary that may be useful to the author. I will fudge a bit when the rejection is purely for lack of merit.

There are happy occasions when an unsolicited manuscript is so clearly on point and so manifestly well researched and written that I will accept the work without further review or consultation. I realize that this practice takes us out of the realm of the refereed journal so valued in other disciplines and of particular merit in academic tenure-stature considerations.

On other occasions, when I do not feel comfortable or very well informed about a topic, yet I believe there is probable cause in favor of publishability, I may ask an appropriate member of our editorial board to review it and give me his or her opinion. On other occasions, I will solicit academics or practitioners not connected with the CLB, but experts in the area, and ask them to provide me with their views on publishability and possible revisions.

I am strongly guided by such opinions and, for example, if an article is deemed publishable but in need of fairly extensive revision, I will communicate those ideas, and then work with the author to achieve publishability. For a proprietary journal that does not pay its authors, a good piece of work is a gem to be valued even if it needs further polishing.

Where I have solicited a manuscript then, quite frankly, I approach the work I receive with a presumption of publishability. This is not to say that I have not been disappointed on occasion, or even ultimately had to reject a manuscript. However, in the great majority of cases in which there is a problem, I will simply work with the author—at times going through three or four exhaustive rewrites—to achieve publishability.

I have thus far actually touched on two distinct roles that I play—or have played—as editor of the *Bulletin*: (1) providing form and content to the *Bulletin* as it moved from a reprint publication to a mainstream proprietary law journal; and (2) soliciting, accepting, and rejecting articles. I also perform a third function, which I will characterize as doing a "soft edit" on the manuscripts.

By "soft edit" I mean that I will mark up the manuscript by substituting one word for another or one sentence for another, do minor punctuation, some sentence revision, and the like. While I may insist that a number of pages be rewritten, I will not undertake revision on that scale. My task is to urge the rewrite and then evaluate how well it was done.

The CLB has a professional staff of copy editors in New York City and they do the "hard edit" and, ultimately, prepare the manuscript for typesetting using their arsenal of slashes, add abbreviations, underlining, and other signals.

Authors receive galley proofs in due course and have the usual opportunities to respond to queries and make some changes at this point. This part of the business is out of my hands and is done with our New York City staff of highly trained professionals.

One of our most attractive features, I am told, is the potential for an extraordinarily quick turnaround, that is, the time from submission to acceptance to actual publication. I must have copy to my New York City editors about three months prior to the particular issue. Thus, on June 1, I must send in the material for our September-October issue, which will be printed and distributed in early September.

I am rather certain that our turnaround time is substantially faster than virtually any law school-connected review (seven or eight months is not unusual there). It is not unusual for social science journals to take a year or more to review and publish an article. Since it is the review process that seems to cause the often inordinate delays in social science publishing, our system of a semi-independent editor is the crucial factor in our ability to move quickly. In addition, many legal topics have a sense of urgency or, at least, timeliness about them, as distinguished from a piece of research and scholarship that seeks an audience but whose message will remain significant despite the lapse of a year.

Many of my social science colleagues express dismay about publication delay and seem particularly dismayed at a review process that may take six months followed by a rejection. In the ordinary course of things, that simply cannot happen with the *Bulletin*.

This, in turn, leads to another aspect of our policy that differs significantly from other journals and other disciplines. While I do not encourage the multiple submission of manuscripts, we certainly do not disqualify anyone who does so. My only grievance with multiple submissions is when that fact is undisclosed. Failure to so disclose, in my mind, borders on an unethical practice by authors, especially when disclosure comes at the point of publication of an article by the *Bulletin*!

However, when I receive an unsolicited manuscript that candidly informs me of multiple submissions, and if that manuscript involves a subject of interest or an author whom we might look upon favorably, then I will actually expedite review of that manuscript. On the other hand, when extensive reading and review is engaged in and I then learn that the author just accepted another offer of publication, it leaves a distinct bad taste; a taste sufficiently bad that I am likely to remember should the same author seek to publish with us in the future.

I strongly believe that any prospective author should know something about the journal in which he or she seeks publication. If you think this is a ridiculously obvious point, then you probably have not done much, if any, work as an editor. I regularly receive manuscripts that are essentially quantitative studies about criminal justice, and that are clearly inappropriate for us. I receive short "I believe" articles that more nearly resemble extended letters to the editor. And I receive lengthy, frequently turgid articles that resemble nothing that we have ever published! Tenure review time seems to have a causal relationship to such submissions. The point is, an author should at least browse through a publication before submitting a manuscript over the transom. If you are responding to an invitation then you probably have the good sense to ask about the deadline, tables and charts, length, number of copies required (an original and one copy is a bare minimum), citation style (although the nature of the journal suggests that will not likely be an issue), and whether a hard copy and a disk are required. It happens that we do not require disks but clearly it is the wave of the future. Also, we do not impose any author charges as is the case with some publications.

But if you are coming to my desk with only a general invitation, then it is imperative that you know as much as possible about your prospective host. As a prospective author, send in the clearest, best-edited copy that you are able to produce. Consider what your reaction would be if you read a paper with several typographical and grammatical errors in the first few pages. This is obviously the moment to put your best foot forward and an "unclean" paper is likely to be on the road to a speedy rejection.

A brief, factual biography also is part of good form along with a brief synopsis of the work. I actually receive unsolicited manuscripts bearing only a name and a street address. There is no professional or academic affiliation noted. (This is usually, although not always, a law student trying to publish an "A" seminar paper. A student is far better off identifying himself or herself and his or her work since we have no rigid rule against publishing "mere" students' work). To exclude work for reasons other than merit strikes me as unthinkingly rigid. To look more closely at law student-authored work strikes me as sensible.

Our masthead includes a group of individuals characterized as contributing editors. While I am not certain what contributing editors do for other publications, ours are regular contributors to the CLB. The *Bulletin's* format includes a regular feature that we call a "Workshop." Our workshop subjects include law and social science (Jim Acker[4]), forensic science, (Edward Imwinklereid[5] and Paul Giannelli[6]), law enforcement (Geoffrey Alpert[7]), and prosecutorial ethics (Bruce Green[8]), evidence (done for so long and so well by Michael H. Graham[9]), and state constitutional developments (Barry Latzer[10]). Some of our contributing editors receive a token honorarium for their good work, but it is clearly a modest honorarium and not even close to the sort of fee persons of their stature might command.

Another contributing editor does a regular feature entitled "From the Legal Literature." Elizabeth Walsh is an attorney, has a graduate degree in criminal justice and regularly reviews important articles and books for us. Her review is in the form of an annotation and seems quite useful to our readers.

We also regularly publish book reviews. They are handled by a book review editor who also receives a token honorarium.

Finally, in each issue, the *Bulletin* includes digests of recent federal and state court decisions involving criminal law and procedure. This material is contracted out to lawyers who prepare their digests and submit them directly to the publisher's New York office. Thus, I have virtually nothing to do with this feature.

Summing up then, I have an unusually long tenure as editor of a journal that has many characteristics not found in the other publications represented in this volume. The *Bulletin* is straightforwardly a law journal; it is proprietary and not membership based; it is subject matter specific; it seeks to publish well-crafted material that is neither cookbook nor cosmic; and it remains in business by remaining profitable.

It may be that our reputation is based on our more scholarly articles while our subscription renewals are based on our more practical articles. Authors tell me that they seek publication in the *Bulletin* when they want to be read and used. A law professor in search of tenure will aim first, and sensibly so, for the mainline, high reputation law school reviews.

We sell ourselves, in part, on extremely fast turnaround, very professional production, and a well-founded belief that to be in the *Bulletin* is to be read and potentially to impact on the area being written about. We are not only fast and professional but also reasonably flexible, even as to length. When I edit an article, it is not to make it over into some standardized CLB format but to accept the author's style and work within those parameters.

Every manuscript we receive is given at least one reading. External review is resorted to only to resolve the subject. Our editorial advisory board and external reviewers are then available. Professor Yale Kamisar of our board deserves special recognition for his interest in the *Bulletin*, his advice, and his generosity in steering worthy prospective authors to the *Bulletin*.

To be the editor of a journal like the *Bulletin* in an era of information overload is actually a privilege. I am able to remain abreast of developments in criminal law and procedure that might otherwise elude me. I may even contribute to the growth and development of the law in my capacity as gatekeeper to the CLB.

In any event, over the years I have begun to feel almost parental—or at least avuncular—about the *Bulletin*. Having confessed to such feelings, readers, I hope, will forgive any conceits they may have detected here.

I do believe that I have become a better and more prolific writer through my experiences as an editor. Just as I strongly believe that one must read in order to write, I believe that editing another's work benefits one's own work.

I will end by again urging those of you who write and seek publications to know as much as possible about your publication outlets, and to come to the editor's table wearing your best clothing.

Notes

1. James Acker, Assistant Professor and Associate Dean, School of Criminal Justice, The University at Albany; Yale Kamisar, Professor of Law, University of Michigan Law School; David B. Wexler, Professor of Law, University of Arizona Law School; and Practicing Attorneys Herald P. Fahringer, Walter L. Gerash, Gerald W. Heller, and Richard H. Kuh.

2. To my knowledge, we have never published anything quite like these hypothetical topics, which are invented purely for illustrative purposes.

3. I do not mean to denigrate the topics or the approach. I mean, again, only to address their appropriateness for the CLB.

4. Assistant Professor and associate dean, School of Criminal Justice, The University at Albany, State University of New York.

5. Professor of Law, University of California, Davis.

6. Weatherhead Professor of Law, School of Law, Case Western Reserve University.

7. Professor, College of Criminal Justice, University of South Carolina.

8. Professor, School of Law, Fordham University.

9. Professor Graham recently announced his "retirement" from the CLB and we have not as yet announced his replacement.

10. Professor, Department of Government and Public Administration, John Jay College of Criminal Justice, The City University of New York.

10

Special Problems in the Editing of "Special Series"

✳

Michael Lewis

Editing belongs to a category of activities whose true nature is rarely if ever revealed to those contemplating their apparent allure. In this way editing is a lot like parenting. If the truth were told to prospective parents, if the joys of parenting were matched with the activity's anxieties and frustrations in those "how to" books, who knows how many planned pregnancies would be planned right out of existence! Since that would have serious consequences, they just don't tell you the truth. And so with editing, it has apparently been assumed by those who know the truth about what really transpires, that if they ever revealed it, more than a few novices would undoubtedly forsake the order of the blue pencil.

When people take on activities without really understanding what's in store for them, their disappointment in the reality they inevitably confront is not merely personal; it has functional consequences as well. It may be, for example, that parenting suffers because the realities of having and rearing children overwhelm and immobilize adults made unready for their responsibilities by falsely euphoric expectations. And thus it may be that the quality of social science editing suffers because even talented scholars become "routineers" or otherwise seek shortcuts when departures of editorial reality from editorial expectation breed cynicism among those who naively embraced a Panglossian version of the latter. A novitiate, informed about editing's troubled reality, may yield a smaller group of serious and competent scholars willing to take on its necessary tasks, but their efforts are less likely to be encumbered by the cynicism that is the probable product of the existing disjuncture between expectation and experience. While second-rate editing would continue to characterize the work of careerist mediocrities, editorial work performed by the most able among our colleagues would have a characteristic vitality that disappointed naivete presently renders exceptional.

Every discipline has its official or semi-official journals. Editors of these publications are usually chosen by the discipline's more prominent communicants and such selection bestows honor even as it imposes burden. If you are going to be an editor, these are clearly the assignments to pursue. They do, or course, have their problems. But they have built-in advantages as well, advantages that render the attendant editorial tasks almost tolerable if not actually enjoyable. First and foremost among these is a surfeit of manuscript submissions. Editors of the official and semi-official journals do not have to worry about having enough publishable material to meet their next deadline. Whereas editors of other scholarly publications may, in confronting a paucity of reasonable papers, perpetrate the "type 1" error of accepting for publication something better suited for the recycling bin. Editors of these journals are more likely to commit the "type 2" error of rejecting a piece that should have been published. A second advantage is the availability of paid staff, a managing editor and a secretary, who can shoulder the burden inherent in everyday operational matters. A third is the bevy of associate editors more than eager to review manuscripts and make publication recommendations as long as they are listed on the masthead or the journal's inner cover.

One of the most difficult and thankless of editorial experiences is that associated with taking on the editorship of a special interest journal or series. Such a publication is usually the product of a rocky marriage between scholar–zealots who feel their particular substantive interest or methodological approaches are insufficiently represented in the pages of the official or semi-official journals, on the one hand, and commercial publishers, usually small to midsized, who look to the library sale market as a source of steady if unspectacular profitability, on the other. The marriage is a source of significant editorial malaise because it introduces that most alien of sensibilities, the bottom line marked either in black or red, into a decision-making process that is supposed to heed nothing except scholarly standards. How often to publish and how many papers ought to be published per issue become decisions not solely determined by scholarly need and the availability of informative materials. Advertising potential and the demand made by most research libraries that they be fed fresh issues on a regular basis have as much or more to do with what gets published and when. Editors of special interest publications are characteristically made vulnerable to an awful, perhaps even shattering truth, to wit: that in order to meet the publisher's insistence on a predictably available product, they have to include papers that are, at best, of dubious quality.

The realities of scholarly publishing are such that the editors of special interest journals and series must commit the type 1 error of accepting that which they ought to reject if their publications are going to survive. All scholars know that they will receive more credit for publishing in the official or semi-official journals of their disciplines (the "leading journals") than they will for publishing in the more narrowly focused and less visible special interest publications. Thus they are more than likely to send their best work to the former. If that work is rejected by the leading journals, they will then send it, together with work they themselves are not terribly enthusiastic about, to the special interest outlets.

Occasionally this process makes a high-quality paper available to the special interest publications (e.g., when the editors of the leading journals make the type 2 error of rejecting papers they ought to accept; or when the authors of a paper underestimate its appeal to the editors of the "better" journals and, out of a desire to get a quick acceptance, send their material directly to a special interest outlet). More often than not the editors of these publications have to pick their way through table scraps, the leftovers already found unpalatable once and sometimes two or three times, or those never even served for fear that discerning tastes will be offended. Pick they must, and pick they do. The publishers don't want to hear that a journal issue or a series volume has to be delayed for any reason, let alone that you can't go to press because you don't have enough papers worthy of publication. In fact, from their point of view, the relative worthiness of a paper is irrelevant to the matter of publication. Since library sales are preordered and prepaid, quality has little or nothing to do with whether subscriptions will be renewed; delays and failure to produce a deliverable product will, however, lead to cancellations. Thus, as long as the editor puts something, virtually anything, within reason, between the covers, the publisher will be happy with this effort while delay in search of quality sufficient to justify the publication's continued existence will not be tolerated.

Editors of special interest publications are unlikely to be surprised by the behavior of their publishers; it more or less conforms to their stereotype of the crass world "out there" where pecuniary gain and only pecuniary gain establishes utility. They are, however, quite likely to be caught offguard and to be disenchanted by the failure of many colleagues to support their editorial efforts; particularly when many of these same colleagues had argued loud and long on behalf of establishing the publications they edit. Whatever may have been said about unmet publication needs that these journals and series would serve, in reality they are never the outlets of choice, at least not for first-line scholars. The editors, confronted with a resource pool mostly constituted of the best work of second- and third-rate scholars on the one hand and the second- and third-rate papers of first-rate scholars on the other, not only have to work harder than they ever imagined to put creditable issues together on a regular basis, but they also have to steel themselves against an understandable propensity to view their colleagues as disloyal self-seekers or, at the very least, a group of "no talent bums"!

At the invitation of a colleague who was acting as a consultant for Johnson Associates Inc. (JAI Press), I agreed to edit the series *Research in Social Problems and Public Policy* during the 1980s. The need for this particular publication might not seem immediately apparent, but I saw several purposes that, if served, would justify its existence.

To begin with, I thought there was a need for a publication whose editorial emphasis would be to subject the goals of public policy, no less than the means of their realization, to a value informed social scientific criticism. *Research in Social Problems and Pubic Policy* would, I hoped "move contemporary policy discourse from the assessment of means given an uncritical acceptance of ends to a wholistic assessment in which both ends and means receive their share of appropriate critical attention."[1]

It seemed, moreover, that the proposed publication might also provide a forum for those who wished to bridge the gap between knowing and doing. Along with JoAnn L. Miller (coeditor for the last two volumes in the series), I later addressed this purpose with a number of questions:

> Is it possible and epistemologically defensible for social scientists to adapt their zeal for discovery to at least *some* of the constraining requirements that policy makers must work within? Is there any legitimacy to the *pragmatic test* wherein the truth value of scholarly claims is determined, at least in part by the degree to which these claims can be translated into innovative

and effective inventions? When claims are made that social science yields little of use in policy venues, do such claims have merit or are they merely defenses invoked by the unnecessarily timid as they confront limitations of dubious reality?[2]

Finally, I saw the proposed publication as a vehicle for stylistic reform in the social sciences. I had long been a critic of the conventional style format in mainstream social science publications, which I viewed (and continue to view) as ill-suited to the necessarily interpretive character of social science scholarship. The twenty-page journal article with its statement of the problem, review of the literature, methods section, findings, and conclusions is all too often an ex post facto creation that reconstructs and frequently misrepresents the research it ostensibly reports. It is a format having no place for an expression of inference anchored in extra-disciplinary sources (a type of inference more than minimally present in social science), a format that, as such, inadvertently censors any allusion to the nonscientific character of the scholarship in question; a format, therefore, that hides material of significance from the critical reader. With the complete editorial control over the proposed series that was offered me, I believed I would have the opportunity to encourage contributors to adopt a variety of expansive formats, encouraging, thereby, more accurate characterizations of each author's scholarship.

Given the purposes the publication was to serve, I rejected an open submission policy for manuscripts in favor of solicitation by invitation. I reasoned open submission would result in my having to plow through many manuscripts not meeting any of the publication's defining purposes; and that seemed like a considerable waste of my energies. Open submission, I convinced myself, puts the editor having a clear purpose in the position of the prospector panning for gold; you have to filter through a lot of mud and silt in order to get to the glitter; and even the glitter may turn out to be something other than gold. I convinced myself that since I was reasonably well respected by my professional peers, I would have little or no difficulty coming up with material for all of the volumes I had agreed to do, including the inaugural one I was then focusing my attention upon.

After too many phone calls and too many letters, I exacted promises from my colleagues to produce ten papers for volume one of *Social Problems and Public Policy.* The same torturous procedure yielded but nine papers per volume for the remainder of the series. The extent to which these papers honored the purposes justifying the existence of the series varied in considerable measures. In volume one, 80 percent of the papers served at least two of the three justifying purposes (e.g., the critical examination of ends as well as means, bridging the gap between knowing and doing, and stylistic reform). Not bad, but even such a relatively high rating indicates that there were instances in which I decided to publish papers that really did not meet what should have been the minimum criteria for inclusion. Volume two saw a significant drop-off in papers clearly serving the publications' defining purposes; only fifty-five percent of the papers served at least two of these purposes. In other words, almost half of the papers included in Volume II probably should not have been published in this series. We were much more successful with volume three where 88 percent of the papers met what should have been the minimum standard for inclusion. Volume four, however, once again saw a major drop-off; only 55 percent of the papers we published met the minimum two-purpose standard.[3] The publication history for the four-volume series shows, in its entirety, the inclusion of three papers that failed to meet any of the defining purposes and eight papers that met but one of these purposes.

While these numbers may not appear to be overwhelming, they do indicate that during my editorial watch about 30 percent of the decisions to publish were unwarranted. I must say it is a relief to conclude that we made the correct decision most of the time. Given the tribulations we regularly confronted, I am a bit surprised that our batting average is as high as it appears to have been. Nevertheless, "type 1" errors were made (i.e., the inclusion of papers that should have been rejected) in the preparation of each volume, and for two of the volumes, erroneous inclusion came very close to being the characteristic editorial judgment.

Looking back, it is easy to see why. First, when prospective authors were approached, authors I had reason to believe would appreciate the publication's purposes, many declined to submit papers. In particular, many of these prospects were wary about the stylistic changes I was seeking. Asking people to abandon the highly structured format they had used with considerable success (the conventional social science paper format noted above) for more expansive and less structured formats that for many represented the unfamiliar, was asking a lot more than I had surmised. Some of those I approached seemed unable to grasp what I was trying to get them to do. Others had no problem understanding my intentions on the issue of stylistic reform, but simply wanted no part of the endeavor because, in their view my purposes were epistemologically erroneous. Seeing themselves as discovers rather than interpreters, as scholars whose inferences were derived from their disciplines and only their disciplines, they viewed the adoption of more expansive formats, allowing the explicit use of extradisciplinary sources of inference, as inappropriate. While they may have shared some of my substantive concerns, we were clearly in different epistemological camps; and as such, they respectfully declined my invitation to participate.

Whatever the reason, the actual list of potential contributors for each volume in the series, always turned out to be considerably smaller then I had assumed. Then, of course, not every author who agreed to deliver a paper informed by the purposes of *Social Problems and Public Policy* actually did so. Intention and execution, as we all know, are not one and the same. Some authors never delivered any kind of paper; while others delivered manuscripts that bore little or no resemblance to what they had promised. Invariably, these were the papers that arrived late and only after their authors had become the targets of sustained, if diplomatic, collection efforts on my part.

Now put yourself in my position. The pool of potential contributors is much more limited than you thought it would be. Of those, from this already limited pool, who agreed to write papers, some just haven't come through. At a certain point, you simply have to give up on them. The publisher is clamoring for the volume. In fact, having announced it in his catalogue, he has already received library orders that he is justifiably anxious to fill. Authors who have submitted acceptable papers more or less on time call about the publication date and voice their understandable chagrin when they are told of delays. Then, after considerable effort to elicit papers from delinquent authors, the three or four papers absolutely necessary to the shaping of a coherent volume, arrive. Hallelujah, you've finally got something to send off to the publisher. You can stop screening your calls. You can go to professional meetings without worrying about running into disgruntled colleagues. Or can you? One or two of the late-arriving papers meet the volume's purposes reasonably well, but the other two are seriously deficient.

You now have a choice to make. On the one hand, you can reject the deficient papers as incompatible with the purposes of the volume, thereby extending the already agonizing delay. You can go back to screening your calls and you can continue to duck behind those large potted plants favored by convention hotels. On the other hand, you can convince yourself that despite their deficiencies the papers are acceptable, if only marginally so. Considering the costs incurred by choosing the former alternative, you really don't take much convincing: particularly since the scholar doing the convincing (yourself) has a wealth of credibility in your eyes. Whoever said that every volume of *Social Problems and Public Policy* had to be a perfect exemplar of its defining purposes anyway.

I'll leave it to the reader to decide whether the compromises I made with my own standards were justified. I, of course, like to argue that they were; that had I not accepted the deficient papers for publication the existence of the series would have been cast into considerable doubt, that the compromises actually saved the series and thereby rescued the opportunity to serve my editorial purposes from the oblivion that would have come with its demise. I find the argument rather persuasive; but then convincing myself too easily created the necessity for the argument in the first place.

The travail experienced in eliciting enough material for each of four volumes was not the only type of difficulty I experienced during my tenure as editor of *Social Problems and Public Policy*. Until I resigned, my editorial experience would, I believe, be best characterized as a synergy of provocative surprises. No sooner had I come to grips with the limited pool of materials from which I would have to select the papers for volume one than the publisher informed me that instead of paying a royalty to authors, he would offer them a flat fee. This meant that I had to contact authors to explain the change. Since the money involved was hardly an astronomical sum under either arrangement, none of the contributors was particularly chagrined at the change. Nevertheless, I felt obliged to offer each of them the opportunity to withdraw his or her contribution to the volume, since the change was both unilateral and ex post facto. One defection probably could have been tolerated; two, would have made it impossible to go ahead without, at that eleventh hour, seeking out more material. Given the difficulties already alluded to, this was not a prospect I could envisage with equanimity.

Just before its release and during the period I was dealing with the scarce resources available for volume two, I had to mediate a dispute between the publisher and one of the contributors to the inaugural volume. The publisher refused to accept financial responsibility for late corrections and the author, noting that the publisher had skipped galley proofs and had instead gone directly to pages, was equally adamant.[4] The dollar amount at stake was hardly something to get bent out of shape over, but it symbolized a fairness issue that could have affected the future of the series. If authors come to feel they are not being treated fairly, they themselves would be loathe to contribute to future volumes and are likely to recommend against participation by others. Since I had by then become acutely aware of the limited pool of materials the series could draw upon, anything that threatened to further reduce this pool had to be considered a matter of consequence.

After the appearance of volume two, the publisher decided that in the future no fee would be offered to authors. He reasoned that since *Social Problems and Public Policy* had been reasonably well received, authors would be willing to contribute without a fee. In effect, he had decided to put the series on a footing with journals that rarely if ever pay fees or royalties. I felt strongly that the two situations were not comparable. Journals are characteristically nonprofit endeavors, while JAI Press was nothing if not a profit-making enterprise. Yet again, the amount of money involved for each author was relatively insignificant. Again the decisions suggested a fairness problem that was inherently troubling, even as it threatened to cast *Social Problems and Public Policy* in a bad light among the already limited pool of potential contributors. I protested, but to no avail.

Driven no doubt by the vanity of my purposes, I continued to edit *Social Problems and Public Policy*, but several other profit-based surprises provoked considerable disappointment. As volume three was being prepared, the publisher complained about the length of volume two; at 282 pages it was, he insisted, too long. When volume three turned out to be even longer at 312 pages, the complaints escalated. Clearly the increased size of each volume meant that production and shipping costs increased as well; although it would seem only marginally. From my perspective, however, any attempt to put a page limit on future volumes constituted an infringement upon the total editorial control I had been promised. If not successfully resisted, I believed, it would have had negative consequences for my efforts to encourage stylistic reform. Page limitations would certainly have made it difficult for me to advocate the adoption of formats that are more expansive than those conventionally in use.

During this period the price per volume of *Social Problems and Public Policy* rose to a point where libraries would have to pay well over $60 (less, of course, a 10 percent discount for standing orders). It seemed to me that the price, very high to begin with, was becoming prohibitive and could only reduce demand. From

the publisher's perspective, this would not necessarily be a negative development. By lowering costs (which had in fact been accomplished by the retreat from royalties and fees and would have
been reduced even further by a page limitation), while raising prices,
the profit margin per unit sold would be increased from both ends.
Thus, reduced sales, while not necessarily desirable, would be
acceptable because the profitability of each sale was being increased.

From my perspective, however, such a development would have
been an unmitigated disaster. None of the scholars involved with
Social Problems and Public Policy was in it for the money. The contributors participated because they had been convinced that the
series would bring exposure to the work they submitted. I had
agreed to participate to push my editorial purposes. Any reduction in library sales would mean a concurrent reduction in acces-
sibility and, consequently, in exposure. Thus, even if I had no
concerns about the legitimacy of the institutional price per se, the
increases were an unwelcome development given my purposes and
those of the authors.

Finally, there was an incident suggesting that in an effort to
reduce costs the publisher was less than aggressive in pursuing
attention for the later volumes in the series. During the preparation of volume four, I noticed a uniform failure to review volume
three. A spot check indicated that *Contemporary Sociology* had never
been sent a review copy. An accident? Perhaps! But the uniform
failure to review volume three, even by journals not known for
their selectivity, suggested something else. Early reviews for the
series had been quite positive. For example, the reviewer in *Choice*
wrote, "The collection is highly recommended to college and university libraries." The reviewer in *Contemporary Sociology* had written,
"The series should attract many readers who are interested in
evaluation research and policy analysis of social problems."

JAI Press made use of these reviews in its promotional copy.
Sending out review copies constitutes an advertising cost. If you
already have reviews that you can use in promoting library sales,
why bother incurring the expense of sending out review copies
for subsequent volumes? This undoubtedly makes good economic
sense, but the failure to get reviewed became a burden for me. As
I have already noted, exposure of one's work is the only motive
for contributing to a series like *Social Problems and Public Policy.*
Anything, therefore, that reduces exposure must make it difficult
to convince potential participants to contribute. Given the existence of a limited pool to begin with, the publisher's failure to

promote volume three aggressively, minimized my persuasiveness with possible contributors to volume four.

Thus, the synergy of surprises lasted until my editor's narcissism, made weak by the claims of reality, could no longer drive me to continue! Only resignation finally halted what seemed like an infernal perpetuity. And I promise never to edit again. Well, maybe not never. . . .

I am convinced no scholar should entertain the possibility of taking on an editorial assignment unless he or she is interpersonally adept. The editor is first and foremost a project manager. Brilliance will be to no avail if the editor is unable to move gracefully among his or her peers. Whether it is a matter of dealing with intradisciplinary politics or disgruntled or dilatory authors, the editor's only hope of success is a disarming personal style combined with the patience of Job. Since these are not qualities easily come by—they are not, for example, picked up in graduate school— I recommend great caution on the part of those who are candidates for the "order of the blue pencil." Don't accept an assignment too easily. You may soon regret that you have.

Finally, I would be remiss if I did not sound an alarm against self-seduction. Scholarly success requires some degree of narcissism. Within limits its presence moves us to activities its absence would render inconceivable. Its presence allows the expenditure of effort in creative but solitary tasks, where its absence would render the experience of solitude a loneliness too painful to endure. Narcissism can, however, render the scholar vulnerable to himself or herself. Too great an appreciation of your scholarly powers can seduce you into editorial activities better avoided and can for too long keep you believing in a task that externalities will prevent you from accomplishing. It is amazing how easily creative energies continue to be squandered when any clear-eyed observer would conclude that the editorial cause is lost. Those who would edit must learn to say "enough" long before they presently do. The narcissistically rooted belief that we can overcome any externally imposed impediments to success not only has significant personal consequences, but it blinds us to the fact that we are doing the bidding of a publishing industry that ought to, but is not, maximizing opportunities for scholars to communicate with their audiences. Saying "enough" to publishers and calling a halt to our editorial activities as soon as it becomes apparent that they do not intend to live up to their promises, would impose a discipline that our narcissism presently allows them to escape.

Notes

1. *Research in Social Problems and Public Policy,* 1 (1979): 224.
2. *Research in Social Problems and Public Policy,* 4 (1987): 237.
3. The final volume I edited, along with coeditor JoAnn L. Miller.
4. The usual arrangement assigns financial responsibility to the publisher during the galley proof state, but requires authors to accept financial responsibility for the corrections they make once a piece is set in pages.

11

Genre in Sociology:
The Case for the Monograph

✳

Teresa A. Sullivan

Since 1988, I have edited the Arnold and Caroline Rose Monograph Series, arguably the most unusual of the official publications of the American Sociological Association.[1] Unlike the periodical publications, the Rose Monograph Series publishes original, book-length basic research in sociology. And unlike the others, which are expected to be self-supporting, the Rose Series is supported by an endowment. The Rose Fund, created by bequests from the late Arnold and Caroline Rose, was established to support the publication of basic sociological research that is otherwise "not commercially viable." The Rose Monograph Series fulfills this mission by subsidizing a university press to publish four to six monographs a year, and by subsidizing the costs of monograph purchases by members of the association. The association also keeps the monographs in print, should the university press discontinue selling the book. The series is rigorously peer-reviewed at two levels. First, a manuscript is blindly refereed by at least two ad hoc referees. At the second stage, the manuscript is read by at least one associate editor and its acceptance is formally voted on by the board of associate editors.[2]

In this chapter, I will discuss three issues that often arise in discussion of the series. The first issue is merely definitional: What constitutes a monograph, and how does it differ from some other genres? The second issue is whether monographs are uniquely suited to some subject matters and approaches within sociology. The third issue is the relative effect on the discipline of monographs (or books) versus articles. To address this third issue, I will introduce data from two samples of articles and books published in 1985 and later traced through the *Social Science Citation Index.*

The Definition of a Monograph

Potential authors are often puzzled by a monograph series, and they ask many questions that ultimately hinge on the issue of genre: What is a monograph? Length was once thought to be the distinguishing factor. Many scholars refer to any article or research report that exceeds one hundred manuscript pages as a "monograph." The final report of a funded research project might be considered a monograph in this sense. The very early Rose monographs, which were published in paperback by the association, sometimes fit this description. Over time, however, the Rose Monographs have become longer and perhaps more complex. Most Rose manuscripts these days are 200 to 400 pages long, and most are organized into chapters. Publishing technology makes binding a manuscript of fewer than 150 typescript pages uneconomical for most university presses, and so the shift to longer manuscripts has suited publishers.

Length is not the only criterion for a monograph, however. I would restrict the term monograph to an integrated, book-length treatment that reports new results of a theoretical or empirical nature. My definition is similar to Caroline Persell's definition of a scholarly book as "one based on systematic original research that addresses a significant problem or makes an important theoretical contribution to the field in question" (Persell, 1985, p. 34).

Both Persell's definition and mine eliminate edited collections with chapters written by many authors. Edited collections are more similar to special issues of journals, with the separate chapters analogous to journal articles. No matter how well edited the collection is, or how well integrated the conclusions, few of them achieve the same sustained attention to a topic that a monograph does. Edited collections and special journal issues play an important role in scholarly publishing, but they are not monographs.

Monographs should also be distinguished from most textbooks. Many texts, especially at the introductory level, are nearly formulaic in their treatment of the sociology canon. They provide a valuable service in synthesizing sociological knowledge and representing the knowledge in a pedagogically appropriate form, but they are not monographs. There is, however, the "monographic textbook," which is an intermediate case. Typically used in upper-division and graduate courses, the monographic textbook reports original results, but does so with sufficient clarity and context that the material becomes accessible to students. A few publishers—but probably a diminishing proportion—will produce monographic textbooks.

The Rose Monograph Series does not publish textbooks, even monographic textbooks. As in the music industry, however, some monographs "cross over" to the textbook market, often as collateral adoptions to supplement a mainstream textbook. This is most likely to happen if the monograph content is topical. Many university presses have crossover monographs, and a few of the Rose Monographs have crossed over into the textbook market. When this happens, I try to encourage the university press that publishes the series to bring out a less-expensive paperback edition that students could afford. On the whole, however, the generalization that the monograph is not a textbook is accurate, and our decisions do not hinge on predictions about possible course adoptions.

Finally, monographs should be distinguished from dissertations. Although most dissertations present original findings on a theoretical or empirical issue, the dissertation genre differs in important respects from the monograph. As one observer has noted: "Dissertations are the ultimate homework, a complex, ritualized caricature of every academic exercise one has done, or should have done, and now, finally, must do. Consequently, most dissertations are marked by pedantry, redundancy, defensiveness, and timidity"(Fox, 1985, p. 10).

Dissertations tend to have elaborate literature reviews with very detailed accounts even of fairly routine methods. There are good reasons for this level of detail, because dissertation writers must convince faculty committees of their expertise and competence. In most monographs, by contrast, references to precedent literature are more focused and the interpretation of statistical tests omits mention of routine issues. Our experience in reviewing unrevised dissertations is that the referees unfailingly identify the manuscript as a dissertation and suggest eliminating much of the literature review and the unnecessary technical elaboration.[3]

Because there is some confusion about what constitutes a monograph, I often spend a fair amount of time simply discussing the writing project with the author. Since I have been editing the series, I have received about fifteen submissions and twenty formal inquiries annually. Formal inquiries are those that require some editorial time, such as reviewing a prospectus or a sample chapter. In addition to the formal inquiries, I receive many more informal inquiries through telephone calls or visits to the Rose Monograph Series displays at professional meetings. About half of our authors are new Ph.D.s seeking a suitable outlet for their dissertations. The other half are established sociologists who know of the series and have explicitly chosen it as a publishing outlet. I steer many inquirers to a different outlet that has a higher probability of publication success, often because their writing project is not really a monograph.

Monographs and Subject Matter

Ida Harper Simpson, a former editor of the Rose Series and of *Contemporary Sociology*, claims that there is a "book sociology" and an "article sociology." The book sociology, she argues, is qualitatively different from the article sociology. I tend to agree with her. Articles, for example, are likely to represent a lower level of ambition than books in terms of the scope of analysis, the synthetic power, and the extent to which nuances of meaning can be explored. In a large research project, for example, it is not unusual for the authors to issue a series of articles reporting findings. After the project has been completed, the researchers write a book to synthesize their findings and evaluate the new state of knowledge. In such a case, the methods and theory of the articles and the book are likely to be similar and the major difference will be the scope of the book. One caveat for the prospective authors is in order: Some book publishers will fear that the articles have preempted the market for the monograph, so the monograph needs to be a demonstrable advance over the collection of articles.

Articles and books may also differ from each other in their subject matter. Some articles are so short and highly specialized that only a few specialists will be interested. There are some indications that sociologists find "article sociology" a little boring. A survey asked respondents whether they agreed or disagreed with the following: "When I look at a new issue of my discipline's major journal, I rarely find an article that interests me." Political scientists were the most likely to agree or to strongly agree with this statement (43 percent), although sociologists were right behind with 41 percent agreeing that articles rarely interest them (Morton & Price, 1989, p. 67).

Although it is a bit of an oversimplification, studies using qualitative methods are more commonly developed in books, and studies using quantitative methods are more commonly developed in articles (Lindsey, 1978, p. 96). Ethnographic and historical/comparative data, for example, often require extensive discussion and development in text. By extension, detailed theoretical discussions often require book length for a complete exposition. If there is a "book sociology," such studies are overrepresented in it. Quantitative data, however, can often be parsimoniously summarized in statistical tables, and statistical models can be written in equations. If there is an "article sociology," quantitative studies are over-represented in it. Indeed, this generalization is the basis for periodic disputes over how representative of the discipline journals such as the *American Sociological Review* are. The Rose Monograph Series encourages any type of subject matter, but it is probably true that in recent years quantitative studies have been less well represented than more qualitative ones. This is a function, I might add, of submission patterns and not of acceptance rates.

Publications and submissions to the Rose Monograph Series vary both by subject matter and method. In terms of topic, there have been one or more monographs published in the following areas since 1986: art and culture, critical interpretation, environment and ecology, organizations, politics, religion, social psychology, stratification, and theory. Methodological approaches have included analysis of administrative data, texts, and historical records; community institutional case studies; comparisons of theoretical models; and survey research.

The coexistence of a book sociology and an article sociology can be a problem when sociologists are being evaluated by academics from other disciplines. A frustrated member of the promotions committee in a liberal arts college once asked me, "Is sociology a book field or an article field?" The question stemmed from a committee meeting in which the members were comparing the scholarly achievements of tenure candidates from various disciplines. Throughout the humanities (languages, history, philosophy), publication of a book is the *sine qua non* for promotion. In such fields, there is considerable debate about how much articles should count, or if they should even count at all. In the biological and physical sciences, articles are the expected scholarly output, and it would be odd for an assistant professor to have published a book. Indeed, in science departments the issue might be raised of whether the book should count. Within the social sciences, economics and psychology lean somewhat more to the articles mode and anthropology somewhat more toward the book mode.

Sociology straddles the book/article divide just as it straddles the humanities/sciences divide, and indeed the standards for promotion vary from one sociology department to another. In departments that embrace the more scientific end of the discipline, articles are prized; in departments with a more humanistic orientation, book are prized. In all sociology departments, one often hears the half-facetious effort to measure productivity phrased as "How many articles equal a book?"[4] It is no surprise, then, that evaluation committee members tend to judge sociologists by the standards of their own disciplines, perhaps because they cannot discern what the standards within sociology are. This means that a sociologist who writes articles may lose the vote of the historian or the philosopher, but the sociologist who writes an ethnographic monograph may lose the vote of the psychologist or the economist. Department chairs and external referees might do well to recall for the committee Ida Simpson's argument that there is both a book sociology and an article sociology.

The issue of genre is an especially pressing one for the young sociologist who may soon face a tenure decision. One question I am frequently asked as an editor is, "Should I try to publish my dissertation?" The answer to this question has both a strategic element and an intellectual element. The strategic element is related to the departmental culture. First of all, some departments consider *any* additional time spent on a dissertation to be wasted, and they will count only postdissertation projects toward tenure. More typically, however, the question of how to publish a dissertation should be considered in light of the genre distinction. If a department views articles as the true sign of professionalism, then the young Ph.D. might be well advised to carve up the chapters of the dissertation into discrete chapters. If the department considers a book the bare minimum for academic respectability, then converting the dissertation to a monograph might be wise. Either way, the new Ph.D. will face considerable work revising the dissertation. In one survey, only 13 percent of sociology respondents had published all or most of their dissertations in book form; three times as many (39 percent) had published part of the dissertation in article form. By contrast, in history 35 percent of respondents had published their dissertations as a book, as had 27 percent of the respondents in classics (Morton & Price, 1989, p. 69).

Besides strategy, there are intellectual reasons for deciding on articles as against a book. I ask dissertation writers to consider how well integrated and interdependent their findings are; to consider how much the arguments and data could be condensed; and to consider how much description of methods and data would be needed to make sense of any of the findings. A cohesive, well-integrated dissertation makes a good book. An episodic dissertation, for example, one in which different data bases are examined in different chapters, is probably more suitable for articles.

Whatever the merits of monographs, however, publication outlets are more scarce for them than for journal articles. About one in four sociologists surveyed reported that more book publishers are needed (Morton & Price, 1989, p. 29). Monographs are expensive to produce, and many trade houses have recently become more conservative in their decisions as a result of their acquisition by profit-hungry parent organizations.[5] Even university presses, traditionally well aware of their not-for-profit status, have become more concerned about the bottom line (American Council of Learned Societies, 1979, p. 94). These pressures may lead to greater variation in the conduct of peer reviews among monographs as compared with journals.[5] A journal editor might take a risk and publish an article for which the reviews indicated some weaknesses, but book editors probably take fewer risks.[6]

The future of monograph publishing is somewhat difficult to forecast (Horowitz & Curtis, 1982). Great economic concentration in the publishing fields, combined with the perception that sociologists are not book buyers, suggests publication of fewer monographs. On the other hand, the advent of inexpensive, high-quality desktop publishing may spur innovations among small, new houses. And although there has been some speculation about electronic journals, very little speculation has so far appeared about electronic monographs.

The Impact of Monographs and Articles

The final issue I would like to address is the relative impact of articles and monographs. Everyone is aware that not all articles have equal impact; articles published in more visible and prestigious journals are likely to have more impact than those published in more specialized or smaller journals. By the same token, there is a hierarchy among book publishers such that some books will become more visible just by virtue of their publishers. But what is the relative impact of a prestigious article compared with a prestigious book?

To answer this question, I needed to develop a sample of articles and a sample of books that would both be prestigious. I selected a random sample of twenty-seven articles published in either *American Sociological Review* or *American Journal of Sociology* in calendar year 1985. Most sociologists would agree that these articles had undergone rigorous review, and that they were located in highly visible journals.

The sample of books was harder to develop. Literally hundreds of books are published in sociology every year (see American Council of Learned Societies, 1979, p. 88), and the prestige hierarchy among presses is not as well defined as that among journals. Moreover, the review processes differ from press to press in terms of rigor and thoroughness. As it happened, however, in 1986 I was the chair of the American Sociological Association committee to pick the Distinguished Scholarly Contribution Award. This award, which was once called the Sorokin Award, is awarded annually to an outstanding book in sociology. (Technically, the award could go to an article or chapter, but in practice only books are competitive for the prize.) Books published during the preceding three years are eligible, so that in 1986, books that had been published in 1983, 1984, and 1985 were nominated. The process of award nomination represented an additional level of selection; of the hundreds of books published in those years, eighty-five had been nominated, most of them from the preceding year, 1985. Consequently, I drew my sample of twenty-seven books randomly from among the nominated books that had been published in 1985. Although Rose Monographs are frequently nominated for this and other book awards, none fell into my sample. The appendix contains bibliographic information for the two samples.

The next problem was measuring the impact of the articles and books. For this I turned to the *Social Science Citation Index*, published annually by the Institute for Scientific Information. The *Index* indicates the citations to published works found in some two thousand social science journals that are included in its data base. Thus, all the references from journal articles become citations, and a work that is widely cited is assumed to have considerable impact. All citations to the published works were counted for five years, 1985–89, and for the first eight months of 1990. Because the sample consisted of works, not authors, this search avoided some of the biases involved when an author's citations are analyzed (Lindsey, 1978, p. 41).

It seems a plausible inference that citations are an indicator of impact (Lindsey, 1978, p. 43), but the meaning of citations is not always clear. For example, not all citations are favorable. Moreover, citations might have differential validity as impact measures for books relative to articles. Books are longer than articles, so that books might garner more total citations, even though citations per page might be considerably lower for books than articles. The usual metric, citation counts, might be skewed in favor of books.

On the other hand, the citation index is asymmetric: it includes only citations from journals, and none from books. For this reason, the *Social Science Citation Index* might contain a bias against monographs. This problem gains added impetus to the extent that "book sociology" represents not merely a different genre, but a different orientation to sociology and to subject matter. Hargens (1991, citing Line, 1981) notes that as many as three-quarters of the citations in sociology books are to other books. The more intellectually segregated book sociology is from article sociology, the more compelling this objection becomes. Suppose, for example, that an area of specialization reaches print exclusively in books; as subsequent books are published, they cite the earlier books in the field. If an author were widely cited in the footnotes of books, but relatively ignored in the journals, the citation index would undercount the author because it reports only citations from journals.

A third possibility suggests a bias in favor of books. Postpublication book reviews continue to highlight the significance of books, often bringing the book to a reader's attention eighteen to thirty-six months after publication. Articles do not have this advantage, because their most important reviews occur before their publication. Table 1 presents descriptive statistics for the two samples. Over the period of five years and a few months in 1990, the twenty-seven books garnered 1,384 citations and the articles garnered 364. The median number of citations for articles was nine and for books it was nineteen. As might be expected, the mean was considerably higher, especially for the books: 13.5 for articles, 51.3 for books. These means are obviously affected by "citation stars," books and articles that received a great deal of attention.

Figure 1 presents the comparison of citations graphically. Even if the index is biased against books, books have demonstrably more impact ($\chi^2 = 15.15$, $p < 0.01$). Given that the index is at least asymmetric, if not biased, in its treatment of books, this finding is all the more remarkable.

The timing of the citations is interesting, as well. Neither books nor articles receive many citations in the year of publication. Figure 1 shows dramatically the lag between publication and the rise in citations. The peak of citations for the sample of books was

Table 1
Descriptive Statistics, Citation Counts for a Sample
of Sociology Books and Articles Published in 1985

	Books (N = 27)	Articles (N = 27)
Total citations	1385	364
1985	8	5
1986	138	35
1987	266	63
1988	336	77
1989	256	97
1990	381	87
Mean	51.3	13.5
Median	19.0	9.0
Range	454.0	60.0
Standard deviation	91.4	12.8

reached in 1988, about three years on average after publication. The peak for articles was reached a year later, in 1989. The shape of the curve, however, might be somewhat misleading, because one-third of 1990 is not included in the 1990 figures. In every year, however, books are more cited than articles. By 1986, the sample of books had received more citations than the peak number of citations achieved by articles in 1989.

The pattern of timing is notable, perhaps, because one reason for developing journals was their greater timeliness compared with books (Osburn, 1984). Greater timeliness is still an advantage with natural science journals, some of which publish on a weekly basis and often cite other articles within days of publication. The advantage of timeliness has been somewhat muted in most social science journals, however, because of their bimonthly, quarterly, or even semiannual publication schedules. In addition, large backlogs often insure that an article (and the citations it contains) will not appear for months after acceptance. Thus, one citation advantage for journals has been diluted.

What explains the greater citation frequency for books? Several possible reasons have already been suggested. The first rea-

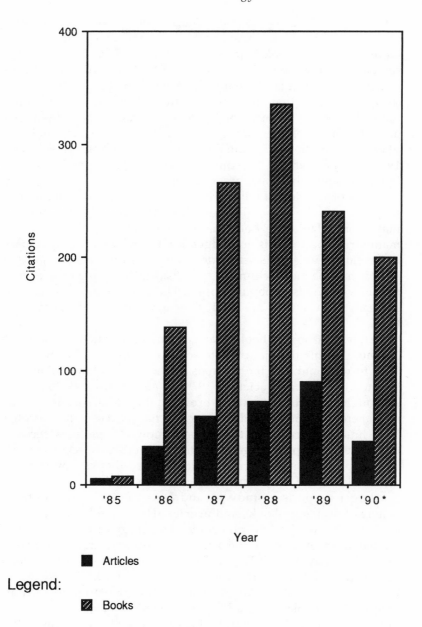

Figure 1: Citations by year for a sample of sociology articles and books published in 1985 (1990 includes January through August only).

son is substantive significance. The broader scope and ambition of the typical book, compared with the typical article, may lead to more citations. A book that serves as the capstone for a large research project is more likely to be cited than the articles that preceded it; indeed, it is likely to eclipse them completely. A possible second reason is that the subject matter of the books, compared with the articles, is hotter. Books represent a considerable investment by the publisher, and some consideration of marketability plays a role in the publishing decisions of most houses (Eisenstein, 1980).[7] "Marketability," in this context, may be a proxy for subfields or topics that have great current interest.

Some proportion of journal articles, then, may be submitted to the journal as the second-best publication outlet. Rejected authors may reorganize some book-length manuscripts into articles. A manuscript topic that is not judged marketable by printing houses represents a far smaller risk for a journal editor, and so journal editors may be more willing to take risks in accepting articles that tout new methods or obscure topics. These riskier articles may not be read; even if they are read, they may not attract many citations.

A third reason that books may garner more citations is that they are more visible than journals to scholars in other fields. Scholars tend to read and cite the journals in their own fields (American Council of Learned Societies, 1979, p. 46; Lindsey, 1978, p. 93). Although other academics may browse a few of the sociology journals, there is an understandable fear that the journals will be written in technical, obscure language. Books, however, perhaps because of editors' concerns with marketability, are often consciously written to appeal to a broader audience, and so they are often more accessible to researchers publishing in other fields.

Hargens reports a study he and David Botts conducted of a cohort of sociology books and articles. They found that "the median number of citations books receive approximately equals the median number going to the articles and research notes published by ASR" (Hargens, 1991, p. 347). A small set of "classic" books garnered a high proportion of all citations, leading Hargens to conclude that sociology displays a general orientation toward an elderly set of books. My study does not contradict Hargens's study, but it also does not corroborate it because only the citations to the cohort of 1985 books were analyzed. But the two studies taken together seem to reinforce the conclusion that book sociology remains lively, vital, and visible.

Conclusion

The citation data indicate that sociologists attend to and cite leading books at even higher rates than they cite leading articles. If citation counts can be taken as a sign of impact, then books continue to make a substantial intellectual impact on sociology. Through careful reviewing and editing, the American Sociological Association seeks to support monographs that can add to the scholarly conversation. Taken in this context, the Rose Monograph Series fills an appropriate intellectual niche in fulfilling its mission.

Notes

1. The Rose Monograph Series, along with all other American Sociological Association publications, requires exclusive submission of manuscripts. This is not the case with many other book publishers (Topkis, 1985: 80; American Council of Learned Societies, 1979: 113–14). Our peer review system is such, however, that networks of professional contacts are not so important as Topkis (1985) and Powell (1985) imply is the case with scholarly publishing. When a manuscript has received at least one positive review, I am very likely to suggest that the author respond in writing to the criticisms raised in the review. I am already familiar with the manuscript and offer suggestions for revisions to the author both in writing and by telephone. Increasingly, these conversations are carried on by electronic mail.

2. I have prepared a one-page handout on the differences between a dissertation and a monograph that is intended to provide information to prospective authors. It is available upon request.

3. Lindsey's (1978: 41) formula gives an article a value of 1, an edited book a value of 2, and a book a value of 5.

4. For a discussion of the takeover of independent publishing houses by conglomerates, see Coser, Kadushin, and Powell (1982).

5. For a discussion of manuscript selection policies, see Powell (1985).

6. Risks will probably not be taken at journals with large numbers of submissions and restricted space, but greater risks probably are taken among the smaller or less established journals.

7. As I mentioned, marketability is not a consideration in the Rose Monograph Series decisions.

References

American Council of Learned Societies. 1979. *Scholarly Communication: The Report of the National Enquiry.* Baltimore: Johns Hopkins University Press.

Coser, Lewis A., Charles Kadushin, & Walter W. Powell. 1982. *Books: The Culture and Commerce of Publishing*. New York: Basic Books.

Eisenstein, Elizabeth L. 1980. *The Printing Revolution in Early Modern Europe*. Cambridge: Cambridge University Press.

Fox, Mary Frank. 1985. "The Transition from Dissertation Student to Publishing Scholar and Professional." Pp. 6–16 in Mary Frank Fox, ed. *Scholarly Writing and Publishing: Issues, Problems, and Solutions*. Boulder: Westview Press.

Hargens, Lowell L. 1991. "Impressions and Misimpressions about Sociology Journals." *Contemporary Sociology* 20 (May): 343–349.

Horowitz, Irving Louis and Mary E. Curtis. 1982. "The Impact of Technology on Scholarly Publishing." *Scholarly Publishing* 13 (April): 211–28.

Lindsey, Duncan. 1978. *The Scientific Publication System in Social Science*. San Francisco: Jossey-Bass.

Line, Maurice B. 1981. "The Structure of Social Science Literature by a Large-Scale Citation Analysis." *Social Science Information Studies* 1: 67–87.

Morton, Herbert C., and Anne J. Price. 1989. *The ACLS Survey of Scholars*. Washington, DC: American Council of Learned Societies.

Osburn, Charles B. 1984. "The Place of the Journal in the Scholarly Communication System." *Library Resources and Technical Services* 28 (October/December): 315–24.

Persell, Caroline Hedges. 1985. "Scholars and Book Publishing." Pp. 33–50 in Mary Frank Fox, ed. *Scholarly Writing and Publishing: Issues, Problems, and Solutions*. Boulder: Westview Press.

Powell, Walter W. 1985. *Getting into Print: The Decision-Making Process in Scholarly Publication*. Chicago: University of Chicago Press.

Topkis, Gladys S. 1985. "Book Publishing: An Editor's-Eye View." Pp. 73–98 in Mary Frank Fox, ed. *Scholarly Writing and Publishing: Issues, Problems, and Solutions*. Boulder: Westview Press.

Appendix: Sample of Sociology Books and Articles Published in 1985

Books:

Alford, Robert R. 1985. *Powers of Theology: Capitalism, the State, and Democracy*. New York: Cambridge University Press.

Banton, Michael P. 1985. *Promoting Racial Harmony*. New York: Cambridge University Press.

Beckford, James A. 1985. *Cult Controversies: The Societal Response to New Religious Movements*. New York: Travistock Publications.

Bellah, Robert N., et al. 1985. *Habits of the Heart: Individualism and Commitment in American Life*. Berkeley: University of California Press.

Bunker, Stephan G. 1985. *Underdeveloping the Amazon: Extraction, Unequal Exchange, and the Failure of the Modern State*. Urbana: University of Illinois Press.

Burstein, Paul. 1985. *Discrimination, Jobs, and Politics: The Struggle for Equal Employment Opportunity in the United States since the New Deal*. Chicago: University of Chicago Press.

Cohn, Samuel. 1985. *The Process of Occupational Sex-Typing: The Feminization of Clerical Labor in Great Britain*. Philadelphia: Temple University Press.

Feldman, Elliot J. 1985. *Concorde and Dissent: Explaining High Technology Project Failures in Britain and France*. New York: Cambridge University Press.

Gerson, Kathleen. 1985. *Hard Choices: How Women Decide about Work, Career, and Motherhood*. Berkeley: University of California Press.

Heimer, Carol Anne. 1985. *Reactive Risk and Rational Action: Managing Moral Hazard in Insurance Contracts*. Berkeley: University of California Press.

Horowitz, Donald L. 1985. *Ethnic Groups in Conflict*. Berkeley: University of California Press.

Konvitz, Josef W. 1985. *The Urban Millennium: The City-Building Process from the Early Middle Ages to the Present*. Carbondale: Southern Illinois University Press.

Lieberson, Stanley. 1985. *Making it Count: Improvement of Social Research and Theory*. Berkeley: University of California Press.

Mirande, Alfredo. 1985. *The Chicano Experience: An Alternative Perspective*. Notre Dame: University of Notre Dame Press.

Naff, Alixa. 1985. *Becoming American: The Early Arab Immigrant Experience*. Carbondale: Southern Illinois University Press.

Pedraza-Bailey, Sylvia. 1985. *Political and Economic Migrants in America: Cubans and Mexicans*. Austin: University of Texas Press.

Pitkin, Donald S. 1985. *The House That Giacomo Built: History of an Italian Family, 1898–1978*. Cambridge: Cambridge University Press.

Rogler, Lloyd H., and Rosemary Santana Cooney. 1985. *Puerto Rican Families in New York City: Intergenerational Processes*. Maplewood, N.J.: Waterfront Press.

Rossi, Alice S. (ed.). 1985. *Gender and the Life Course*. New York: Aldine Publishing Company.

Rozman, Gilbert. 1985. *A Mirror for Socialism: Soviet Criticisms of China.* Princeton: Princeton University Press.

Shkilnyk, Anastasia M. *A Poison Stronger Than Love: The Destruction of an Ojibwa Community.* New Haven: Yale University Press.

Stichter, Sharon. 1985. *Migrant Laborers.* New York: Cambridge University Press.

Thomas, Robert J. 1985. *Citizenship, Gender, and Work: The Social Organization of Industrial Agriculture.* Berkeley: University of California Press.

Vesperi, Maria D. 1985. *City of Green Benches: Growing Old in a New Downtown.* Ithaca: Cornell University Press.

Weitzman, Lenore J. 1985. *The Divorce Revolution: The Unexpected Social and Economic Consequences for Women and Children in America.* New York: Free Press.

Wilson, James Q., and Richard J. Herrnstein. 1985. *Crime and Human Nature.* New York: Simon and Schuster.

Zelizer, Viviana A. Rotman. 1985. *Pricing the Priceless Child: The Changing Social Value of Children.* New York: Basic Books.

Articles:

American Journal of Sociology

Amsterdamska, Olga. 1985 "Institutions and Schools of Thought: The Neogrammarians." AJS 91(1): 332-358.

Blum, Terry. 1985. "Structural Constraints on Interpersonal Relations: A Test of Blau's Macrosociological Theory." AJS 91(1): 511–521.

Carroll, Glenn. 1985. "Concentration and Specialization: Dynamics of Niche Width in Populations of Organizations." AJS 90(4): 1262–1283.

Duncan, Otis Dudley. 1985. "New Light on the 16-fold Table." AJS 91(1): 88–128.

Greenberg, David F. 1985. "Age, Crime, and Social Explanation." AJS 91(1): 1–21.

Hogan, Dennis P., and Evelyn M. Kitagawa. 1985. "The Impact of Social Status, Family Structure, and Neighborhood on the Fertility of Balck Adolescents." AJS 90(4): 825–855.

Miller, Joanne, et al. 1985. "Continuity of Learning-Generalization: The Effect of Job on Men's Intellective Process in the United States and Poland." AJS 91(1): 593–615.

Naoi, Atsushi, and Carmi Schooler. 1985. "Occupational Conditions and Psychological Functioning in Japan." AJS 90(4): 729–752.

Nyden, Philip W. 1985. "Democratizing Organizations: A Case Study of a Union Reform Movement." AJS 90(4): 1179–1203.

Ridgeway, Cecelia L., Joseph Berger, and LeRoy Smith, 1985. "Nonverbal Cues and Status: An Expectation States Approach." AJS 90(4): 955–978.

Robinson, Robert V., and Maurice A. Garnier. 1985. "Class Reproduction among Men and Women in France: Reproduction Theory on Its Home Ground." AJS 91(1): 250–280.

Rosenthal, Naomi, et al. 1985. "Social Movements and Network Analysis: A Case Study of Nineteenth-Century Women's Reform." AJS 90(4): 1022–1054.

American Sociological Review

Alexander, Karl L. et al., 1985. "Schooling and Cognitive Performance." ASR 50(3): 409–420.

Baron, James N., and Peter C. Reiss. 1985. "Mass Media and Violent Behavior." ASR 50(3): 347–363.

Bradshaw, York W. 1985. "Dependent Development in Black Africa." ASR 50(2): 195–206.

Devine, Joel A. 1985. "State and State Expenditure." ASR 50(2): 150–165.

Galaskiewicz, Joseph. 1985. "Professional Networks." ASR 50(5): 639–658.

Hagan, John, and Patricia Parker. 1985. "White-Collar Crime and Punishment." ASR 50(3): 302–316.

Haller, Max, et al. 1985. "Career Mobility and Structural Positions." ASR 50(5): 579–602.

Humphrey, Ronald. 1985. "Work Roles and Perception." ASR 50(2): 242–252.

Lauman, Edward O., et al. 1985. "An Organizational Approach to State Policy Formation." ASR 50(1): 1–19.

Markoff, John. 1985. "Rural Revolt and the French Revolution." ASR 50(6): 761–781.

Markovsky, Barry, 1985. "Multilevel Justice Theory." ASR 50(6): 822–839.

Muller, Edward N., 1985. "Income Inequality, Regime Repressiveness, and Political Violence." ASR 50(1): 47–61.

Robinson, Patricia. 1985. "Language Retention." ASR 50(4): 515–529.

Weil, Frederick. 1985. "Education and Liberalism." ASR 50(4): 458–474.

White, Lynn K., and Alan Booth. 1985. "Stepchildren in Remarriages." ASR 50(5): 689–698.

Part III

University and Commercial Press
Editors and Directors

12

University Press Editing and Publishing

*

Carole S. Appel

I recently came across a letter my mother wrote to her sister in Brooklyn in the 1940s when I was a few months into the first grade in Philadelphia: "Carole has learned to read," my mother reported, "and now it's all she wants to do." The letter is consistent with my own memory of the delight in books that transformed my childhood. By the time I was seven, I found I was not alone in this passion. My friends and I would play ball and jump rope together and trade Bobbsey Twins, Nancy Drew, and Beverly Gray books. Older girls, our occasional baby-sitters in those dreamy days before television occupied summer vacations, would bring me *Little Women* or *A Tree Grows in Brooklyn*, and we would read for hours on shady porches and talk about the characters.

I pictured myself growing up to be a writer or a librarian. Had a prophet appeared on Lebanon Avenue then to announce that I could become a publisher if I liked, I would have seized that opportunity too. It bemuses me sometimes to see how closely my work now fulfills that dream, though I could not have understood then the daily responsibilities that being an editor and publisher entail.

I am an acquisitions editor in the humanities and social sciences for a scholarly publishing house, the University of Illinois Press. My primary editorial responsibilities are in women's studies. I am also the press's journals manager and oversee the publication and distribution of twelve scholarly journals. Wearing my editorial hat, I work with scores of authors whose books I would like to publish or who hope to publish with us. As journals manager, I speak frequently with the editors of scholarly journals and with the officers of learned societies whose publications we distribute. I spend a great deal of time reading about new technologies for journal publication, in hopes of containing journal costs (particularly through computer typesetting from author-supplied disks) and wondering how CD-ROM and other innovations may transform our profession.

The editors of this volume have asked "How do editors see their role? How did they become editors? What gets published and why?" I hope that the answers I explore here will illuminate the editorial process both for scholars who want to know what happens to the manuscripts they entrust to us and for individuals who have contemplated editorial careers for themselves. I think that the answer to "what gets published and why" is very much wrapped up in the facts of who we editors are as individuals, what interests us, what publishing risks have succeeded for us in the past, and what publishing opportunities our experience has taught us are golden rings to grab as quickly we can.

My route to my current career, despite my early joy in books, was indirect, though, in retrospect, appropriate at every stage. I entered college as a journalism student, wild about anything that had to do with newspapers and intent upon becoming a reporter. I worked for a weekly newspaper, wrote for the Temple University *News*, went to classes. Not until the end of my freshman year did I realize that there was more to college than preparing for a job. Truly, no one in my high school had pointed out that simple truth and my family, professionally oriented, did not discuss such matters. The journalism curriculum required history, economics, English, and political science courses, and the electives provided plenty of opportunities to explore other courses in the humanities. I cannot think of a single course I took as an undergraduate that has not been an important resource to me as an editor, whether it was a business school offering in marketing or an English department course in Chaucer. It is hard to serve your authors and your employers well without thinking about the eternal marketing questions: Who will buy this book? Who will want to read it? What will it cost us to publish it? What will the price have to be? And while an editor cannot be an expert in every field in which a press publishes, the more you have been exposed to at least the rudiments of a field, the easier it is to understand manuscripts and prospectuses and to ask reasonable questions about them.

The undergraduate journalism curriculum at Temple permitted me to concentrate my electives in English literature and language and to qualify for graduate work in linguistics, which is where my growing fascination with the history of written and spoken English took me next. After graduate school and several years teaching freshman rhetoric and English as a second language, I was offered a position as a copy editor at the University of Illinois Press. I am amused when I recall one of the questions Rita Simon posed when she told me about the mission she and James Fyfe had for this book: for editors to write personal essays relating their "great notions" about the books they wanted to publish. I have such notions now. I want to publish serious, important books about women and social history and psychology, in a manner that is considerate of the needs of the authors and the press; and I want some of my books to win major awards and more than a few of them to be financially rewarding to the press. I want to publish scholarly journals that are respected in their disciplines, distributed at prices that libraries and individuals can afford to pay. When I first became a copy editor, in 1969, however, my greatest hope was to learn not to overlook authors' misspellings and not to let embarrassing grammatical errors slip by me. I was thrilled to be in book publishing, but I had only a small understanding of the process by which the manuscripts I worked on came to my desk.

I recently asked a few other university press editors how they arrived at this career, and the responses are not particularly different from mine. Kate Torrey, who is now director at North Carolina, became fascinated with publishing during a stint as an editorial assistant at Indiana University, where she was working on a dissertation in history; Joan Catapano of Indiana University Press told me that she read history extensively as a child and later, as an undergraduate, "wanted to change the world through psychology." She started to work in university publishing as a marketing assistant while a graduate student in history. Like many of us, she saw the acquisition of manuscripts as a way of making a difference. Richard Wentworth, now director at Illinois, discovered the University of Oklahoma Press on his beat as a college newspaper reporter and won a fellowship for the press's training program in publishing. Three other men who are now directors of university presses were also fellows in the Oklahoma program: John Kyle of Texas, Donald Ellegood of Washington, and Stephen Cox of Arizona. Other editors I know have moved into acquisitions from jacket copy writing or from the sales force. When students are referred to me for information about publishing as a career,

I recommend the publishing institutes offered by the University of Chicago, the University of Denver, Howard University, Radcliffe College, New York University, and Stanford University. I receive numerous letters from people applying for journals copyediting positions, and I pay attention to a résumé that shows experience at another press or attendance at a publishing institute.

When I started work as an assistant editor, the University of Illinois Press was much smaller than it is now—we published twenty-five new books that year. I look at the 1969 catalog and don't perceive that the small staff at that time had great visions either, except to provide competent services to the university community, locally and nationally. No single thread tied together the varied titles on that list, and though it includes some excellent works—some classics still in print—I suspect those books were published because the authors were from our campus and were satisfied to offer their manuscripts to a conveniently located publishing house whose editors were careful and accommodating.

The planning and vision that permitted the press's expansion and dominance in several well-defined areas—American history and literature, women's studies, black studies, and American music—would come a few years later, as many American scholarly presses began to grow, to specialize, and to compete for manuscripts by promising authors. I was fortunate to be on the staff when this expansion began and to learn firsthand from an aggressive editor how a press carves out an area for itself. I was equally fortunate to be trained as a copy editor by a managing editor whose first instruction to me upon handing over a manuscript was to read the correspondence file to understand how the press came to be publishing this book and what the manuscript's outside readers expected from it.

Several interesting events of the earlier 1970s propelled me into the editorial position I now so dearly cherish, and the women's movement was a focus of all of them. One Sunday in about 1971, the *New York Times Magazine* featured on its cover a photograph of three women marching in a women's liberation demonstration in New York. The women triumphantly carried a banner that read "Male Chauvinists Beware," and they looked so enraptured that I cut out the picture and put it on the wall above my desk. This small act seemed to single me out as the office feminist and to prompt anyone with a sympathetic word or a gripe about feminism to direct it to me.

Concurrently, in the newly opened Chicago branch of the press, the acquiring editor had been advised by a historian that women's history was a coming thing, and he began to write various scholars for advice on which classics in women's history were worth reprinting for a modern audience. His quest brought us some important books, like Charlotte Perkins Gilman's *The Home: Its Work and Influence* and Jane Addams's *The Spirit of Youth and the City Streets*; it also brought him good advice to look for fresh scholarship. As a result of my clear interest in feminism, I was given some of these studies to copyedit, and my delight in those books led to a trip to an inaugural Berkshire conference on women's history in 1973, where I took my first tentative steps as an acquirer of book manuscripts.

If I knew then what I know now, I would have signed up every one of the panelists to publish a book with us. I listened to scholars give papers, talked with them and others at communal meals, and forged friendships with women historians that I have valued ever since, personally and professionally. Through the manuscripts I was copyediting, such as Berenice Carroll's *Liberating Women's History: Theoretical and Critical Essays*, and the conference papers I heard, I learned what issues in women's history were important to scholars in the forefront of the new research. I became better prepared to decide which manuscript proposals were worth pursuing and which invited manuscripts deserved to be sent beyond my desk to outside readers. I learned, too, the kinds of questions I needed to ask outside consultants in order to receive from them the most useful critiques possible.

It is appropriate for me to write here about the evaluation process at the University of Illinois Press (which is typical of that at most presses) and about the interaction between authors, editors, outside readers, and a press's director and faculty board.

Manuscripts arrive at our office because we have been pursuing them or because the authors have written or called us on their own. Our job as editors is to obtain outside reports on the most promising manuscripts, to return as soon as possible the manuscripts that don't seem appropriate for us, and to move into production in a timely manner those works that have been accepted for publication. All manuscripts that we publish require the approval of a faculty board, appointed by the university administration. The board meets three times a year and reads dossiers consisting of descriptions and critiques of each manuscript.

In the course of events, most of the manuscripts the editors think should be published are approved; works that have received weak recommendations do not go before the board. We can issue contracts before a manuscript goes before the board, so long as the authors know that publication is based on board approval. Editorial decisions are made at every step: whether to issue a contract early, on the basis of a prospectus and sample chapters; or to wait until a manuscript is completed and reviewed; whether to make commitments contingent on minor (or major) revisions; whether to seek press board approval early in the evaluation process or only when the last report on the last set of revisions is in hand. There are manuscripts by acknowledged scholarly stars we would want to sign on the spot, studies by authors who prefer to wait until the book is complete before signing a contract, and work by authors, junior or accomplished, who are more comfortable finishing a book with a publishing agreement (and its attendant deadlines) in their files.

In the old days—the seventies, for me—I might spend most of a day reading a new manuscript to see whether the press should invest in an outside report. Not only did I dread wasting the press's money and a reader's time on a weak study, but I wanted never to be embarrassed by a report that might question why anyone would want to publish a certain work. The competition of the 1990s, and the tight budgets that make us all want to produce more books in the same amount of work time as we took for fewer books, make this kind of comfortable on-premises reading rare. We learn to characterize a book's possibilities in an hour at work, or in a few hours on a weekend at home. Sometimes I find myself spending more time with a manuscript after I have received critiques than I did before I sent it out, time to reconcile conflicting reports, or to decide whether a manuscript that received a mildly positive recommendation should be sent out to a second reader. As a result, sometimes I don't meet my goal of swiftly returning inappropriate or weak manuscripts.

The flow of incoming work is not easy to control. One may solicit three or four manuscripts a week (at a conference or by mail) only to have many months of encouraging letters bear fruit all in the same two week period. Editors learn how to make quick decisions, and we try not to grieve too long over the manuscripts we lose because of wrong decisions. Roger Cohen, writing in the *New York Times*, quotes George Brett, the publisher of Macmillan, in advice given at the turn of the century to the founder of the University of Chicago Press: "This is for your private ear only. It is sometimes better for a mistake to be made with the possibility of rapid decision than slow action."[1] Comforting advice if we think about books of ours that sank without a ripple after publication; comforting as well when we recall fast decisions that produced rousingly successful titles for our list; and discomforting when we notice the age of several letters waiting for response.

That brings me to a piece of advice for authors: if you haven't heard from a publisher after a few weeks have gone by, call, for your sake and the publisher's. An important letter can get buried when an editor is away at scholarly meetings or on vacation or just plain busy. Risk setting a deadline for a response. It may mean writing off a good publisher who is too swamped to deal with your proposal at the time, but it will speed you onto the next possibility, and may also speed a response from the first publisher. I would give the same advice to anyone whose manuscript is in the evaluation process. Do not nag a publisher after only a few weeks, it can easily take that long to find an outside reader, but after three months, if you haven't heard anything, call. If the manuscript is with readers, you should know the deadlines they have been given, if readers haven't been found, you need to know that too. Occasionally, after spending hours on the phone and by letter trying to find a qualified, objective reader for a manuscript (someone who is willing *and* available), I have waited six months or more for a report I expected (and was promised) in eight weeks. Readers can get bogged down in their own academic work; elderly parents become ill, children get the flu, a reader's own book proofs arrive early, all these reasons have been give to me by well-meaning scholars who agreed to read manuscripts and probably wished afterward that they hadn't.

The questions I ask of readers can be summarized in a handy few that I learned as a novice editor from Richard Wentworth, editor-in-chief at Illinois since 1971. "Was the topic worth researching and was it done well? Will publishing the manuscript distinguish the author and the press? Should we publish it essentially as is, with optional revisions, essential revisions, or not publish it at all?" At Illinois, we prefer readers' reports in letter form, and we have found it useful to provide readers with a list of questions as a guide. (One should realize that these questions do not have equal weight in our evaluation of the critique; a negative response to the question about the potential for interest abroad is not likely to hurt a manuscript's chances with us, although a positive response would be fine.) These are the questions:

1. Please describe briefly what this work sets out to do and for whom it is intended.

2.   Does this manuscript make a truly significant contribution to the field? Why or why not?

3.   Is the scholarship sound? Has the author gone to all the right sources and made the best use of them? Do the conclusions flow from the evidence presented?

4.   How do you rate the manuscript's organization?

5.   How do you rate the writing? Is it clear, free of jargon, and interesting? Is the style appropriate for the subject and the intended audience?

6.   Will this work prove useful to interested readers outside this field, whether scholars in other disciplines or lay readers? If so, to whom and to what extent?

7.   How does this work compete with, complement, or otherwise compare with other available books? Please comment briefly on the titles you cite.

8.   Does this have classroom potential? If so, for what kinds of classes and at what level?

9.   Would there be potential interest in this work abroad?

10.   If in your opinion the manuscript needs further work:

   (a) Does it show enough potential that we should encourage the authors to undertake the necessary revisions?

   (b) Do you feel that the author is capable of making these revisions?

   (c) Is the manuscript longer (or shorter) than it needs to be to make its case most effectively?

   (d) What are your general and specific suggestions for revision?

11.   Did you find this manuscript stimulating? Did you enjoy reading it? Is this something you would recommend to others?

12.   In sum:

   [ ] I strongly recommend publication.

   [ ] I recommend publication and have suggested optional revisions.

   [ ] I recommend publication only if the specified revisions are satisfactorily completed.

   [ ] I do not recommend publication.

For a collection of essays, especially by different authors, it is important to know whether the essays form a cohesive, unified whole or whether the argument can be made that the authors should publish the essays individually as journal articles. I have learned the hard way that one of the most important questions I must ask the collection's editors is whether they are prepared to drop weak essays and to insist that contributors of chapters that need revision really do that work. Editors of collections must edit and instruct; it is not enough that they compile interesting conference papers.

Most acquisitions editors I know are eager to publish important scholarly monographs and try not to overload their lists with collections of essays, reprinted articles, or anthologies. Edited collections, however, serve a purpose and are often financially successful. They can get work in progress on a single topic into print quickly while the contributors complete longer studies. And the best of them, adapted as classroom readers by teachers in the field, can support some of the scholarly monographs we are proud to publish because of their excellence, even though we are aware that the potential sales will barely cover costs and may even require a third-party subsidy.

One of the books I am happiest to have published is a collection entitled *Lesbian Psychologies: Explorations and Challenges,* edited by the Boston Lesbian Psychologies Collective. I think of it as a project on which I did everything right, and remembering that can soften my regrets on those dreary days when I learn that a manuscript I should have landed has slipped away from me.

The prospectus for *Lesbian Psychologies* arrived on a winter day early in 1985. I had been looking for good manuscripts in lesbian studies for a few years, ever since the first papers on the history and writing of lesbians in America were presented at meetings of the National Women's Studies Association and at the Berkshire conference. I opened the manila envelope with a Boston address and knew as soon as I saw the table of contents that this was the kind of book I wanted to publish. The letter of inquiry had been sent by Loraine Obler. I read her proposal and immediately called to ask her to send the complete manuscript. I took the chapter abstracts home with me that night, read them all, and the next day asked a lesbian friend of mine from the Illinois campus if the proposed manuscript interested her as much as it did me. Not to my surprise, she shared my enthusiasm. The topics ranged from questions of lesbian identity to issues of food obsession, alcoholism, interracial relationships, and community life.

Eventually the complete manuscript arrived from Boston and I immediately started calling potential outside readers. Since many of the chapters had been written by practicing therapists and some had been written by practicing academics, I had decided that I would seek therapists connected with universities to review the manuscript. My initial telephone calls to readers were unsuccessful in a remarkably illuminating way. Had the manuscript been in history, my primary field, I would have known a dozen or more qualified scholars to approach, starting with the editors of our series Women in American History. But my acquisitions in psychology had been in child development and learning disabilities, and in 1985, I did not yet have a network of consultants in adult psychology. I started my quest by calling the counseling center at Illinois, asking to speak to a person expert on lesbian relationships. The person in charge could think of no one. Next I called the author of two books I had published; she was a professor of child development in the psychology department of a New England university and I asked her who in her department was an expert on gay and lesbian topics or who at her university's counseling center would be a good reader for my manuscript. She laughed at my question, saying that her colleagues seemed not to have noticed that homosexuality was worth studying and that the university counseling center was unlikely to have such a specialist. I called a local psychiatrist in private practice, who, trying to be helpful, suggested the names of two authors of "books on perversion." The more I struck out in finding a reader, the more I knew that this book needed to be published.

In the course of several days of what seemed like constant phone calls, or waiting for calls to be returned, I was directed, through a chain of referrals, to two women who agreed to read the manuscript: a university counselor in Chicago who had published articles on the psychology of women, and a social worker and therapist in New York who had published on lesbian topics. Then I had to wait some six weeks to find out if my instincts as a publisher would be seconded by these two professionals: Would the book really be useful? Were the ideas new and properly grounded in theory and method? The critiques arrived; both readers were favorable to the project as a whole and to the majority of the papers, though each had suggestions to make about needed improvements for individual essays. I sent the critiques to the editors and included contract terms for publication of the book.

I was not the only publisher to make an offer; I had to make a case for why the collective should choose Illinois. I had been planning a short vacation on Cape Cod that spring, and decided to make a detour to Boston to visit the editors. I talked with them about the introduction to the volume and how it could be made more effective. We discussed marketing plans, trade discounts, paperback possibilities. They were satisfied with the comments of the two readers. The group caucused privately and then announced that they would publish the book with Illinois. I left Boston delighted, and with a job ahead of me: to read and comment on each paper so as to resolve differences between the two readers and add my own opinions.

As is typical with large projects, it took a year for the contributors to return the revised chapters and the editors (who innocently thought that their main editorial task was completed when they sent me the collected and edited papers they had already worked on for several months) to review the revised chapters and to send me the final compilation. Our press board had approved this project at an early stage, and the manuscript could go to a copy editor as soon as I looked it over myself to confirm that the revisions had been competently executed. The press decided to bring the book out in cloth and paperback simultaneously. I suggested an initial printing of 500 clothbound copies, for library purchasers, and 2,500 paperbacks, intended for classroom use and bookstore sales; the sales manager suggested printing 1,000 hardbound copies and 3,000 paperbacks. We sold out the first printing of the paperback within five months and have thus far sold more than 17,000 copies of the book, including some 800 in cloth. The book received excellent reviews in scholarly journals and in gay and lesbian newspapers, and it won the 1988 Distinguished Publication Award of the Association for Women in Psychology. The editors have contributed their royalties to scholarships for students in psychology, and the press's proceeds from sales have helped to fund other worthy books that, despite their excellence have small markets. I have continued to solicit manuscripts in gay and lesbian studies and have signed up several that have been published or are about to be.

In the course of bringing *Lesbian Psychologies* into print, I spent numerous hours communicating with the editors by telephone and mail. As is the case with most collaborative efforts, the editors designated one of their number to deal exclusively with me for each stage of the editorial process. I enjoyed my conversations with them as the manuscript traveled through our copyediting department and as they began to communicate with our marketing department to plan book signings and other special promotional events.

Theoretically, once the acquisitions editor turns a manuscript over to the managing editor for assignment to a copy editor, an author can be "handed over" from copy editor to marketing director without needing again to confer with the acquiring editor.

In fact, this sometimes happens. But more often than not, especially for me in the area of women's studies, friendships form between editor and author, and future academic meetings become a time of renewed professional and social acquaintance. We frequently call upon our published authors to act as readers for manuscripts under consideration, and I think that we all hope a satisfied author will recommend us to colleagues who are ready to publish manuscripts. A fellow editor once reminded me that authors are our main resource and that we should treat them well. I certainly think about that truth as I look at our press's monthly production reports, to make sure that my own books are moving along well and to seek the reason for any delays I notice.

Acquiring a monographic study by a single author is similar to acquiring a collection of original essays except that with a monograph there are no third-party contributors of individual chapters. The editors of collections often feel a loyalty to those contributors whose papers they have solicited, especially if some of the papers have been on hand for a long time while the editors waited for the remainder to arrive. It is difficult, though often necessary, for the acquisitions editor to insist that some of them be dropped, let go perhaps because they just do not fit well with the rest of the book or because the author is recalcitrant about following a referee's advice to revise. With a monograph, though, as long as an author is capable of revising, questions of third-person diplomacy seldom arise. Some authors of very long works (say five hundred pages or more) have trouble cutting chapters they have worked so hard to write even though editor and readers believe the work will be better focused (or more affordable) if trimmed.

Many monographs submitted to us by junior faculty members started life as dissertations, I estimate that roughly a fifth of the monographs we published in 1991 were in this category. Most editors I know wish that nobody would send us a dissertation until the work had been rewritten as a book. Note that I use the word "rewritten," here, not "revised." I always advise new Doctors of Philosophy to banish the word "revise" from their vocabulary when talking about the next stages of their thesis. To think about revising the dissertation can lead one into mere tinkering with the document that was produced to earn the Ph.D., moving around some chapters, dropping some footnotes, sprucing up the introduction.

But a thesis is not a book. There is a fine publication that explains exactly why: *The Thesis and the Book*, edited by Eleanor

Harman and Ian Montagnes.[2] There is a difference between the scholarly exercise carried out to show you know the field and are qualified to teach in it and the work of *author*ity that customers will actually pay money to buy. My final word to those who plan to write a book based on their dissertation research is to treat the dissertation like a treatise from which the work's author will permit you to borrow heavily. Put the dissertation aside and think about the *book* that should be written on this topic. Outline that book and start to write it, taking a word, a phrase, or even whole paragraphs from the dissertation whose author is so close to you.

I look at unchanged dissertations more often that I would like, mainly because authors of some of the most remarkable dissertations know that their work is in demand by competitive publishers, and I would not want to miss my chance to make a publishing offer on a work in my specialty. I am happy when some confident dissertation authors write their books before sending their manuscripts out for evaluation.

When the University of Illinois Press was smaller, and when I seemed to be the only junior person to care about the women's movement, I considered women's studies my editorial domain and I handled just about any prospectus dealing with women's issues that was sent to me, whether in literature or history or any other discipline (though I concentrated heavily in American history, a strong feature of our list). By the mid-1980s, it was clear that in almost all the disciplines, authors were writing to my colleagues to tell them about manuscripts dealing with women: women as composers, poets, writers, founders of religions and religious orders, subjects for anthropologists, psychologists, political scientists, sociologists. All acquisitions editors at Illinois expect to publish books on women or studies that examine issues of gender (as well as race, class, and other issues of importance to contemporary scholars), and I have kept after them, to the annoyance of some, perhaps, to make sure that collections of essays reflect the diversity of human life or of the population of scholars. For example, it would bother me to see a collection of essays on American poets that considered only men (unless the book were titled *Essays on Male Poets*) or an anthology of works on the South that listed only male writers (or only white writers, for that matter). I have listened to and participated in the dialogues about canon formation in the academy and agree with those who feel that the works we call classics are so defined because they suited the expectations of a relative handful of individuals, entirely men, who were making such choices in the past and simply ignored important work by women or by people of color.

I have also watched with interest the differing career paths of men and women in publishing. To discuss that aspect of the profession would require a chapter in itself. The women I have talked to tend to believe that women are promoted on their accomplishments, men on their potential. It is not unheard of for a position to be advertised at one level, say, senior editor for acquisitions, and filled, by a man, at another level, say editor-in-chief, much to the surprise of the women on the staff. Perhaps this is typical for corporate America, not just for scholarly publishing.

Of eighty press directors listed in the 1992 directory of the Association of American University Presses, ten were women, and a great many acquiring editors and some editors-in-chief were women. It will be interesting to see how these percentages change by the end of the nineties. As early as 1987, my colleagues in the organization Women in Scholarly Publishing could name at least three men who became press directors after having been asked to leave their former jobs. Obviously, some individuals and some search committees are not abashed by the circumstances under which male applicants have left previous jobs. But in the end, men and women at presses usually get along with each other. They have to, if the best books are to be published and the organization is to thrive.

I mentioned earlier that sponsoring manuscripts is a way editors feel they can have an influence on their world, make a difference, a way not only of facilitating the dissemination of scholarship by others but also of helping to define the direction that scholarship takes. I have provided a case study of one particular book that was a pleasure for me to handle from beginning to end. I am equally pleased with the entire list of books I have sponsored in our women's history series. My work with the consulting editors on this series, Mari Jo Buhle of Brown University and Anne Firor Scott and Nancy Hewitt of Duke University, has been gratifying and an education in itself. As the facilitator of written dialogues among the editors (who earlier included Jacquelyn D. Hall of the University of North Carolina), I have been able to see how each formulates her opinion of a submitted manuscript. I've learned what matters most to them about historical monographs and what kinds of interpretive powers they expect from authors. Since it is Illinois's custom to print in each new volume the entire list of books in the series, the arrival of the advance copy of each title is especially exciting for me, for I can look at a growing body of work and realize that a difference really has been made.

Notes

1. Roger Cohen, "When a Best Seller Is at Stake, Publishers Can Lose Control," *New York Times*, May 12, 1991, "Week in Review." For another view of the world of the trade press editor, see Gerald Howard, "Mistah Perkins—He Dead: Publishing Today," *American Scholar* (Summer 1989). An excellent description of the acquisitions process in scholarly publishing is presented by Paul Parsons in *Getting Published: The Acquisition Process at University Presses* (Knoxville: University of Tennessee Press, 1989).

2. Toronto: University of Toronto Press, 1976.

13

A Formula for Successful Scholarly Publishing: Policy-Oriented Research and the Humanities

✳

Richard C. Rowson

I remember, in the late 1960s walking out of the lobby of one of those wonderful old high-ceiling buildings with huge, double-slung windows on Fourth Avenue in the used-bookstore area on the fringes of New York's Greenwich Village after an interview with a publisher and saying to myself, "I think this is the place where I'll end up working."

And so I did. After spending twelve years in the field of world affairs education with the Foreign Policy Association (FPA) and six with Radio Free Europe (RFE) in international political communications, I was about to become a publisher. "But why," I asked the president of Praeger at the end of the hiring interview during which I was offered the directorship of Praeger Special Studies (PSS), "do you want me; I know nothing about publishing?" "Oh Mr. Rawson" (he always turned over his "o's" into "a's" with his distinctive Viennese accent), he replied, "You know where the good authors are! We will teach you about the other parts of publishing!"

I had just been instructed on one of the most important lessons in publishing, namely, that the heart of the business lies in the kind and quality of manuscripts one acquires. Or put another way, the key to good publishing is knowing what subjects are important and where good authors writing on them can be found. My new boss saw immediately that my experience as a research and policy director for Radio Free Europe demonstrated that I knew what constituted sound policy analysis and good writing, and that I was hooked into the network of authors in the lucrative field of "policy-oriented research." All I needed to do, as he saw it, was transfer that know-how to the acquisition of good books for his company, and apply the lessons of effective communication, which I had learned at RFE and FPA, to book marketing. Then I'd be a publisher.

Obviously, it was not that simple. And, indeed, I soon discovered that my publisher-colleagues looked askance at my credentials; even after becoming president of the company some years later, they considered me somewhat of an outsider.

Publishing Policy Studies Commercially

But none of this really mattered as I plunged into the process of acquiring and publishing a wide variety of specialized works on contemporary domestic and international policy issues, many of them written by former associates from abroad, and from academe, government, think tanks, and the like with whom I had relations.

I cite this bit of personal history to make two important points: first, a good acquisitions capability is the *sine qua non* of a good editor or of good publishing, and second, in performing the "gatekeeping" function, it is very useful to have an association with or knowledge of the field in which acquisitions are being sought, both from the standpoint of making sound judgments as to what is publishable and in terms of bringing the works selected for publication before the right groups of potential readers.

I learned another lesson about publishing and performance of the gatekeeping function from my new chief: "Mr. 'Rawson,'" he said, "Never spend more than fifteen minutes on any manuscript you are reviewing for publication." And he went on to say, "If you're not convinced it's publishable by then, drop it and go on to the next project." By following that rule, I was able to survey vast numbers of manuscripts in a minimum amount of time. In fact, eventually one of my colleagues took pity on me in my daily struggle to stuff several manuscripts into my inadequate briefcase for reviewing at home each evening and on the subway en route, and bought me one of those large, canvas sling bags I once used when delivering newspapers as a kid, in which I could transport the potentially publishable largesse.

Of course, I learned very soon that sometimes it was *not* wise to reject a manuscript outright on my own recognizance; from time to time, it paid to seek the reading of an outside expert. And I say "from time to time" because in the commercial field of publishing scholarly and professional research (the field I was in), there usually was little time for the kind of "peer review" practiced by university presses. I had to make the basic publishing decisions myself, subject, of course to approval by our internal editorial board (actually the president of Praeger). It was only later in my career in university press publishing, that I learned to appreciate the key role the peer review process plays in noncommercial scholarly publishing.

My publishing experience at Praeger offered several lessons for the intellectual gatekeeper. First, as a publisher of specialized and scholarly studies for a commercial enterprise, we set out to prove that there was a viable place in the market of ideas for books that warranted only small printings. In the early 1970s at Praeger, the average printrun was around 1,500 and it dropped to half that by the end of the decade. Further, we had to demonstrate that we could sell at comparatively high retail prices. Our sales did demonstrate the validity of this readership and that there was a place in the publishing spectrum for the serious, clearly written, high-priced, specialized book that met a real need. Testimony to this fact was the emulation by competitors of the successful Praeger Special Studies publishing formula.

Second, we set out to prove that good, worthy books with these small audiences of buyers, could be published profitably. By the late 1970s we were realizing an 18.5 percent net operating profit. We were achieving that high rate of financial return by avoiding all "frills." Our books were either "red," "green," or "blue" and front-stamped with "one-hit" gold lettering with virtually identical internal and external design, and never jacketed. Also, by limiting our marketing to cost-effective direct mail, pinpointed advertising (only in specialized journals), generous offerings of complimentary review copies, vigorous foreign marketing by an overseas company (we sold them rights to all of our titles at a generous 75 percent discount, nonreturnable), and selective exhibiting at scholarly meetings, we were able to mount our promotion to our target audiences at an affordable cost.

Third, we sought to ensure that our role as "gate-openers" to scholars and experts seeking to publish specialized research (at a time when other publishers considered such works unpublishable, commercially) did not run counter to our equally important role as gatekeepers responsible for publishing only the best quality work.

We achieved this by limiting our program to books that brought new information and analysis to policy issues, that is, we became specialists in the publication of what we termed policy-oriented research of the type with which I had gained more than passing familiarity at RFE. We specifically avoided the publication of historical or humanistic studies, which by definition did not have immediate policy relevance.

Furthermore, related to our pursuit of quality, we instituted the practice of carefully copyediting and proofreading all of our titles. We avoided the temptation of accepting camera-ready copy from our authors unless we were allowed to copy edit and proofread such manuscripts ourselves or were satisfied that only the highest standards of editing were employed by others.

Still, I believe we only partially realized our goal of opening the gates to the manuscripts deserving of publication. Both the publishing field and the authors it served, were too strongly committed to the belief that only "good-looking" books that carried substantial printruns and sold for much lower prices than were feasible for specialized works, could possibly be real books or books of genuine quality. Yet our authors who, despite this perception, enjoyed good reviews and who enhanced their reputations through our publication of their so-called arcane studies, knew otherwise. When they saw the fruits of their research being utilized in government and business to resolve real problems or as a basis for further research by their peers, they, as we, knew a useful publishing service was being performed. Many a young unknown (and an equal number of established scholars) gained recognition and advancement in his or her chosen field through publication in PSS or in one of its later cousins, Pergamon Policy Studies (PPS) or Duke Press Policy Studies.

Linking Policy-Oriented Research to Publishing in the Arts and Humanities at Duke

One of the frustrating aspects of commercial publication of contemporary issues manuscripts was the limitation placed on it by the need to make a profit. What this meant was that though we were offered excellent manuscripts on history and the other humanities, relevant to the resolution of policy issues, our bosses did not believe that there was a market large enough to warrant publication of such works on a cost-effective basis. Such theoretical

treatments were not thought to meet the here and now requirements of those interested in policy-oriented research.

What a joy it was when I entered the field of university press
publishing in 1981 as Director at Duke to be in a position to challenge the validity of that assumption. Besides, Duke Press needed
a means of jump-starting a new publishing program at a point
when the old one had atrophied for lack of adequate university
support. So, when the administration at Duke decided to place
scholarly publishing, once again, at the top of its academic priorities following an exhaustive assessment of Duke's overall academic
program, and invited me to lead the effort, it was agreed that the
link between the humanities and policy studies should become
our hallmark. The "engine" for the initial revitalization process
would become the publication of policy-oriented research. Once
that process had gotten things rolling again, the press could shift
its priorities more toward the humanities publishing area. Thus,
Duke Press Policy Studies (DPPS) was created.

Our effort to link policy with humanities publishing, was illustrated by a book that I had turned down while at Pergamon
Press (where I served as president for three years after leaving
Praeger when it was sold to CBS). That rejection was based on the
economic infeasibility argument noted above (i.e., publication would
not potentially contribute to program profitability). This book was
entitled *To Helsinki*. This title, which paraphrased Lenin's rallying
cry "To Finland Station!" uttered on his departure for St. Peters-
burg in 1917 to mount the Bolshevik Revolution, was derived from
the book's treatment of the landmark East-West summit, the Conference on Security and Cooperation in Europe (CSCE), held in
Helsinki, Finland, 1973–75. It was a firsthand historical account
by John F. Maresca, the one American who took part in the entire
span of these historic negotiations.

What emerged from the publication of this book, and the initiation of the DPPS of which it was a part, was the demonstration
that *historical* treatments of policy issues sell well. We sold out the
cloth edition and reissued the book in paperback. By linking history and current policy, the author helped point the way for the
publication of other humanities titles within our DPPS framework,
and eventually outside of it. This book exposed the key role played
by the peer review process. A tough-minded Duke professor who
insisted that what he viewed as a good manuscript could become
an outstanding book if it were properly revised, so hammered at
the author that the latter spent his entire summer holiday on Cape

Cod cutting the manuscript to half its original size and otherwise tightening up his analysis. The reader's advice was sound; the very strong reviews and sales substantiated that fact.

In 1986, five years after we began our effort to breath new life into the press, *fifty-seven* books had been published in Duke Press Policy Studies, and our emphasis had shifted heavily in favor of the humanities, as was evident from the following introduction to our winter 1986–87 catalogue:

> "Above All Nations Is Humanity"—This inscription at the main entrance to Duke University is our hallmark for publishing at Duke University Press:
>
> We endeavor to link basic values in the humanities with contemporary research in Duke Press Policy Studies, a book series begun in 1982; its fifty-seventh title, HELSINKI, HUMAN RIGHTS, AND EUROPEAN SECURITY, by Vojtech Mastny, is announced in this catalog and personifies our effort to focus on the importance of human values in world politics.

Through our strategy of utilizing Duke Press Policy Studies to revitalize scholarly publishing at Duke, a foundation was laid for expanding beyond DPPS into the fields of history, literature, and the arts, and for delving more deeply into political theory, philosophy, and psychology. All of these new publishing directions were given new momentum, by the "critical mass" (in terms of titles published annually), the marketing presence, sales growth, and author recognition that DPPS brought to the press. What form this growth took will be shown next.

The Results: Growth in Titles Published and Service to our Scholarly Mission

The application of the editorial and publishing concept linking policy studies and the humanities brought dramatic growth to the press between 1981 and 1990. In terms of the numbers of titles published, the press grew in nine years from twelve to seventy books published annually and we expanded our list of journals from six to nineteen. Our sales expanded from $700 thousand annually to $2.75 million and our operating subsidy from the university declined to 1.5 percent of our sales from the nearly 50 percent subsidy we were receiving when we initiated this new approach in 1981.

We endeavored to base this growth on the publication of quality scholarship by adhering to three principles enunciated so eloquently by an eminent Yale professor, Jaroslav Pelikan. Professor Pelikan had served as chair of the Yale University Publications Committee, when his remarks at an annual meeting of The Association of American University Publishers were published under the title, "Scholarship: A Sacred Vocation."[1]

First: "It is one of our obligations, both as scholars and publishers, to introduce each succeeding generation of scholars to their intellectual ancestors" rather than learning the latest trendy jargon or newest hypothesis "so as to instill scientific and scholarly discipline as an intellectual virtue, without which scholarship would be only a job, not a sacred vocation."

Adhering to this edict of Professor Pelikan, we at Duke sought in our publications to convey to the reader not only *who* his or her intellectual ancestors were, but *why* they merited such distinction and *how* their ideas evolved.

Second, Pelikan spoke of the need for "imagination" in the interpretation of data and in determining the meaning of findings across and among disciplines. Imagination, he argued, is the essential difference between "significant and trivial research."
So, we sought out the scholar who went beyond the normal standards of good research and brought to his findings a new vision of his subject and its importance, as Professor Pelikan advised.

Pelikan added an extremely important corollary to this point which we took to heart in our acquisitions and editorial work: "Scholars and presses need to become themselves the communicators of the outcome of research . . . don't leave this task to the authors of textbooks, to trade publishers, and to the *New York Times Magazine*." We interpreted this to mean that a scholarly author, should keep it simple, and utilize language comprehensible to the widest possible readership. We always tried, again as professor Pelikan advised, to select the scholarly work that spoke to a broader audience in understandable language over the one that treated the same subject with the same level of scholarship, but limited its readership by the use of unnecessarily complex means of presentation.

Third, Pelikan linked this need for imagination and clarity to the responsibilities of the scholar as a *teacher*. He argued that the need to publish need not conflict with the obligation to teach, quite the contrary. "The difference between bad scholarship and good scholarship," he said, "is the result of what we do in graduate school, but the difference between good scholarship and great

scholarship is the result of what we do in college." For this reason, he stated that it is the responsibility of the accomplished, senior
scholar to teach the freshman survey course and to bring to the
undergraduate, thereby, the fruits of his or her research and publication.

At Duke, we did not always find that good teachers were good
writers, but they invariably were good *authors* in the sense that
their ideas had been tested and shaped before a demanding audience, students in a university classroom setting.

Finally, "Publish or perish!" wrote Pelikan, "is a fundamental,
psychological, indeed physiological, imperative that is rooted in
the very metabolism of scholarship as a vocation." To Pelikan, a
community of scholars in critical dialogue with one another is the
sine qua non of any university.

Therefore, at Duke, we argued that publishing is not only integral to the scholarly activities of the university, but constitutes an
essential part of its organic wholeness.

Did these ambitious guidelines work in practice? Did the DPPS
list live up to these demanding standards? Naturally, every title
we published could not meet all these criteria and even the best
would fall short of the mark in one way or another. But I can offer
two examples from my experience at Duke that, to my mind, sub-
stantiate the wisdom of a policy that required us to aspire to these
standards and consciously to apply them in judging what and what
not to publish.

My first example concerns a phone call I received after I had
spoken at a Duke faculty meeting, from a James B. Duke Professor of Physiology, Charles Tanford. He had earlier taught at Harvard
and was about to submit his manuscript to the press there. But
after hearing in the course of an address I made to the Faculty
Council at Duke that we were interested in books that introduced
our readers to our intellectual ancestors and presented difficult
material in plain English, he decided to approach us. We ended
up publishing his remarkable monograph, *Ben Franklin Stilled the
Waves: An Informal History of Pouring Oil on Water with Reflections
on the Ups and Downs of Scientific Life in General*. It was a gem and
came as close to Professor Pelikan's standards as one could wish.
But it is important to remember that it was a public enunciation to
our faculty of our publishing criteria that brought this fine author
to our doors in the first place.

The second example of our effort to apply these standards to
the works of our authors is brought to mind by what I must admit
was my somewhat indelicate handling of a manuscript from the

then president of Harvard, Derek Bok. He had delivered the Terry Sanford Lecture at Duke, which he had edited for book publication. The reviewers recommended further revisions. I knew that President Bok had worked diligently to put his manuscript into publishable shape, but in a somewhat overzealous effort to maintain the integrity of the review process and our editorial standards, I wrote him indicating the need for further additions and changes. I stated that the Harvard president's postlecture editing efforts obviously were appreciated by the reader, but that when it came to his joining his theoretical argument with current practice, the reviewer believed, as I rather crudely paraphrased it that the author had "come up short." Well, it would have been wiser to let the review speak for itself! Nonetheless, my editorial board while rapping me on the back of the knuckles for "unnecessary roughness," did support the need for further revision. The author responded ably to this appeal and a very fine book, *Universities and the Future of America* (1990), was the result. It was excerpted in the *Chronicle of Higher Education* and was very well received by a wide cross-section of readers.

General Lessons

How would I relate my experience in scholarly publishing to the editor's intellectual gatekeeping function, the subject of this book? Here are a few personal guidelines:

• *Stay on top of developments:* Keep abreast of major trends in public thinking, new cultural developments, and basic issues of policy. Reading *The New York Times* daily is a must, in my opinion. And, also reading the local paper published in the community in which you reside and work also is most important. Keep in mind that these two exercises are not for background purposes only. I recall coming across the names of two scholars of women's studies, Professors Barbara Harris and JoAnn McNamara, in a *New York Times* news article on the 1980 fifth Berkshire Conference for Women. I wrote them suggesting a book that would bring together the best ideas from that meeting. *Women and the Structure of Society* published by Duke in 1984 was the result. And now a second book, *Sainted Women of the Dark Ages* by one of the authors, JoAnn McNamara, is about to be published by Duke. It is a fascinating study based on translations of the Latin texts, analyzing the criteria for women's sainthood as applied in those early days.

Another good way to keep abreast of new intellectual trends

and who is leading them (i.e., to identify who's doing new work and who are your potential authors) is to join their societies, peruse their journals (you can hardly read them all!), and attend their meetings. And don't forget should you be a university press publisher, the best intelligence of all is right under you nose, among your colleagues on campus.

For example, at Duke, the Institute for Policy Sciences and Public Affairs was invaluable in the initiation of our DPPS program. And when we expanded into the arts, the Duke Museum of Arts provided us with a series of magnificent manuscripts around which a copublishing venture with them was built.

• *Build an acquisitions network*: At a university press, your editorial board and your faculty are the place to start. I also found that establishing a board of visitors composed of leading intellectual and publishing figures, who are well connected in the right circles, from outside the campus community, was a tremendously important help in this respect. Even more important is the fact that such a board helps establish your press credentials with the administration of your university or institution.

Your authors are an equally important part of your acquisitions network. Their recommendations as to publishable works in their respective fields can be invaluable. And oftentimes, a satisfied author will bring a second or third book to you. Don't forget to tap your reviewers for manuscripts and for ideas on new authors. We always made it a practice to send a copy of our catalogue along with a manuscript being offered for review (to show our wares), and we encouraged our reviewers to select books at half-price from our list in lieu of a cash payment reader's fee.

• *Meet your public*: Whether I was an editor, a manager of a department, or president of the publishing house, I always made a point of attending, personally, academic and professional meetings where our books and journals were being exhibited. I tried to review each conference program in advance for clues as to prospective acquisitions, and oftentimes would write a note to author prospects. And it's important to follow up your discussions at such meetings confirming in writing points of agreement and proposed follow-up actions.

At these conferences, try to spend as much time as possible at the exhibit in order to learn of audience reaction to what you have published. Even more important is to listen to what the visiting scholars have to say about new work in their respective fields. Often this will lead you to new authors. For example, when someone walks into your exhibit, don't say, "May I help you?" Rather ask, "What is your field?" You will be surprised how often that leads to a discussion of work in progress by the visitor or by another scholar, which in turn can lead to a manuscript proposal that otherwise might never have been discovered.

And finally, to authors, actual or potential, who may be reading these words,

- *Some editorial and publishing guidelines:*

1. Think of the first test to which an author should subject his or her work: "Does it tell the informed scholar something he or she doesn't know?" For example, excessive documentation, the parading of one's knowledge of the existing literature, and the like, may be considered impressive by the author but only a bore to the reader.

2. It is most important that an author evaluate which scholarly presses specialize in his or her field and go straight to those, avoiding broadside submissions. Always write to a person, not to a title, and while it is useful to pick a specific editor who concentrates on the particular field of the work being submitted, keep in mind that at many presses, especially university presses, the director often handles some of these portfolios personally. So, if you are not certain as to whom to write, the director, or head of the house is recommended, especially if you have chosen a good press whose director can be counted on to direct your work to the proper editor. Specific information (names, addresses, phone numbers, description of the publication list, etc.) can be found in *Literary Market Place*, available in most libraries.

3. On the initial go-round, an author is advised never to send a manuscript unsolicited, but rather to write a straightforward letter descriptive of the work (a page or so), and to enclose a table of contents and biographical sketch or "C.V." Be sure you inform the editor or publisher of the projected or actual length and completion date of your manuscript. Should the editor be interested in your proposed work, you should be sent an "Author's Questionnaire" (AQ), which allows you to expand further on the nature of your work and its potential readership. Subsequently, should the manuscript be accepted for publication, you should receive a "Marketing Questionnaire" requesting further information on potential readers and how to reach them. Expect your publisher to request a prompt return of this AQ with the manuscript if that is desired. It is always advisable to include a preface and introduction with the manuscript as this constitutes an important statement of the genesis of your book and enables your editor/publisher (and the reviewers to whom your manuscript is sent) to get a feel

for your work, as well as a summary of its main arguments. Be sure that the manuscript sent to you is paginated consecutively from the first to the last page, that it includes a title page, and that the table of contents indicates where the chapters begin. Oftentimes, when I have had doubts about a work's suitability for our list, what has tipped the balance toward rejection has been a sloppily prepared manuscript, especially one that does not allow the readers to locate the beginning page of one of the chapters in which they happened to be especially interested, simply because the table of contents had not also been paginated! And once, one of my reviewers accidentally dropped a manuscript that had been paginated chapter by chapter rather than consecutively from beginning to end, on the floor, and returned it unread, frustrated by his inability to put it back together again.

4. It is perfectly proper for you as author to suggest scholarly reviewers whom you know to be objective authorities in the field and who are not among those from whom you solicited critiques. Such suggestions can be most helpful, especially if your field is a narrow or unusually specialized one. Furthermore, if you are in a position to indicate which reviewers in the field can be relied upon and have the time to undertake the review process, that is especially useful information to the editor or publisher. Indicate titles, affiliations, addresses, and telephone numbers, if possible. Finally, it is also helpful that two copies of your manuscript be sent as that enables the editor or publisher, should he or she wish to do so, to send the manuscript out for simultaneous reviews, thereby saving valuable time in the review process.

5. After your work has been reviewed and your editor has made a careful assessment of it, that assessment should be sent to you along with the "sanitized" review from which all identifying marks or unnecessarily critical or offensive comments, should have been removed. Submit promptly your written reaction to the review, take care to respond to each point of criticism indicating what action is intended or offer sound reasons why you consider certain criticisms specious.

Once the manuscript has been revised (if that is called for), you should accompany its return to the publisher with a letter explaining what has been or will subsequently be revised and why, in direct response to the reviewers' specific points of criticism. This assists the re-review process (your letter along with the revised manuscript will in all probability be sent to the reviewer, who will appreciate being reminded of requested revisions). Also such a letter is most important to the editorial board of the press, the body that makes the final publishing decision.

Conclusion

Finally, may I offer to authors (I hope with editors and publishers reading over their shoulders) advice as to what I consider the proper attitude authors should take toward their editor/publisher. This comes from a chapter I contributed entitled "The Scholar and the Art of Publishing," to *The Academic's Handbook* (Duke, 1988):[2]

In your dealings with your editor and publisher, keep in mind that you have entered a form of partnership in which each party is very important to the other. This is not the place to discuss in detail the business side of publishing but keep in mind that you are working with a professional who is, in his/her line of business, just as expert as your are in your chosen field of scholarship. So while it is your responsibility to place in your publisher's hands all relevant information regarding the potential readership (the market) for your book, it is the publisher's responsibility to translate this into a suitable book price, an economically sound print-run, a decision as to cloth and/or paperback editions, a marketing budget, an attractive book design, and the like. You place your life's work in his or her hands, he or she places at risk the publishing firm's financial resources, professional time (and that of your peer reviewers), as well as the publishing reputation of the house, when placing the name of the press on your work.

So, the old adage pertains, "A rising tide lifts all boats." In short, publishing is a teamwork process. Consider your publisher your partner, not your protagonist.

Also keep in mind that you (and all authors) are your publisher's most important asset; how your publisher handles your work is obviously of crucial importance to you personally and to your career. Through the medium of scholarship and your publisher's appreciation of its significance, you may even become close friends. Many times I have met authors years after our initial association by mail and have felt an instant rapport despite the absence of any previous personal contact.

A final word is in order concerning the responsibility of the scholar for peer review of other scholars' work on behalf of a publisher. Publishers, as well as potential authors, must rely on the expertise and the goodwill of scholarly colleagues for the execution of this useful, sometimes satisfying, but often difficult task. It is as important for you as a scholar to be responsive to a reasonable request from a publisher for review of a work relevant to your field or discipline, as it is for you to have your own work reviewed for prospective publication. When you are next approached with the request for a review and accept, keep in mind how important it would be to your own work to have that review completed promptly by the deadline indicated by the publisher. Consider also how valuable a careful, intelligent, and constructively critical review will be to the author. Most important of all, your effort in reviewing the work of your peers will have made a vital contribution to scholarship and to the all-important process of its dissemination.

With these thoughts, I conclude this effort to set forth the link I see between policy-oriented research and the humanities—my own personal formula for successful scholarly publishing. But, I urge you in reading and weighing these words, to keep firmly in mind an overriding consideration, central to all editorial and publishing efforts: the essence is in the personal relationship and the marvelously creative symbiosis between author and publisher. So, while formulas are useful, in the final analysis, it is the people involved and their mutual respect, their enthusiasm for the task at hand, and their commitment to quality and timely publication, who stand above all else in this exceedingly personal endeavor called scholarly publishing.

Notes

1. "Scholarship: A Sacred Vocation," in *Scholarly Only Writing: A Journal for Authors and Only Writers*, Vol. 16, No. 1, October 1984, University of Toronto Press, Toronto, Canada.

2. Denoff, A. Leigh, Goodwin, Crawford, and McCrorte, Ellen Storm, Editors. *The Academic's Handbook*, Durham, N.C.: Duke University Press, 1988.

14

Listbuilding at University Presses

*

Sanford G. Thatcher

Why do university presses publish what they do? How has the nature of their publishing changed over time? Which parts of their environment, within their own universities and within the wider world of publishing, influence the shaping of presses' lists? What is the role of editors in the publishing process at the university presses?

These are the principal questions I shall address in this essay, drawing from my experience as an editor at Princeton University Press for twenty-two years (1967–1989) and as director of the Penn State Press since then. The comparison between these two types of presses—one a prestigious large press at a leading private institution and the other a less well known small press at a major state university—will figure importantly in what I have to say.

There are two general observations that I want to make at the outset, however, and they need to be kept in mind as constants framing the overall working environment of editors at university presses—and probably at publishing houses of all types. First, it readily becomes clear to any editor who has been acquiring manuscripts for a few years that there is always a relatively small pool of absolutely first-rate books waiting to be published compared with the very much larger pool of perfectly competent, useful, but not brilliant books. The significance of this fact reveals itself in the often fierce competition that exists for the few best books and also in the dilution of quality in a press's list when it attempts a major expansion in its annual output of titles; one cannot expect to publish twice as many books in a given field without accepting proportionately more second- than first-rate books.[1] Second, the role of serendipity in publishing should never be underestimated. Any experienced editor will be able to cite examples of successes that are primarily attributable to sheer luck—being in the right place at the right time, taking advantage of coincidences, finding one manuscript when looking for another, and so on. A good editor will also be able to make these successes look, in retrospect, as though they were planned. What Walter Powell (1985) says of the commercial scholarly publishers he studied in *Getting into Print* is equally true of university presses: "The dynamics of acquiring manuscripts include chance elements that appear to have been rationally calculated only after a manuscript has been secured; rationales are then constructed to explain events" (p. 97).[2] Luck can play a particularly salient role early in a publisher's efforts to enter a new field where the publisher has no prominent backlist and well-established reputation to serve as a magnet for attracting unsolicited submissions.

The Role of an Editor

Editors at university presses today typically perform one or the other of two distinctively different functions: finding books to publish or copyediting manuscripts once they have been put under contract. Even as late as the early 1980s, it was not uncommon to have these two jobs carried out by the same individual in some houses. At Princeton University Press, for instance, almost all acquiring editors used to do some copyediting, and some though not all copy editors did some acquiring; a few editors even had their jobs formally structured so that they spent half of their time on each type of editing. One advantage of this arrangement was to make acquiring editors more sensitive than they would be otherwise to the problems—hence extra costs—that some manuscripts would entail for copyediting and production, and that awareness could then enter more directly into the decision whether to pursue publication of a book in the first place. Increasingly, though, as specialization has affected the organization of university presses, these different editorial duties have been strictly separated; now at many presses (including both Princeton and Penn State) the people doing these jobs are not even members of the same department, the copy editors working within the production rather than the editorial department. Acquiring editors do continue to do some hands-on editing of a large-scale, structural type that is often called "developmental," and I shall have more to say about this part of an acquiring editor's work later.

It should be understood in what follows that I am talking about the role of acquiring editors in this more specialized sense and not about the role that copy editors play in university presses, important though that is. To the extent that copyediting considerations enter into the editorial decision-making process now, they do mainly by way of reports that full-time copy editors prepare on manuscripts after they have been approved for publication by a press's editorial board but before they have been put under contract; these reports are part of the procedure of gathering information (including estimates of manufacturing costs) that can affect the way in which terms of the contract are written (regarding, for instance, subsidies or royalties or requirements for preparation of the manuscript prior to copyediting)—and even, in rare instances, whether a contract is offered at all. Some acquiring editors still begin their careers as copy editors (as I did) and carry that kind of skill with them into their decision making, but it would be unusual nowadays to require an applicant for a position in editorial acquisitions to pass a copyediting test as a condition for employment.

I have so far used the term "acquiring editor" to designate that special type of editorial work that will be the focus of our attention here. This is a popular label that has the advantage of being straightforwardly descriptive of what an editor holding this position does.[3] Other labels commonly used are "soliciting," "procuring," and "sponsoring" editor. August Frugé (1984), former director of the University of California Press, provides a good argument for preferring the latter: "In our early innocence we proposed to call them soliciting or procuring editors; after being told that we were stealing the terminology of another profession, we named them sponsoring editors, and encouraged each one to think of his/her books as lists within the larger list" (p. 173).

"Sponsoring editor" has the advantage of directing attention to the important roles as overseer, cheerleader, and liaison that an editor performs. As Paul Parsons (1989b) points out in *Getting Published*, "On agreeing to sponsor a manuscript, the editor becomes an unabashed advocate of the work throughout its passage toward publication" (p. 79). Walter Powell (1985) quotes the editor-in-chief of Plum Press as saying: "'The sponsoring editor has the broadest, most general responsibility for each book, from the time that it is signed to the time that it is declared out of print. To a very unusual degree, our editors work with other departments. Almost everything done by other departments, from ad copy to the jacket design, *has* to be approved by the book's sponsoring editor"(p. 132).

The term I personally prefer, however, is "listbuilder" or "listbuilding editor," which we used at Princeton University Press. The significance of this name is partly revealed by August Frugé in his quote above, where he speaks of an editor's developing "a list within the larger list." Though not so frequently employed as the other labels, this one captures best what I consider to be the highest accomplishment to which any acquiring editor can aspire, namely, the development of a group of books that relate to each other in an intellectually coherent way such that they form a whole— a list—greater than the sum of the individual parts, or titles. A good analogy would be the bibliophile who buys rare books to constitute a collection by virtue of the unifying conception that has gone into the identification of each book as relating to the others in some intellectually accountable manner.

The bibliophile's collection or the editor's list makes a statement about the importance of this group of books that signals its intellectual value, which translates more or less directly into prestige and financial value: for the successful bibliophile, the enhancement of personal wealth and reputation; for the successful editor, the strengthening of the press's image and presence in the fields the list covers, the ability to market the press's books in these fields more effectively, and the attractiveness of the press to new authors of the best (and often best-selling) books.

A good illustration of what it means to build a list from my own experience may be found in the development of Latin American studies at Princeton University Press over a twenty-year period. For many years before I became social science editor in 1969, Princeton had been publishing books sponsored by the Rand Corporation. It happened that Rand had a vigorous program of research about Latin America under way at that time, and the Press because of its strong prior association with Rand became a natural outlet for a number of its book-length studies. I acquired, more or less passively in this way, three books on Latin America that were published in the early 1970s: Alfred Stepan's *The Military in Politics: Changing Patterns in Brazil* (1971), Richard Nelson et al.'s *Structural Change in a Developing Economy: Colombia's Problems and Prospects* (1971), and Herbert Goldhamer's *The Foreign Powers in Latin America* (1972). I had very little familiarity with Latin American studies before becoming involved with these books; I had never taken any courses in the field in college, nor had I even read much about that area of the world except in newspapers and magazines. But this fortuitous appearance of a trio of books in a short span of time gave me reason to learn more, and it gradually dawned on me that this field was spawning a whole new generation of young scholars who were at the forefront of the developing theoretical literature in the social sciences.

The previous generation, I was aware, had made political development the paradigm for research on the Third World, very largely through their case studies of African (and, to a lesser extent, Asian) countries. Many of the books resulting from this research were published by Princeton, which had a formal arrangement with the Committee on Comparative Politics of the Social Science Research Council to issue the edited volumes produced under its auspices.[4] For various reasons, including the adverse reaction of African governments to social science research and the changing priorities of U.S. foundations, the focus of theoretical interest had begun to shift to Latin America.[5] Already Latin American social scientists, influenced by Marxist theoretical currents flowing from Europe, had produced a significant body of writing about the dependent relationship of Latin American countries to the core advanced industrial states, especially the United States, and the stage was therefore set for a fruitful mixing of North American empirical modes of research with the fairly abstract theorizing typical of the approach taken by South American social scientists.

"Dependency theory" became the new paradigm, explicitly set forth as a kind of dialectical critique of the earlier political development literature. Once I became attuned to the inner dynamic driving this new generation of scholarship, I began vigorously to pursue the brightest of the young researchers for their books, many of which were revisions of their dissertations. Among the most successful of these, in part because it was one of the earliest to appear, was Peter Evans's *Dependent Development: The Alliance of Multinational, State, and Local Capital in Brazil* (1979).[6]

What is striking about this work, and about the work of this generation of scholars in general, is its strong interdisciplinary character; one would not know from reading it that this was the writing of a sociologist rather than a political scientist or an economist. Much of the intellectual excitement and appeal of this new literature in Latin American studies was due to its revival of political economy in its original form, prior to disciplinary specialization, in the era of Adam Smith or—more to the point here—Karl

Marx. This interdisciplinary flavor also characterized the work of anthropologists and historians doing research on Latin America, and as I developed the program at Princeton, we began adding books in those areas, too. A notable example of a book by a historian strongly influenced by anthropology was Nancy Farriss's *Maya Society under Colonial Rule* (1984), which went on to win three major academic book awards. The active dialogue and cross-fertilization of ideas among scholars in all of these presumptively separate disciplines within the overarching field of Latin American studies made its conventions, publications, and networks fertile ground for an editor to till, and because of its unifying themes and approaches a list of books built upon it could have a very real identity and impact.

I took particular pride in developing this list for Princeton because that press had hardly published any books on Latin America before and because it became a natural extension, on a theoretical level, of the strong backlist the press had earlier developed on studies of political development in African and Asian countries.[7] One particularly satisfying testimony to the success of my efforts came from a historian whose book on nineteenth-century Peru, written in part as a critique of the dependency approach, had been accepted for publication before my departure from Princeton but was published afterward. He wrote to a former colleague: "I do hope that Princeton University Press will continue its strong tradition in Latin American studies; if you took a vote among Latin Americanists, I'm convinced that Princeton's would come out now as the top list in the world." Whether he meant it that way or not, I was especially gratified by his use of the word "list" in this context, which confirms my view that listbuilding is the best term to describe what an editor does.

If listbuilder is the most satisfactory name to use overall, still there are aspects of an editor's role that can be more precisely delimited by other names, and I shall briefly try to highlight these special dimensions of what editorial work involves by focusing on the editor as hunter, selector, shaper, linker, stimulator, shepherd, promoter, ally, and reticulator.

Hunter

Hunting for new manuscripts is a principal activity of any editor, and this term nicely captures the elements of aggressiveness, risk, suspense, competitiveness, and survival that are involved in listbuilding. The days when editors could afford to stay at their desks and just handle manuscripts arriving over the transom or respond to letters of inquiry are long gone. The competition among university presses, and between them and some commercial publishers, that intensified in the 1970s has made it necessary for press editors to engage in aggressive acquiring behavior, including frequent travel to conventions and college campuses, to track down and capture the always scarce quarry of first-rate authors in order to ensure the survival and prosperity of their houses.

An interesting, though perhaps not typical, example from my own recent experience is a book about the currently much discussed topic of date rape. A panel on this subject was held at the Pacific Division meeting of the American Philosophical Association in 1991. The principal speaker was the author of a paper that had been chosen as winner of the Fred Berger Memorial Prize by the APA Committee on Philosophy and Law; the commentators included two law professors and a philosophy professor. I attended the session as much out of personal curiosity as anything else, but while listening to the speakers became persuaded that their talks could form the basis for a very good book on the subject. I spoke with some of the panelists afterward, suggested the idea then, and followed up in correspondence with them later. The volume, as of this writing, is still in the process of being completed, but I am confident that it will be both a timely and pedagogically valuable work for use by teachers in college courses. This is a topic all college students care about, and a good book probing the philosophical and legal dimensions of the issue could help them appreciate the value of learning how to think about it critically.

Selector

Once editors have succeeded in ferreting out and securing submission of manuscripts, their next job is to select the ones that will contribute the most to enhance their press's list by way of prestige, profit, or preferably both. This is what many call the gatekeeping function that university presses carry out in identifying what most deserves to be widely disseminated and in legitimating its status as a genuine advance in scholarly knowledge. So central is this function, in fact, that it is sometimes argued that "gatekeeping is the one indispensable function they perform" (Goellner, 1990b, p. 8).

The decision making that editors undertake at this stage may appear to outsiders as though it reflects complete editorial autonomy, but in fact there is a variety of constraints affecting the decisions that editors reach. Some take the form of explicit rules. At some presses manuscripts exceeding a certain length must be rejected, regardless of their merits; or at least these manuscripts cannot be sent out for formal review by experts without authorization from the editor-in-chief or director. The need for a subsidy to publish a particular book may affect how it gets reviewed and will certainly determine how the contract gets written. Editors at some houses have to operate within a formal system of quotas, whereby they are required to sign up a minimum number of titles with sales potential of over, say, three thousand copies and are not allowed to sign up any more than a certain number of titles with sales potential less than, say, one thousand copies. For some presses the faculty at their own universities have privileges not accorded to authors from other universities; for example, editors cannot reject a faculty member's manuscript without soliciting one or more external reviews and without having the decision formally approved by the press's editorial board. Prior obligations, such as a press's standing agreement with a series editor or a sponsoring organization, may further limit the flexibility an editor has in conducting the review of a manuscript.

Other constraints take a more subtle form—what Walter Powell calls "unobtrusive controls" (1985, pp. 144–58). These have to do with the traditions, or "personality," of a publishing house—the accumulated weight of past editorial decisions that have already given a distinctive character to the press's list and make some types of books more appropriate for it than others. Just as the press's image in a certain field serves as a signal to communicate with prospective authors looking for the right publisher, so too does it lead editors to look most favorably on those manuscripts that best complement what the press has already published; and it becomes a heavy burden for a new press director who may want to steer the house in a different direction!

Besides these more or less overt constraints, which operate constantly to frame and guide editorial decisions, there are other elements of gatekeeping that can pose special challenges from time to time. Some situations pose "political problems"(cf. Powell 1985, p. 113). An editor may want to reject a manuscript recommended by a member of the editorial board, or one written by an author whose previous books the press has published, or one solicited from an influential senior scholar that turns out to be disappointing. In such circumstances an editor—especially one without a long track record from working in the field that has provided that editor with some independent credibility—may choose to manipulate the review process in such a way as to lead to the desired outcome without appearing to be the direct cause of it, either by selecting readers not expected to be particularly sympathetic to the author's work or by passing the buck to the editorial board, which can make the final decision on the basis of the editor's recommendation and thus appear to the author to be the arbiter of his or her fate (cf. Powell, 1985, p. 107).

Manipulation can also work in favor of an author. When an editor is predisposed to want a book published, choosing the right readers can make all the difference in the outcome, especially when the book has a strong ideological slant. This cannot be done too blatantly, however, for any good editorial board will rightly raise questions about the choice of readers and, if bias appears to play too obviously a predetermining role, will ask for additional review by a less partisan reader; in fact, excessive enthusiasm from readers can serve, in the eyes of editorial board members, to undermine the credibility of their reports.[8]

Another problem that can arise is relying too much on the same readers. Editors understandably like to use readers who have proven themselves prompt and responsible on past occasions. But they run a risk—the same associated with a series edited by a single scholar—of becoming too much the captive of those readers' own enthusiasms and biases. This problem becomes exacerbated when one relies on the same reader to review, time and again, the work of a prolific author. There is much to be said for an editor's nurturing an author's loyalty to a press, and few satisfactions for an editor can match the pleasure that comes from a close working relationship with an author developed over the course of publishing two, three, four, or more books; but if the editor always has that author's work evaluated by the same one or two reviewers, who are consistently enthusiastic about it, there may be a danger of favoritism that can backfire. Here, or course, it is more important than ever for an editor who succumbs to this temptation to use the reviews subsequently published in professional journals as a check to see whether the prepublication reader's opinion reflects a consensus or an idiosyncratic viewpoint.

Finally, there is the inevitable disgruntled author that an editor must handle, as tactfully as possible. In my experience, fewer authors express displeasure with the review process, or even the production of their books, than with the marketing (or, as they would say, the lack of it) that follows publication. But there are enough who run afoul of procrastinating readers, or mixed reviews, or other circumstances that can hinder steady progress toward a prompt decision to require an editor always to be prepared to respond to complaints.

At Princeton in the late 1970s and early 1980s, the press faced a problem with disgruntled authors that grew to such proportions that it caused real damage to the press's reputation—exacerbated, I suspect, by the readiness of editors at other presses to take advantage of Princeton's situation.[9] The press's director, not wanting to let the list grow too rapidly and sacrifice quality to quantity, set a target for the number of new books to be accepted each year. That target was then used to determine how many manuscripts, on average, the editorial board could be allowed to approve at each of its meetings. During this period, however, the press came to have such a productive group of editors that very often the agenda for the board's meetings would contain as many as 25 percent more manuscripts than the quota would permit the board to accept. Consequently, the press over time developed the reputation of stringing authors along, encouraging them with favorable reviews solicited by the editors, and then rejecting their books at the very last stage—because the editorial board could not approve all the manuscripts recommended by the staff. The authors who got burned in this way naturally vented their frustration not only at the press but to their friends and colleagues in the profession; and the press's editors eventually found themselves having to work at damage control in persuading authors to submit manuscripts in the first place and not to withdraw them at later stages of the review process.

The tension in the system was finally relieved, when I became editor-in-chief, by a change from having an overall quota for the press to having each editor work within the constraints of a personal quota, thus encouraging editors to monitor their own lists more closely in a quantitative as well as qualitative way and put fewer manuscripts into the pipeline for review at the outset. This adjustment to the system helped achieve greater balance, in a more planned manner, among the areas in which the press published, as an additional benefit. It also helped improve staff morale, which had been affected negatively by the internal competition among editors that the earlier way of operating had promoted and also, of course, by the rising chorus of complaints from rejected authors. Although this was a special case of an editorial system gone awry, owing to the unusual productivity of Princeton's acquisitions staff at this time, it highlights the importance generally of not being cavalier about rejecting manuscripts—at any stage in the process of review, early or late. As Walter Powell (1985) affirms, "an inap-

propriate or thoughtless rejection letter can . . . have dire consequences. . . . Academics have well-organized grapevines; word gets
around the academic community very quickly" (p. 112). The editors at Princeton, by force of circumstance, became especially adept
at writing rejection letters during this period!

Shaper

The editor's work is not done when the manuscript has finally
cleared the hurdle of approval by the editorial board and a contract has been signed. Even sometimes before acceptance, and even
on occasion before a manuscript is sent out for its first review by
an expert, an editor has an opportunity—limited, naturally, by the
scarcity of time available to any productive editor—to help shape
a manuscript by engaging in what has usually been called "developmental" or "structural" editing, as distinct from line-by-line
copyediting. This is editing that assists an author in dealing with
such problems as the sequence of chapters, the proper role and
content of a preface, introduction, and conclusion, the relationship
of evidence to argument, the use or misuse of footnotes, omissions
of important relevant literature from the bibliography, and general stylistic shortcomings such as the overuse of the passive voice,
sexist language, too heavy reliance on quotations from other authorities, and broad-scale inconsistencies of a type that require more
than simple copyediting to resolve. Developmental editing can cover
a wide spectrum of advice, from basic instruction on how to go
about successfully transforming a dissertation into a book, to the
gentle offer of suggestions about fine-tuning an argument or element of style.[10]

To give a better idea of the type of interaction with the author
this kind of editing involves, I quote from a letter by a Princeton
author, David Norton, written to a third party about the work I
had done on his book *Personal Destinies* (1977):[11]

> My acquaintance with Mr. Thatcher consists in our close work-
> ing relationship of four years, toward the publication of my book.
> . . . Sent to my files by the talk of writing this letter I found
> there no less than 100 pages of detailed commentary to Mr.
> Thatcher upon each chapter and each page, as well as upon the
> organization and development of the book as a whole. I recall
> very vividly my awareness, in the early stages, that by his re-
> solve nothing was going to appear in print that was less than
> the best humanly possible. This resolve proved contagious, and

I girded myself to emulate it. Subsequently and to this end the book—600 typewritten pages—was rewritten once from beginning to end, and twice more partially, all under the continuous chapter-by-chapter scrutiny of Mr. Thatcher. Not an argument or developmental opportunity was left unexamined by him. . . . What his initial response forcibly indicated was his remarkable ability to lend himself to it, to see it from the "inside," and discern unerringly where it was going. From that point on, his every move was given to the purpose of fulfilling its intrinsic aim. . . . He discerned the inner criteriology of the work—often to a degree surpassing my own perception of it—and held the book to the fulfillment of its own promise. Had he not done this the book would not be published, for its internal criteriology is a departure from today's fashion. And in holding the book to its own promise, he was tough and relentless.

Needless to say, this kind of deep engagement with a book is the exception rather than the rule, and no editor could afford the luxury of spending this much time on more than a very few books. For me, it happened to be a book I found particularly stimulating, and my own background in philosophy gave me greater resources on which to draw in advising the author and getting "inside" his argument than I would otherwise have had. But, at one extreme, this example does show what, in an ideal world with unlimited time, an editor could contribute to many books.

Linker

Editors rarely specialize in a subject to the extent that scholars, by necessity, must; indeed, dilettante is a word that is sometimes used to characterize an editor by contrast with the scholar as an expert. What editors lack in depth, however, they compensate for by having a wider vision of the terrain of scholarship, which can provide advantages in espying links among different areas of ongoing scholarly activity.

One example of the kind of linkage that an editor can accomplish is provided in the same letter by David Norton quoted earlier:

I consider myself to be rather widely read, but I soon found that his scope far surpassed my own, particularly with respect to new and recent work, and work in progress both in our country and abroad. My education began with his recommendations of current work on themes treated in *Personal Destinies*, and of which

PD should take account. But gradually I became aware that he was lending his resourcefulness not only to the book but to its author. He has repeatedly provoked me to think about themes which are outgrowths of the book, but which on my own I had failed to recognize or had managed successfully to neglect. Likewise thanks to his initiatives I am in touch with a continuously expanding circle of theorists whose current work bears upon my own, but of whom I was unaware. Without question my recent development owes much to Mr. Thatcher.

The links here were mostly within the field of philosophy and involved both associations among ideas and associations among people. Editors, with their antennae always extended to pick up early signals of new ideas and their extensive networks of individual contacts, play a meiotic role in making connections among different strands of intellectual development and among the different scholars pursuing them.

Another example of editorial midwifery, also within one field, resulted not only in two scholars establishing contact with one another about their work but also in their collaborating as coauthors of a book. In the mid-1980s, while discussing his ideas for a book about the modern intelligence community with Bruce Berkowitz, then a political scientist at the University of Minnesota, I received an inquiry from Allan Goodman, associate dean of the School of Foreign Service at Georgetown University, who proposed a book of a similar kind. In fact, both individuals had in mind writing a book that would perform the service for today's world that Sherman Kent's classic study *Strategic Intelligence for American World Policy* (Princeton, 1949) had provided for the immediate postwar world. Once made aware of each other's plans through my good offices, Berkowitz and Goodman immediately saw the advantages from collaborating and ended up writing *Strategic Intelligence for American National Security* (1989). Indeed, their collaboration continued, again with my encouragement, as they joined forces in helping the Penn State Press to launch its series of publications emanating from the CIA's Historical Review Program, the first two volumes of which, with their introduction and commentary, appeared in 1990 and 1992.[12]

But an editor's ability to force links is not limited to activity within a single discipline. Because many editors have responsibility for acquisitions in a number of fields, they have a vantage point not available to most scholars of being able to juxtapose and relate developments going on within different disciplines.[13] Work-

ing in philosophy and political science, I recall vividly how striking it was in the mid-1970s to observe political scientists engaged
in fierce debates about scientific methodology that were considered old hat by philosophers at that time. There was a cultural lag
of about ten years between these two fields, and in talking with
political scientists, I had the advantage of knowing the philosophical
literature well enough to point out what answers had already been
given to many of the questions political scientists were then discussing. I also could see real differences in the ways that political
philosophy was done in these two disciplines—one much more
historical and contextual in its approach, probing authorial intention and patterns of influence, the other much more concerned with
analysis of arguments for their own sake, independent of historical origin, and with rational reconstructions of classic positions
like utilitarianism or social contract theory.[14]

But editors themselves wear disciplinary blinders, less restrict-
ing though they may be than the ones that make many scholars so
myopic. As sponsoring editor for Richard Rorty's now famous
Philosophy and the Mirror of Nature (1979), I was oblivious to the
tremendous appeal this book would have to scholars in literary
criticism because, while vaguely aware of names like Derrida, I
did not work in that field as an editor and was not intimately in
touch with the currents of Continental theory that were beginning
to sweep over departments of English and comparative literature.
To his credit, Lindsay Waters, then an editor at the University of
Minnesota Press who had taught literature and was handling that
field as well as philosophy at the press, did appreciate the significance of Rorty's work for literary theory, and when I declined to
encourage submission of Rorty's collection of essays, Walters leaped
upon it eagerly and *The Consequences of Pragmatism* (Minnesota,
1982) was the result.[15] This was part of Waters's strategy to make
Minnesota the preeminent American publisher of Continental literary and philosophical theory, which he accomplished with great
success before moving on to become a general editor at Harvard
University Press.

This lesson was not lost on me, however, and I have made amends
at the Penn State Press by working closely with my fellow editor
Philip Winsor, who knows literary criticism from years of experience in the field, in establishing a new series in literature and
philosophy edited by Anthony Cascardi of Berkeley's Department
of Comparative Literature. One of the early products of that series
will be a volume of original essays introducing the work of the
well-known analytic philosopher Donald Davidson to literary theo-

rists and, in turn, showing philosophers how Davidson's work has relevance to literary theory. There is a real irony here in that, as Reed Way Dasenbrock explains in his introduction to this volume,

> there is a sense in which literary theorists have absorbed analytic philosophy primarily through being interested in the reaction against it. The work of Richard Rorty has been an important agent in this contradictory process: *Philosophy and the Mirror of Nature* tells us . . . that analytic philosophy has self-deconstructed, yet *Philosophy and the Mirror of Nature* was also the first detailed introduction to contemporary analytic philosophy for many literary theorists.

Having been partly responsible for leading literary theorists down the garden path, I feel some special obligation to set them straight again!

Because of their broad view of the scholarly horizon, editors have a special fondness for interdisciplinary work, and it is no accident that university presses publish a great deal of it, perhaps out of proportion to the importance it has within individual disciplines (as judged, for instance, by tenure committees). This meiotic role is usually not very visible to the outsider but, I suggest, it is valuable in stimulating scholars to pursue lines of inquiry that the structures of reward in their own specialized fields might not otherwise justify. As Paul Parsons (1989a) observes,

> University presses, as a leading vehicle for intellectual discourse, seldom serve as passive gatekeepers. Instead, they actively shape the cultural agenda by defining their role in the scholarly enterprise through listbuilding and aggressive acquisition methods. By being on the frontiers of scholarship, a press can help direct the cultural agenda, rather than merely reenforce existing values, beliefs, and practices. (p. 175)

Stimulator

Just as editors can help shape the cultural agenda by forging links among people and ideas, so too can they influence the direction of scholarship by stimulating the production of certain kinds of writing. Editors at university presses, unlike their counterparts at some commercial houses (especially those involved with textbook and reference book publishing), rarely commission books, it is true; their primary job is to keep abreast of the latest advances in scholarly knowledge and encourage the writing of books embodying these new ideas. But sometimes editors have opportunities to provide incentives for scholars to consider writing a certain kind of book they might not otherwise have thought about.

Several examples of this kind of initiative come to mind. Even before he left Princeton University Press (where I succeeded him as social science editor in 1969), William McClung had begun to work on promoting the concept of the short book as a vehicle for the expression of ideas that would offer an outlet for writing at a length beyond what most journals would accept for publication as an article yet shorter than what most publishers normally consider to constitute a book—say, between 60 and 120 printed pages. He laid out his thinking in an article for the very first issue of *Scholarly Publishing*, which he began with a telling quote from Harold J. Laski: "One sixteen-page tract by a George Bernard Shaw will do more good than all of the Ph.D. theses of Harvard, Yale, and Princeton combined"(1969, pp. 45–52). After joining the editorial staff at the University of California Press, he implemented this idea by founding a new series of short books called "Quantum Books" and set about signing up authors to write them. The first, by Chalmers Johnson entitled *Autopsy on People's War*, appeared in 1974. To date, a total of forty-one have been published, including such notable titles as Robert Dahl's *A Preface to Economic Democracy* (1985) and Michael Foucault's *This Is Not a Pipe* (1982), which has so far held the record for total sales of three thousand in hardback and twenty thousand in paperback.

The short book, I can testify from my own experience, has a special appeal. As McClung points out, it "can be read as a unit, at a single sitting, as a singular and coherent intellectual experience"(p. 46). Among my favorite books at Princeton were two of this kind, *The Passions and the Interests* (1977) and *Shifting Involvements* (1982), both by Albert O. Hirschman, who is an acknowledged master of this genre, an essayist in the tradition of Montaigne.

Placing more emphasis on speed of publication and timeliness of the topic than on the brevity of presentation was Yale's "Fastback" series, launched in 1969 with the publication of an edited volume, *Black Studies in the University*. Perhaps the most famous book to appear in this series so far was *Impeachment* (1974) written by noted constitutional scholar Charles Black. To educate the public about the process of impeachment, at a time when it looked as though President Richard Nixon might be subjected to it, Black completed the manuscript in three weeks, and the Yale Press rushed it through production in twenty-eight days—an all-time record for the series. The book sold some sixteen thousand copies very quickly, and then, once Nixon resigned, stopped selling almost instantly. Another Yale Fastback that has once again taken on new interest and relevance is Catherine MacKinnon's *Sexual Harassment* (1979). The fortieth title in this now well-established and successful line was published late in the fall of 1991: *What Is to Be Done? Proposals for the Soviet Transition to the Market*. Although some of the books in the series might well have been written and published anyway, its existence certainly provided a stimulus—no more clearly so than in the case of Black's overnight sensation.

A final example comes from the late 1960s when the confluence of several events provided the stimulus for the founding of the journal *Philosophy and Public Affairs* in 1971. Within philosophy there had gradually come into being during the late 1960s a renewed interest in political philosophy, which had prematurely been declared dead in the 1950s.[16] Most influential in this movement probably was the work of John Rawls, whose *Theory of Justice* when finally published by Harvard University Press in 1971 immediately set in motion a whole new industry.[17] At the same time, the growing opposition to the Vietnam War, which heightened political consciousness on college campuses everywhere, threw into question the emphasis on "value-free" social science that had been the hallmark of the so-called behavioral revolution in the early 1960s.

Drawing on these two currents, a group calling itself the Society of Philosophy and Public Policy was formed in May 1969. Its initial efforts focused on drafting resolutions—on the My Lai massacre, the invasion of Cambodia, the shootings at Kent State—and gathering signatures on them to submit to the government. But it quickly became clear that if the society were to wield any real influence, it would not be by passing resolutions and engaging in direct political action, but rather by doing what philosophers do best—promoting critical thinking.

Eventually, with Marshall Cohen and Thomas Nagel leading the way, some of the founding members of the society suggested starting a new journal to provide a vehicle for creative philosophical debate about important public issues. As a member of the society since October 1969, I was privy to these discussions and invited Marshall Cohen to submit a proposal to Princeton University Press. The first issue came out in the fall of 1971, and it quickly established itself as the premier journal in the field. Later, again at my invitation, Cohen became editor of a series of books for Princeton called "Studies in Moral, Political, and Legal Philosophy." Together the journal and the series have provided an outlet for a major renaissance in the field of political philosophy.

Shepherd

Within any publishing house the editor represents the author to all other departments, oversees the passage of the manuscript through the various stages of production in a general way, and seeks to coordinate all the work that staff copyediting, design, and marketing do to ensure that the book receives the best treatment that is appropriate for it. In this sense, the editor serves to shepherd the book on its way toward publication, watching over it carefully though not tending personally to every detail. The importance of this role cannot be emphasized enough because, without one person to guide the process on the author's behalf, inevitable mistakes will be made by personnel in other departments that an alert and responsible editor could have forestalled—such as forgetting to send the book to a particular convention's exhibit, to submit it for an appropriate prize, or to make sure that the jacket design accords with the author's expectations, at least in a general way.

Promoter

The editor's work does not end with the appearance of a book in print. However well produced a book may be, and however much the editor has done to ensure its scholarly quality, no book can succeed in accomplishing its purpose unless it reaches the audiences for which it is intended. Although the marketing department has the chief responsibility for promotion, a good editor will function also as the author's cheerleader, first within the house by stimulating enthusiasm for the book among other staff and then later by actively helping carry out the marketing department's plans.[18] Contacts that an editor has developed with book review editors at major media, for instance, can be called into play for titles that have genuine trade potential. Or an editor, knowledgeable about different organizations with special interests, might be aware of a prize that one of these organizations sponsors for which the book could be submitted.

An example of such promotion is a publication party I helped arrange for two authors of new Penn State Press books who happen to be colleagues and friends at Lafayette College in Easton,

Pennsylvania.[19] Taking advantage of my prior acquaintance with the new president of Lafayette, Robert Rotberg, we arranged the party at the Easton Bookshop for a time when he could attend. Such a celebration can serve a variety of purposes: pleasing two young authors who are just beginning what look to be very promising scholarly careers; highlighting the visibility of the Penn State Press as a potential publisher for other Lafayette authors; and establishing good relations with a local bookstore.

Ally

The loyalty of an author to a publishing house is a value that no editor should underestimate. There was a time when commercial publishers such as Scribner's would rate their long-term relationships with authors, such as Fitzgerald, Hemingway, and Wolfe, developed by the legendary editor Maxwell Perkins, as one of their greatest achievements. The conglomeratization of commercial publishing has made this a fading tradition, unfortunately, although it still remains alive in some British houses. For university presses, which do not have the financial resources to offer sizable advances and other economic lures to authors, the possibility of fostering loyalty by other means continues to be a realizable goal to which editors can aspire. The advantages to a press come not only from the author's own productive output, which may number a half-dozen or more books over the course of a career, but from that author's good will in referring other authors to the press and, generally, serving as a cheerleader for the press, too.[20] What was said earlier about the rapid spread of negative information about a publisher through the academic grapevine is equally true for positive information; loyal authors are primary allies of any publisher in creating a good public image.

As an ally of the author, an editor makes the author's project, which may take many years and several books to accomplish, in some ways his or her own. This does not necessarily mean that the editor shares the author's intellectual agenda or ideological point of view; it only means that the editor believes that the author has something important to say, worth disseminating to as wide a public as the publisher can reach. Most editors probably have the fundamental faith that I do in John Stuart Mill's concept of the "marketplace of ideas," and it is to help enrich that marketplace as much as possible that we dedicate our efforts as editors.

As much as I have an identifiable personal ideology, I would describe myself as a Millian liberal; yet several of the authors with whom I have developed long-term relationships are identified in the public eye as "conservative" thinkers—Hadley Arkes, Julian Simon, and Thomas Sowell. Testimony from the author's side of what this kind of relationship involves I can offer here from two of these people, both from letters written to me in 1990 after I had already moved to Penn State. Arkes wrote gratifyingly of the wonderful reactions he was receiving to *First Things* (1986), the third of four books I sponsored for him at Princeton, from many quarters both within and outside academe. He said:

> as these reports have come in over the past year, I've kept thinking of you. It was your backing that became critical, decisive, for the publication of all of my books; and with these reactions to *First Things*, I've felt that we've finally had the kind of sustained reaction that can establish a justification for these projects. If the book managed to touch many thoughtful people in an enduring way, what better confirmation could we have for the decision to produce these books.

And Simon, author of three books for Princeton, two of which I handled, wrote:

> If it had not been for S. Thatcher and PUP, my 1977 book probably would still be looking for a publisher. . . . And if the 1977 book had not come out, all the rest on population would not have happened, also. The dissemination of radically new ideas hangs on a much thinner thread than most people believe, even in a pluralistic society. DNA would have been discovered in a few months even without Watson and Crick, but in the social sciences, one editor and one press can be decisive for a long time.

Allies like these, it should be added, also often end up being good friends.

Reticulator

"To reticulate," according to the Random House dictionary, is "to form a network." A major activity of editors is building networks— networks of advisors, whether they are authors or not, who can keep an editor informed of new developments in a field, refer an editor to work in progress by colleagues, provide early leads to the best and brightest of the graduate students whose dissertations may be worth transforming into books, and even serve as reviewers of completed manuscripts. Paul Parsons (1989b) says, simply, "networking is essential" (p. 59). Walter Powell (1985) affirms that "the primary means for editors to keep *au courant* of the professional disciplines in which they work is through building and maintaining a wide and active personal network" (p. 74). I agree with Parsons, but I think Powell goes too far; while essential and *a* primary source of information for editors, I would not describe networking as *the* "primary means" without qualification.

Editors are individuals who work in different ways, preferring some methods more than others, to achieve the same ends; not all would place networking at the top of the list, though I am confident that all would concur in its importance at some level as essential for their success. A network, in a sense, is an expanded alliance: allies are those authors with whom an editor has developed the closest working relationships over the longest period of time; members of a network include allies but also many other scholars with whom an editor maintains sufficient contact to keep the pipeline of information open. Senior editors are valuable not only because of the experience they have acquired but also because of the networks they are plugged into; a publisher hiring a senior editor gains the benefit of both the experience and the network the editor has developed.

All nine of these specific roles that I have discussed as parts of the listbuilder's job show what editors contribute as "value added" to the book as product in the process of publication and, more broadly, to the system of scholarly communication. Those who currently speak about electronic publishing as the wave of the future, putting the author directly in touch with the reader, often are oblivious to these many and varied contributions that editors make.

Characteristics of Presses

Although editors at university presses continue to wield the greatest influence on what gets published, in contrast with the waning influence of their counterparts in commercial publishing, they nevertheless find their decision making channeled in a variety of ways, not only by operating rules within the house itself of the kind mentioned earlier but also by features of the press that are defined by the nature of the university to which it is attached, its own size and reputation, the strengths of its parent university, the character of its backlist and publishing tradition, the background and interests of its director, and the policies and procedures of its editorial board.

State vs. private

Almost all university presses function as departments of their universities, with the director reporting to the dean of the graduate school, a vice president for academic affairs, or the provost.[21] The exact positioning of the press within the university's overall bureaucratic structure can have some effect on how it operates and what it tries to achieve, but probably more important in influencing editorial decisions is the status of the press's parent university as either private or public.[22] Of the current regular members of the Association of American University Presses that are attached to universities located in the United States, forty-nine are at public universities and twenty-four at private institutions.[23]

It is no accident that those presses situated within public universities have pioneered in the publishing of books of regional interest, whereas hardly any of the presses connected with private universities have engaged in it to any significant extent.[24] At Princeton, for instance, regional publishing meant issuing an occasional book focusing on some aspect of the university's or the town's history; it was taken for granted that books about any other area of the state would go to Rutgers University Press as their natural publisher. Some regional publishing is done within the framework of series. Illinois has its Prairie State Books; Florida has Sand Dollar Books.

At Penn State, we identify some titles as Keystone Books to distinguish these publications, mainly aimed at entertaining and informing a broad range of citizens within the state, from works of primary scholarship that have a major academic contribution to make even though they happen to focus on one or another aspect of the state's history, politics, environment, or culture. Two titles issued late in 1992 illustrate the difference. *The Allegheny River: Watershed of the Nation* is a heavily illustrated, coffee-table book that is sold to the general public through retail bookstores and advertised in popular magazines. *Harrisburg Industrializes: The Coming of Factories to an American Community,* by contrast, though also illustrated, is an ambitious work of revisionist scholarship that will have its main impact through reviews in professional journals and should influence the way academic studies of urban history are done in the future.[25]

Presses in the South and the Southwest have been especially active and innovative in regional publishing. A fine example of the genre is the *Encyclopedia of Southern Culture* published in 1989 by the University of North Carolina Press, which pioneered in the publication of regional books beginning in the 1930s. The University of New Mexico Press, publisher of many books about the Southwest Indian life and culture including best-seller *The Education of Little Tree*, claims to derive fully 60 percent of its income from sales of regional titles.[26] The strength of regional ties even accounts in part for the advent in popularity of fiction publishing at university presses; it began to grow significantly in the wake of the major success of *The Confederacy of Dunces*, published by the LSU Press in 1980 (after it had been rejected by over forty commercial publishers).

Size and reputation

A press's size and its reputation both can have an important impact on the kind of publishing program it undertakes. Here a direct contrast between Princeton and Penn State may be helpful because they differ significantly in these two respects. In 1990 Princeton published 205 new titles, the largest output that year for any American university press; Penn State issued 32, placing it within the smallest quartile (though toward the upper end). Princeton, founded in 1905, has long been regarded as one of the most prestigious academic publishers in the world; Penn State, founded in 1956, has acquired a solid reputation in a few fields—especially art history and literary criticism—but it is not yet regarded by many scholars outside those fields as having any special prestige attached to its imprint, and even within those fields Princeton would undoubtedly be considered the more prestigious publisher by most scholars. What effect does their different status have on these presses' publishing programs?

Size makes a difference because a larger press with a more substantial backlist has a better chance of being able to generate a surplus over operating costs from sales and thus of being less dependent on external subsidies, either from its own university or from other sources. This gives it greater flexibility to undertake long-term, large-scale projects requiring a lot more capital investment than a small press can muster. Hence, Princeton could afford to take on the multivolume writings of Henry David Thoreau, the complete works of W. H. Auden, Kierkegaard's writings, the papers of Thomas Jefferson and of Woodrow Wilson, and such hugely expensive single-volume projects as the *Atlas of Early American History* (printed in six colors), which would be well beyond the means of a press the size of Penn State.

Size also is partly the reason that not more presses are involved in science publishing. Only twenty presses publish in the physical sciences, for instance, and only eleven in mathematics.[27] Princeton is one of the very few presses that has invested significant effort in science publishing and maintained a program covering a broad range of the sciences. It can succeed in this area, as Penn State cannot hope to do (despite the strength of the university's College of Science), for several reasons, almost all having to do with the greater financial resources at Princeton's disposal. First, good listbuilding editors in science are scarce and, consequently, command higher salaries than editors in other fields; they also need large travel budgets because, with scientists not having the same incentives as scholars in the humanities and social sciences to write books, editors are obliged to track them down in their offices and labs and persuade them that writing a book can be a good use of their time. Second, as part of this effort at persuasion, editors are under pressure to offer sizable monetary advances against high royalty rates if they want to sign up the best authors; and yet many of these books put under contract (almost half, in my experience at Princeton) are never finally completed and submitted for publication, leaving the publisher with no possibility of making any return on the initial investment. Third, most science books contain a lot of technical matter that requires special skills of a copy editor and places extra demands on the production department; and the expectations of scientists who put a premium on speedy communication mean that their books usually have to be given faster schedules than other kinds of books. Finally, even if presses otherwise could afford to pay these high costs of science publishing, they would have to be prepared to face stiff competition from commercial publishers— Elsevier, Pergamon, Springer Verlag, and Wiley—that have large investments in scientific publishing, in both books and journals, and have more capital resources at their disposal than even the largest university presses.

The different rates of submission of manuscripts are also partly attributable to differences in size. With three times the number of acquiring editors, Princeton would naturally be expected to attract more manuscripts than Penn State. In 1988, 870 manuscripts were submitted to Princeton, down from a high of 1,147 in 1982; Penn State in 1990 handled 185 submissions. Interestingly, although Princeton and Penn State receive roughly the same proportion of unsolicited manuscripts, about 75 percent, the quality of those submitted over the transom at Penn State is significantly higher: over four times as many unsolicited manuscripts are accepted at Penn State as at Princeton.[28]

This difference cannot be explained by any difference in the rigor of the review process at the two presses, which both operate similarly in this respect. My guess is that many more scholars, especially those early in their careers with dissertations to peddle, are attracted by Princeton's prestige, whereas those who submit manuscripts to Penn State do so for special reasons besides the lure of the press's imprint—because, for instance, they or their colleagues have appreciated the quality of personal attention and care their books have received at the press.[29] As a result, the advantage that comes from having a manuscript solicited by Penn State does not seem so great as compared with a solicitation by Princeton: solicited manuscripts at Princeton are twice as likely to be accepted as submitted manuscripts overall, whereas the odds at Penn State only improve by 25 percent for solicited manuscripts. One benefit for Penn State in receiving fewer unsolicited manuscripts of lower quality is that less time is spent separating the wheat from the chaff and the sheer cost of processing manuscripts that will not bring any return on the investment of handling them is less than it is at Princeton.

The ability of a press to offer service of high quality is a function of size, too, in both negative and positive senses. Larger presses tend to have greater marketing capabilities, for instance, and here economies of scale can make a real difference in spreading costs over a large number of titles.[30] What smaller presses lack in sheer economic clout and market presence, however, they can often make up for by, like Avis, "trying harder." Tender, loving care—while certainly not absent in larger houses—is often easier to achieve in smaller houses where most attention can be devoted to individual titles across the board, not just the front list of lead titles. As Herbert S. Bailey, Jr., former director of Princeton University Press (1991, p. 2) says, "because publishing is such a personal activity, publishing houses need to be small" if they are to develop a distinctive style and offer the best of personalized service to their authors.

In a large house, which by necessity has to develop elaborate bureaucratic structures, more time is spent on paperwork and in staff meetings to accomplish the intricate coordination among the work of many people all involved with different aspects of publishing the same book, and less time is thus available to go the extra mile for an author and do the little things that make the experience of publishing truly satisfying and rewarding. Editors at large houses usually have a higher quota of books they are expected to get under contract than editors of small presses, and handling many titles hampers their ability to pay close personal attention to any one of them. It also limits what they can do to oversee the coordination of work by staff in different departments, increasing the likelihood that some detail or other will be missed— a preference of the author not communicated to the designer, a book not sent to a particular convention or submitted in time for a certain award, and so on.[31] Such coordination is easier to achieve more informally in a less bureaucratically encumbered organization, and this gives the smaller press an advantage in appealing to an author's desire for the personal touch in publishing.[32] While different from the prestige of the imprint, this kind of reputation can help a small press compete with much larger houses, especially when a monetary advance is not a major factor in an author's decision.

The difference between these two kinds of reputation can explain an otherwise puzzling phenomenon: why a small press like Penn State can have a better chance of publishing a book for a senior than for a junior scholar. It is well known that tenure committees judge the significance of a book as much by the prestige of the publisher's imprint as by the quality of the content, and the same book published at Princeton (or Harvard, Chicago, Yale, California, etc.) would be accorded higher marks than it would with the imprint of Penn State (or Fordham, Wayne State, Tennessee, Utah, etc.). Not surprisingly, therefore, the imprint is usually a much more important factor in a junior scholar's decision about publication than it is for a senior scholar, who may place more weight on the quality of service a publisher can provide.[33]

Strengths of the university

Deciding what to publish is more complicated in some ways for a university press than a commercial publisher because, in addition to the business considerations involved (costs of entry into a market, level of competition to be expected, etc.), a press is faced with interpreting its obligations to its parent university in making decisions about where to concentrate its editorial efforts. All presses to some degree feel a responsibility to reflect strengths of their universities' faculty, but how far they go in making their list a mirror of their university differs considerably from press to press. No press, of course, can expect to publish in all fields encompassed within a university's curriculum and still hope to survive as a business; success as a publisher requires specialization. And smaller presses cannot be expected, correspondingly, to represent as many of their universities' strengths as larger ones.

The special difficulties of publishing in some fields limit what presses can do. Although the Penn State Press had tried fitfully for years to establish a program in science and engineering that would do justice to the university's stake in those areas, it had failed to build any real momentum, for reasons that are easy to understand, as discussed above. As the new director, I knew it would be fruitless to make the effort again. At the same time, wanting to build the press's list in the social sciences and history, I saw an opportunity to do worthwhile publishing *about* science rather than *in* science by developing a list of studies in the inter-disciplinary field of "science, technology, and society," where the university has long been a leader with its highly regarded Science, Technology and Society Program.

Intellectual trends have their own dynamic and can lead a press to enter a field even when its own university is not especially outstanding in it. The development of Latin American studies at Princeton described earlier is a good example. Among area studies at the university it was not the strongest or best known, yet the directions in which social science theory was moving made it sensible for the press to concentrate its editorial energies there. It is only fair to point out, however, that the press is also a leading publisher in Middle Eastern and East Asian studies, areas in which Princeton University is preeminent.

While it is generally true, then, that a university press's list will be strong in many of the same areas in which its parent university's faculty is strong, the pressures of succeeding as a business enterprise as well as the attractions of exciting new intellectual developments will tend to make the correspondence between the two less than one-to-one.

Backlist and tradition

The investment that a press has already made in building a list in a particular field is a major determinant of editorial decisions. As Walter Powell (1985) says, "when editors are in the process of signing books, the list that is already in print will impose its own logic on them, in both obvious and imperceptible ways"(p. 153).

Marketing considerations are an important factor here. Continuing a strong list in a certain field provides the opportunity, with the advertising of new titles, to do more promotion of the backlist, which helps to keep those older titles selling steadily over many years. But editorial considerations are equally important: once one has gained momentum in a field, it takes much less effort to sustain it than it does to invest time and energy in entering a field where the press has not published before.

When I arrived at Penn State, the press had a well-developed list in both art history and literary criticism as well as a growing list in religious studies. With an experienced editor already hard at work in these fields, it only made sense to continue building the press's program in these areas. Outside these fields, the press's list was quite thin; there were titles scattered across a wide range of fields in history, the social sciences, and other areas of the humanities as well as in science and engineering.

Given the press's size, it could not expect to publish successfully in all of these fields in the future, so decisions had to be made to bring more focus to the program. The move into studies in science, technology, and society has already been explained. My familiarity with philosophy, political science, and sociology as well as Latin American studies made it sensible to focus on these fields, and the press already had some backlist in all of these areas. I hired an editor from Wesleyan University Press to take charge of listbuilding in history and to help out with some of the social sciences. His expertise in medieval religious history gave us a quick entree' into that field. It soon became apparent that the three of us had sufficiently overlapping interests to make it natural for us to cooperate in various interdisciplinary fields, such as women's studies. And because the focus of our existing lists in art history and literary criticism were already strongly American and European, it was logical to concentrate our efforts in history and the social sciences along these geographical lines, too—with Latin American studies, because of that area's strong historical ties with Europe and America, being a perfect complement to this focus.

One way in which we sought to strengthen the interdisciplinary orientation of our list was by launching a number of series: "Literature and Philosophy" will help build bridges between those two fields for us, while "Hermeneutics: Studies in the History of Religions" will bring our efforts in history and religious studies more closely into relation with each other. Series for many presses are a major vehicle for focusing the list and providing a steady stream of submissions. Series editors, as Walter Powell (1985) points out, can even play a role for presses "that is in certain respects equivalent to the role of literary agents in trade publishing"(p. 50). Some presses prefer organizing their lists along the lines of series more than other presses do, but every press has at least a few series that over time help create an identity for its list and become a part of its tradition.

Another element of a press's tradition can influence editorial decision making, too. Those presses that publish journals (currently, thirty-nine of the U.S. presses that are regular members of the AAUP) have an additional incentive to bring out books that complement their journal publications. The existence of the *Journal of Policy History* at Penn State was a major reason why the press decided to begin publishing books in policy history; indeed, a series was launched in 1992 to make available paperbacks for course adoption in conjunction with the journal's publication of a special thematic issue every year. At Princeton the success of *Philosophy and Public Affairs* led eventually to establishing a series of books called "Studies in Moral, Political, and Legal Philosophy" edited by the journal's editor, Marshall Cohen. All of the journals at Princeton and at Penn State, too, are now closely integrated with the book publishing program. In 1991 Penn State added two journals in American literature (one of them also in women's studies) in part because of the effort under way to build the press's list of book titles in American studies. This symbiosis between book and journal publishing is especially visible at those presses that publish fewer than a dozen journals, but it even exists to some extent at the houses with major journals operations, like Chicago and Johns Hopkins.

Background and interests of the director

The educational training and the special interests that editors have, naturally enter into their listbuilding plans and decisions. At Princeton, for instance, I got the press involved for the first time in a sustained way in publishing in philosophy because that was the field I knew best from my own undergraduate and graduate training, and the press was wise enough to take advantage of it.[34] When I moved to Penn State, it was natural to continue acquiring in philosophy for this reason alone—but also because the university has a strong Philosophy Department and the press already was publishing two journals in philosophy edited by members of the department. Editors when they move carry their networks with them, and presses who hire them do so in part because of the benefit these connections bring.

That I came to Penn State as the new director made my background and interests all the more determinative of the directions the press would take editorially. Indeed, since the vast majority of directors at presses spent their earlier careers as editors (unlike the heads of commercial houses, who today more often come from backgrounds in business, law, or marketing), it is only reasonable to expect that their editorial tastes will have a great deal to do with what their presses publish. Princeton has a major commitment to science publishing in large part because its director from 1954 to 1986, Herbert S. Bailey, Jr., was science editor before he became director; and his crowning achievement as director was to launch the project to publish in some fifty volumes the complete works of Albert Einstein (Bailey, 1989). (Surely one reason that not more presses are involved in science publishing is that few press directors have had any direct exposure to science.) Bailey's successor at Princeton, Walter Lippincott, is an opera lover—and now the press not only publishes books on opera but has a series devoted to it. And if you look at the presses that have strong programs in poetry, you will find many of the directors to be poets themselves—Paul Zimmer at Iowa and Miller Williams at Arkansas, for example.

Policies and procedures of the editorial board

Enough has already been written about the role that the faculty editorial board plays to require little additional comment here (Parsons 1989a; Goellner 1990a). Paul Parsons (1989b, p. 200) usefully points out how the tendency of editorial boards to be conservative (because membership on them is usually reserved for senior scholars) is counterbalanced by editors' desire to position their presses at the cutting edge of the advance of scholarship. As a first approximation to reality, this is a valid observation, but it glosses over some of the subtleties of editorial board operations.

At Princeton a tradition initiated by one editorial board continued for many years: giving explicit recognition to what were called "risk" books, which were seen to depart in various ways from the model of the standard scholarly monograph but were regarded as sufficiently well grounded in scholarship to merit publication by a university press even though, in some respects, they were more like trade books. Julian Simon's *The Ultimate Resource* (1981), an attack on the arguments of the ecological doomsayers like Paul Ehrlich, who so dominated public discourse in the 1970s, was treated as a risk book by Princeton's editorial board, which recognized it to be based on Simon's more academic research, some of it previously published by the press in *The Economics of Population Growth* (1977). The risk here partly had to do with the ideological and political uses to which the book could be put (and Simon did become a favorite with neoconservative groups) and also with its direct challenge to some of the academic scholarship emanating from Princeton's own Office of Population Research (various members of whose faculty made their displeasure known to the university's administration after the book was published). If this was conservatism on the part of Princeton's editorial board, it was not such in the sense that it constrained the press in any way from publishing a controversial book. (While issuing some titles of a neoconservative persuasion, the press was also busily building up a reputation during this period of being a leading publisher of Marxist-influenced scholarship.)

Its openness to taking risks of this kind, however, was not for a while reflected in its approach to feminist studies. One major book by a feminist philosopher, which went on to establish itself as an early classic in the field, was rejected by the editorial board (consisting entirely of male faculty at this time) even after a third report specifically requested by the board recommended publication, as had two earlier readers enthusiastically. That was the most blatant exercise of prejudice I can recall from all of my years in scholarly publishing—and the author has never forgotten it!

This occurred during the time when Princeton was acquiring its bad reputation for turning down well-supported manuscripts at the last stage. Because of the surfeit of books on its agenda and the quota of acceptances that it was being asked to enforce, the editorial board adopted a special procedure whereby all projects not approved by consensus on the first pass through the agenda (which could take several hours of intensive discussion to reach) would be bundled for reconsideration at the end. The members of the board would then rank-order their preferences for manuscripts in the bundle, and the final selection up to the limit of the quota would proceed accordingly. As it happened, this procedure—adopted by necessity given the framework for decision making imposed on the board—exacerbated the tendency of board members to allow their own biases free reign and heightened the role of subjectivity in the whole process.

Policies and procedures like these, not usually visible to observers outside a press, can play a significant role not only in determining what kinds of books get published but also how decisions about them are reached.

Conditions and Changes in the External Environment

University presses simultaneously inhabit two worlds, the world of higher education and the world of publishing, and conditions and changes in these wider environments can have an effect on what presses publish that is often as influential as their own internal character and their relationship with their parent university. Any thorough discussion of these environments would fill many pages, but at least we can point here to some of the main sources of external influence and the way in which such influence manifests itself in presses' editorial programs.

Declining markets

Sales to libraries have always been the solid base on which the economics of scholarly book publishing rests, but that base has been eroding rapidly over the past twenty-five years. In the late sixties, the ratio of expenditures on books compared with journals was 2:1, but even by the mid-1970s it had dropped to 1:1 and has been continuing to decline since then as the prices of journals, primarily in scientific and technical fields, have soared to levels that are finally beginning to provoke librarians into canceling subscriptions.[35]

The effect of this trend on the market for scholarly monographs has been devastating. For example, at Princeton, hardback books that were on average selling 1,660 copies over a five-year period as of 1969 were only selling 931 copies by 1986—a decline of 44 percent. Between 1985 and 1990, a recent study shows, the purchase of monographs by major research libraries dropped by 16 percent, or nearly $23 million (Okerson & Stubbs, 1991, p. 36). With manufacturing costs rising steadily, exerting upward pressure on prices, presses have found themselves in a bind: although buying by libraries is not very price-sensitive, buying by individuals is, and presses realize that faculty salaries and graduate fellowships have not kept pace with inflation sufficiently to make offsetting lost sales to libraries possible through sharp price increases without affecting sales to individuals.

Most U.S. presses have resisted the temptation to which European academic publishers long ago succumbed to forget about sales to individuals and just charge exorbitant prices to libraries to cover costs on very small printruns. They have therefore responded to this cost–price squeeze by trying to effect savings in production through use of computer technology (the misnamed "desktop publishing"), placing more emphasis on publishing shorter books, diversifying the mix of books on their lists, seeking to expand their search for subsidies from external sources, and—if all else fails— withdrawing from some fields of scholarly publication altogether where the market is not large enough to sustain minimally acceptable sales. Signs of this latter trend, leading to endangered species in scholarly publishing, are already beginning to appear and will surely intensify over the coming decade.[36] Fields particularly in jeopardy include literary criticism, music, African studies, and European history.

Conglomeratization in commercial publishing

While university presses were watching their sales to libraries decline, as larger percentages of library budgets went to maintaining subscriptions to expensive scientific and technical journals issued mostly by commercial houses, mergers among large companies in the communications industry, both domestically (such as Time and Warner) and internationally (such as the Bertelsmann takeover of Bantam/Doubleday/Dell), were changing the face of commercial book publishing. Corporate pressures increased for houses to find and milk for all their worth blockbuster books by the best-known authors (Stephen King, Danielle Steel, Bill Cosby, etc.), who commanded ever greater monetary advances. Writers of first novels, poetry, and serious nonfiction works with less than spectacular sales potential found less of a welcome than ever at the houses that had been absorbed in these media conglomerates (including many of the traditionally distinguished houses like Scribner's and Knopf) and turned in increasing numbers to university presses as well as to the newly emerging and robust so-called independent publishers.[37]

This development helped presses in their efforts to diversify their lists, and many more presses began publishing fiction and general trade books than ever had before. Some press directors sought to justify this diversification by reinterpreting their mandate as giving university-based publishing a much more expansive cultural role than it had traditionally borne.[38] Sharp disagreements continue to exist within the university press community over the publishing of fiction, and to a lesser extent poetry (partly because poetry was entrenched within press publishing programs much earlier than general fiction publishing was), but almost all presses have come to appreciate the opportunity to do more publishing of the kind of midlist trade book that commercial houses have been rapidly abandoning.[39] The appeal of these new areas of publishing, however, carries with it the danger that presses will give lesser priority to the publication of scholarly monographs, adding further to the problem of endangered species (Thatcher, 1990).

Competition among presses

As commercial publishers have cut back on their publication of midlist titles, competition among university presses for them has intensified, further reinforcing a trend that already was beginning to manifest itself by the mid-1970s.[40] One possible explanation for this rise in competitiveness among presses is the increase in the number of press directors who began their careers in commercial publishing; for example, the current directors at California, Princeton, and Yale all got their start in the 1960s working in the college department of Harper and Row.

Whatever the cause, the effects of heightened competition on the traditional way of doing business in university press publishing have been substantial. Use of advance and conditional contracts has proliferated, meaning that offers are more often being made when only partial manuscripts, or manuscripts in need of major revision, or sometimes even just outlines are submitted for review. Presses have more and more resorted to special enticements to lure authors away from competitors—enticements such as high royalty rates, monetary advances, fast production schedules, expensive design (such as four-color jackets), extra (especially major media) promotion, simultaneous paperback publication, and so on. Presses, too, have opened themselves up to multiple submission of manuscripts, a practice common in commercial book publishing but once very rare in university press publishing (and still anathema for most professional journals).[41] Whether competition has actually resulted in an erosion of scholarly standards and rigor in the review process is a debatable point, but there can be no question that it has exacted a toll in the waste of scarce resources: only one press can win, and all the time and money that losing presses expend subtract from the resources available for them to publish other books.

Conditions in academia

Many aspects of academic life impinge on the activities of presses, and a whole chapter alone could be devoted to this topic. But a few points especially pertinent to the activities of listbuilding editors are worth making here. Every editor is aware that one can no longer concentrate just on the most prestigious, elite universities in the search for good manuscripts. It may continue to be true that the best authors of academic books receive their graduate training at the top research universities, but owing to the squeeze on jobs during the 1970s and 1980s, the graduates of these institutions were obliged to find work wherever they could, and many ended up at relatively obscure colleges in out-of-the-way places or even abandoned academia altogether in favor of more secure, better-paying jobs in government, business, or law—where some have nevertheless remained intent on writing and publishing important works of scholarship.[42]

Perhaps partly because of this dispersion, and also a growing awareness among college administrators of faculty's needs for publishing support, it has become more common for universities without presses of their own to provide subsidies for authors from their faculty to help them get their books published; and even some universities that do have presses make such subsidies available to their faculty who publish elsewhere. As the problem of endangered species becomes more acute and subsidies are more often required as a condition of publication, it is likely that authors from institutions that have such policies in place will have an advantage in securing contracts over authors at campuses where no support of this kind is forthcoming.

Finally, it needs to be emphasized how sensitive presses are to trends in academic life. Probably the most extraordinary example in recent times is the rapid growth of presses' interest in publishing in women's studies. As Paul Parsons (1991) notes, "remarkably, after only two decades of intensive intellectual pursuit, women's studies is now the second-leading area of specialization at university presses," with fully 78 percent of presses having programs in the field (pp. 45, 47). African-American studies, once very active in the early 1970s before going into a decade-long eclipse, has recently rebounded, in part because of the general movement toward emphasizing the value of multiculturalism in college curricula.

Foundations

The earlier interest in black and ethnic studies in general was attributable in part to the encouragement provided to the field by substantial financial backing from the Ford Foundation. This is just one of many examples of the key role that foundation funding has played in setting the intellectual agenda for higher education and, in turn, stimulating the production of books for presses to publish. The turn away from African toward Latin American studies, mentioned earlier, is another example; a number of foundations, Tinker and Howard Heinz in particular, have been primary supporters of research on Latin America over the years. The Getty grant program has been crucial to the vitality of research and publishing in art history. And the Japan Foundation in 1989 launched a program of awards administered by the AAUP to foster the publication by presses of more books about Japan. Some foundations, notably Mellon, have even given substantial grants directly to individual presses to help subsidize publications in the humanities, but in recent times, Mellon and other foundations have not shown much inclination to continue this kind of support.

Government

Like foundations, government agencies have been sometimes indispensable sources of support for publishing projects undertaken by university presses. The papers of Washington, Jefferson, Madison, Adams, and others could not have been made available in meticulously edited and elegantly produced series without the backing of the National Historical Publications and Records Commission. The project to publish the complete works of Albert Einstein at Princeton would have gone nowhere without major funding from the National Science Foundation. The National Endowment for the Arts has provided both matching grant funds and individual title subsidies to help those presses involved in the publishing of poetry and fiction. And the National Endowment for the Humanities has been a crucial player for many years in enabling presses to publish many first-rate monographs in all areas of the humanities, including history and the more humanistically oriented branches of the social sciences.

Changes in government programs can also make a significant difference in what university presses publish, however. The NEH, for instance, moved in 1988 from subsidizing scholarly monographs with low sales potential, providing grants of different amounts in relation to the financial requirements of each title, to emphasizing works of broader public interest by offering a standard grant of $7,000 to each title approved for support. It appears from evidence to date that presses are not radically altering the kinds of books they are seeking NEH support for, and therefore the change in NEH's criteria is having only a limited impact.[43] Still, by this shift NEH is not perceived as helping with the problem of endangered species but only contributing to making it worse.

All of the foregoing examples have referred to the role of the U.S. government. But increasingly significant, too, is the role that foreign governments have begun to play in fostering and subsidizing publication of books about their own country's history and culture. A number of governments—French, German, and Italian— are active in providing support for translation into English of works originally published in those languages. Even more ambitious is the program that the Spanish Ministry of Culture launched in 1984; besides subsidizing translations, it offers grants to presses to help with publication of any books having to do with Spain's heritage, including books about colonial Latin America. The existence of this program was one important factor in our decision at the Penn State Press to begin a new series of Penn State Studies in Romance Literatures, and so far four books in the series have received subsidies from the program. The availability of foreign government funding of this kind will likely have a considerable influence on where presses concentrate their efforts, and no one will be surprised if more books are published on Spain than on other European countries in the future.

The internationalization of publishing

While interactions with foreign governments are increasingly important in this way, so too are relationships with foreign publishers. In commercial publishing, many of the mergers have brought houses based in different countries under the umbrella of conglomerates with operations extending worldwide. Bertelsmann, the world's largest publishing company, for example, has 48,780 employees scattered over thirty countries.[44] One effect has been to stimulate editors at houses in different countries to cooperate with each other on projects to publish books simultaneously in several languages.

Although this phenomenon has not yet been much in evidence at university presses, there is greater activity than ever in copublishing, especially between U.S. and British publishers. In fact, Penn State owes much of its early success in establishing visibility quickly in history and the social sciences to the close working relationship it has developed with Polity Press in Cambridge, England, which is undoubtedly one of the leading commercial publishers of academic books in the world today, with a list representing the best and most exciting work of European scholarship. The prominence of Minnesota's list in literary theory, feminist studies, and Continental philosophy also owes much to its connection with Polity.

Just now we are beginning to see signs of the emergence of scholarly publishing along traditional university press lines in

Eastern Europe. The University of Nebraska Press contributed to
the launching of a press at Charles University in Prague, Czecho-
slovakia, by arranging for Apple to donate computer equipment
and providing training in how to use it in a publishing operation
(Wanek, 1990/91). As ties are forged between new presses in this
part of the world and American presses, we can expect cooperation in editorial activities to follow.

Computer technology

Not only is computer technology helping presses in Eastern
Europe to get off the ground, it also has since the early 1980s revo-
lutionized the way publishing is carried out in this country. Business operations were the first to benefit, with the availability of
sophisticated spreadsheet and database programs, but computerization has since spread into nearly every aspect of publishing,
from editing and design to marketing and royalty payments, not
only saving money but also contributing greatly to efficiency and
productivity. Our designer at Penn State, for instance, estimates
that with the help of computers in designing jackets he has been
able to produce better designs in half of the time. Now that almost all authors are producing their manuscripts on word proces-
sors, some presses like Princeton have developed the capability to
take floppy disks from authors, edit them on screen, enter format-
ting codes, and use them to drive typesetting equipment.

All of these uses of computers have helped presses provide better
service to authors. Still in its infancy, however, is actual electronic
publishing at university presses. Oxford University Press established an Electronic Publishing Division a few years ago to begin
making available some of its major reference works, such as the
Oxford English Dictionary, in computer-readable form. In 1991 Columbia University Press issued its *Granger's World of Poetry* as a
CD-ROM.[45] Other such projects, probably with emphasis on reference works to begin with, will be undertaken at an increasing
number of presses in years to come, though the scarcity of capital
resources available to presses will limit the extent to which they
can enter this field and compete effectively with commercial publishers. Most likely, presses will start to develop relationships with
commercial firms that can convert to electronic form and market
the copyrighted materials that presses license them to produce and
distribute. Already there is a company called Context Editions at
work in creating electronic data bases of the critical editions of
the writings of the classic philosophers; negotiations for inputting

editions of Spinoza's and Hume's works was under way at Princeton before I left.

The Future

In less than a decade, advances in computer technology, combined with other recent innovations, such as the fax machine and the rapid growth of the Internet, have opened up possibilities for overhauling the entire system of scholarly communication. Some librarians have latched onto technology as a means of salvation for their problems, especially for spiraling costs of subscriptions to scientific and technical journals, and have envisioned a restructured system in which commercial publishers would be left out or given a much reduced role. One of the outspoken advocates of this change, Patricia Battin, said in 1984: "The electronic revolution provides the potential for developing university controlled publishing enterprises through scholarly networks supported either by individual institutions of consortia" (p. 175). The Association of Research Libraries is currently "encouraging experimentation with electronic journals and new technologies" operated by groups of scholars connected through university computer networks like BITNET (Okerson & Stubbs 1991, p. 37).[46] Even more visionary is the hope of creating "a single electronic database that includes all edited and refereed scholarly publication" linked to "the National Research and Education Network currently under development in the United States" (Smith, 1991, pp. 88–89; see also Smith, 1992).

What such visions of a brave new world of scholarly communication usually overlook is the question of "who will keep the gates?" Patricia Battin (1984) did give some recognition to this concern when she admitted, "the lacking ingredient is the organizational capacity for on-line refereeing, editing, and distribution, as well as the necessary modifications in the process of assessing publications for promotion and tenure"(p. 175). This question of gatekeeping is one that must be confronted by those who see electronic technology as making possible direct scholar-to-scholar exchange of information, perhaps with the library as intermediary offering bibliographical assistance and access to some major textual databases.[47]

It is the university press that has traditionally performed this function, through its careful screening of submitted proposals and manuscripts and the elaborate review procedures it undertakes to make sure that what is published has been validated as a genuinely significant contribution to knowledge. If technology is viewed as cost-saving because it makes possible elimination of the role of the traditional publisher, then how does one take care of the problem of separating what is *worth* disseminating from what is merely disseminated? As Kenneth Boulding has pointed out, "We must be very careful not to confuse information with knowledge. In many respects, information is the enemy of knowledge. Piling information on information merely produces noise."[48] At least with print publishing there is now a system in place that helps scholars distinguish knowledge from information. And, as argued above, the publishing process at university presses, beginning with the multifaceted role of the listbuilding editor, provides significant value added to the work of scholars that would be lost in a system of direct scholar-to-scholar electronic communication.

With all that said, however, there is no doubt that we are entering a period when major changes in the system of scholarly communication will have to be made, in response not only to the challenges of computer technology but also to such increasing problems as those affecting endangered species.[49] A hint of what is to come is provided in a letter sent to me in 1991 by a former member of Princeton's editorial board, Lionel Gossman, with which it seems appropriate to conclude:

> I have advocated for a long time that those of us who cannot or do not wish to enter the university press system ought to work out a way of communicating our ideas using the many reproduction opportunities—desktop publishing, I guess—now available. We shouldn't need all that expensive production anyway in order to reach a couple of hundred people in the world who might be interested in reading us. And things do get around using informal circuits. If a highly specialized paper had something in it of more general interest, I am fairly confident that there are informal networks of communication out there that would ensure its dissemination. The presses themselves might benefit from such a system, since they would be able to pick up for more elegant production and more effective distribution work that had already proven itself, as it were, in the cheap, informal circuit. A change of this kind wouldn't necessarily make it harder to get tenure. People (not only tenure committees but individual scholars) might become less fixated on the Book, which would be a good thing all round, and more attention might be paid to the substance of a scholar's work than to the material form in which it appeared. Above all, we would be rid of the

artificial constraints of the book (which the scientists have never had to endure) and free to invent the forms of communication that seem most appropriate to what we have to say.

Notes

1. A parallel can be noted with faculty appointments: the "stars" in any field are few, competition for them intense, and a department expanding rapidly cannot reasonably expect to succeed in capturing very many of them.

2. Powell provides some examples of serendipity experienced by these publishers' editors on page 94. This element of luck is one reason why he describes the decision-making process in scholarly publishing as a variety of semirational behavior known among organizational theorists as "loose coupling."

3. Walter Powell (1985) quotes publishing industry historian John Tebbel as observing that "the widely used term 'acquisitions editor' is an indicator that today's editors seldom edit" (p. 11). Powell goes on to say (pp. 11–12):

> Editors used to be generalists who did everything. Now the time of an acquisitions editor is considered too valuable to be spent on working with an author. In the past, editors read manuscripts, worked with authors, assisted them, and edited their manuscripts to whatever extent was required. Today's editors spend much more time talking, arranging deals, and consulting with lawyers, corporate managers, and marketing and subsidiary-rights directors. This not only signals a power shift within publishing houses— one in which editors are on the decline and others are in ascendance; it has also led to a restructuring of the relationship between authors and editors.

As we shall see, this description does not apply, in nearly the same measure, to university press editors who still operate free of many of the pressures that burden their commercial colleagues. For current comments on the neglect of editing by acquiring editors in commercial publishing today, see Weisberg (1991). This article produced a storm of controversy; some of the reactions appear in *The New Republic* from July 15 and 22 under the heading "Revenge of the Book People." See also the more nuanced and illuminating piece by the veteran editor Ted Solotaroff (1991), who helps place Weisberg's article in context of the evolution of commercial publishing in recent years. As Solotaroff says, Weisberg's "indictment of publishers and editors is about 60 percent right and 60 percent wrong. He has got the crime—the decline of editorial standards—mostly right but the perpetrators and motive mostly wrong. . . . He has missed virtually all of the extenuating circumstances, not to mention the distinctions, comparisons and conflicts, that form the real interest and drama of the case" (p. 399).

4. The first in the series "Studies in Political Development," *Communications and Political Development* edited by Lucian W. Pye, was published in 1963; the ninth and final volume, *Crises of Political Development in Europe and the United States* edited by Raymond Grew, appeared in 1978.

5. In a letter to me dated May 25, 1983, Princeton political scientist Henry S. Bienen (now dean of the Woodrow Wilson School there) elaborated on these reasons:

> The turn away from Africa has been caused by many things. There is the inhospitability to research by host governments as you mention. There is the drying up of Ford Foundation and other funds. There is the depressing reality after the utopian hopes of the 1960s. Also, Latin America, it is thought, can teach us more about our own past and Latin American studies can be informed by our understanding of European and American histories. And, the USA has had deeper economic and political involvements in Latin America. Thus people who wanted to explore these involvements are drawn to Latin America.

6. Unlike some of my fellow editors at university presses, I have always looked favorably on dissertations as potentially good books. They frequently need significant revision to realize their potential, it is true, but the effort is often worth making. Compared with authors who hold down full-time teaching jobs and have many administrative responsibilities as well, not to mention families to take care of, writers of dissertations can concentrate virtually all of their time and effort on this single project; what they may lack in maturity of judgment or range of vision, they can make up for by the intensity and depth of their research, including often very richly rewarding field work (if they are social scientists). The image dissertations have of being dull, dry, and too narrow to interest anyone besides the author's thesis committee is belied by the success of such books as Evans's, which sold over one thousand in hardback and seventeen thousand in paperback in ten years—a sale that would delight any commercial scholarly publisher.

7. Once entrenched within Latin American studies, political economy extended its influence outward to other area studies, and I pursued this trend by acquiring such titles as Francine Frankel's *India's Political Economy, 1947–1977* (1978), Andrew Jano's *The Politics of Backwardness in Hungary, 1825–1945* (1982), John Waterbury's *The Egypt of Nasser and Sadat: The Political Economy of Two Regimes* (1983), Ronald Libby's *The Politics of Economic Power in Southern Africa* (1987), Thomas Biersteker's *Multinationals, the State, and Control of the Nigerian Economy* (1987), and *Manufacturing Miracles: Paths of Industrialization in Latin America and East Asia* (1990) edited by Gary Gereffi and Donald Wyman

8. This happened in the case of the work by a feminist philoso-

pher cited below in the section on policies and procedures of the editorial board.

9. See Parsons (1989b, pp. 101–102) for another account of Princeton's editorial process at this time.

10. On transforming a thesis into a book, the best guide is still Harman and Montagnes (1976).

11. This letter was written on June 16, 1977, and submitted to Robert Gottlieb of Knopf as part of my application for the Tony Godwin Memorial Award in that year.

12. Arthur B. Darling, *The Central Intelligence Agency: An Instrument of Government, to 1950* (1990); Ludwell Lee Montague, *General Walter Bedell Smith as Director of Central Intelligence, October 1950–February 1953* (1992).

13. It is in large part this exposure to intellectual currents in other disciplines that explains why faculty who serve on press editorial boards frequently cite this experience as the most rewarding of any they have in doing committee work for their university.

14. Comparison of political philosophy as done by analytic philosophers in *Philosophy and Public Affairs* and by political scientists in *Political Theory* will immediately reveal the differences in the two disciplines' approaches.

15. The decision not to pursue publication of Rorty's collection was made in the context of a new program, "Princeton Series of Collected Essays," that the press was promoting at the time whereby previously published essays by well-known scholars would be photoreproduced from their original printed source, the object being to make these collections of essays available to students in relatively inexpensive paperback format. Since this method of publication made revision of the essays impossible and Rorty wanted to revise some of his essays before republication, the series could not accommodate his collection. In such manner can press policies lead to unwise decisions!

16. See Peter Laslett's introduction to his edited volume *Philosophy, Politics, and Society* (Oxford: Basil Blackwell, 1957) wherein appears the since oft-quoted statement: "For the moment, anyway, political philosophy is dead." Compare the more upbeat introduction he and W. G. Runciman wrote for the second volume in this series, published in 1962, where they remark that already "the mood is very different and very much more favorable than it was six years ago"—although the volume begins with an essay by Isaiah Berlin entitled "Does Political Theory Still Exist?"

17. Rawls's work was, for me, the "big one that got away." Rawls earned his Ph.D. at Princeton and had close connections with people in the Philosophy Department there. Moreover, he was one of four Princeton-connected philosophers I had approached early in my efforts to build the press's list in philosophy with an invitation to publish a collection of his essays. (The others were Joel Feinberg, Stuart Hampshire, and Gregory Vlastos—all former teachers of mine at

Princeton—for each of whom the press did publish a collection.) Rawls begged off because he was in the final stages of completing his *Theory of Justice* and did not want to take time away from it to devote to preparing a collection. My efforts to persuade him to submit that work to Princeton nearly succeeded, and I was later told that Harvard's editor-in-chief had to get on her hands and knees and plead with Rawls to give his book to Harvard. Harvard had the advantage of proximity, which was important to Rawls, who had a reputation for constant fine-tuning of his work and might well have wanted to insert changes in proofs at the very last minute. Also, it must be admitted, I was still very much a junior editor at the time, with the results of my efforts in acquisitions only just then beginning to show themselves in print, and Rawls had little visible evidence to see of how strong a program in philosophy Princeton would come to develop. Rawls's Harvard colleague, Robert Nozick, also a Princeton Ph.D., was another philosopher I courted in those early years, hoping to get his *Anarchy, State, and Utopia* (1974), which subsequently won a National Book Award; but his close personal relationship with the editor of Basic Books made that also an ultimately fruitless effort.

18. If Walter Powell's testimony is to be believed, this is not an activity that comes naturally to editors. "Editors," he claims, "are structurally conditioned not to pay much attention to books that are currently being released" (1985, p. 57).

19. The authors and their books are Joshua Miller, *The Rise and Fall of Democracy in Early America, 1630–1789: The Legacy for Contemporary Politics* (1991) and Eric J. Ziolkowski, *The Sanctification of Don Quixote: From Hildago to Priest* (1991).

20. On the advantages that accrue to publishers from authors' loyalty, see Powell (1985, pp. 50, 156, 181). For comments on the particular problem that can arise when author loyalty conflicts with house loyalty, see Powell (1985: p. 76.)

21. Princeton University Press is an exception, unique in this country to my knowledge, in being a separately constituted corporation, linked with its university only through the representation of faculty, administrators, and alumni on its board of trustees and through the control that its faculty editorial board exerts over use of the university's imprint. Penn State Press is more typical in its being positioned as a unit within the university's graduate school to whose dean I as director of the press report.

22. Some presses suffer from the misfortune of being regarded as auxiliary services on a par with the university bookstore, which is expected to pay its own way entirely from income generated by sales. Harvard University Press's director, for instance, used to report to the vice president for grounds and buildings, and this awkward placement within the university's bureaucracy had the effect of generating a lot of friction that led to the firing of the press's director in 1970.

23. Presses at public universities are more exposed to the vagaries of state politics than presses at private universities, and the legislatures in some states have even been known to wield a heavy hand directly in the funding of presses at their state universities, which has required defensive lobbying by the presses' directors.

24. One exception is Syracuse University Press, which publishes "New York Classics."

25. Despite its strong regional appeal, Joe Paterno's book about his life as Penn State's football coach was not published by the Penn State Press but by Random House.

26. See *Publishers Weekly*, September 23, 1988, p. 18.

27. See Parsons (1991, p. 47) for a table displaying areas of specialization of North American university presses, 1990–91.

28. The comparisons here and in the rest of this paragraph are based on data for Princeton covering the years 1971–1982 and for Penn State covering just the year 1990. I have no reason to believe that data for the remaining years of the 1980s for Princeton, if compiled, would show any significant differences from what is reported here.

29. F. James Davis, author of the prize-winning *Who Is Black? One Nation's Definition* (1991), explained to me that one reason he submitted his manuscript over the transom to Penn State was that his colleague in the Sociology Department at Illinois State University, Richard Stivers, had had a good experience with the press in publishing his book *A Hair of the Dog: Irish Drinking and American Stereotype* (1976).

30. For comment on some diseconomies of scale in publishing, see Powell (1985, p. 21).

31. I experienced the difference dramatically in moving from Princeton, where in my final year I signed up fifty-one titles, to Penn State, where I have been acquiring about fifteen titles a year. (Of course, as director, I have much else to do besides acquire new books.) Most university press editors handle about twenty-five titles a year all the way through to signing of a contract. Powell (1985, p. 222) cites a range of between twenty-five and thirty-five titles as "a rough average of the annual work load for the senior editors" at the two commercial scholarly publishing houses he studied. There are presses, however, where the expected productivity is much higher: at Cambridge University Press, which issues around 1,000 books annually, I am told that editors are supposed to acquire fifty titles a year.

32. Walter Powell (1985) notes that "part of the success of the small, more specialized houses is due to the declining quality of author–publisher relations in the larger houses, along with the exceptionally high rejection rate for manuscripts that is characteristic of almost any publishing house of significant size"(p. 19).

33. Walter Powell (1985) notes some other ways in which a publisher's "prestige is a valuable currency." It is particularly important to the fortunes of books by little-known authors. The books of highly visible

scholars are typically sent out for review regardless of who their publisher is. But when the book review editor does not know an author's
work, the prestige of the publisher can be a major factor in whether or
not the book receives a review (p. 206). Not only are book review editors
influenced by the imprint, but also "librarians and booksellers often
base their decisions about which new books to order on a publisher's
editorial and marketing reputation"(p. 218).

34. This experience of mine, as well as the advantage his training
in medieval history has given our history editor at Penn State in getting off to a fast start, leads me to question Walter Powell's claim that
"knowledge of a particular discipline . . . does not seem to be a particularly valued asset in scholarly publishing"(1985, p. 57). But it is
true that such knowledge is not a prerequisite for success. At Princeton,
my classmate Edward Tenner enjoyed a very successful career as science editor at the press even though he got his Ph.D. in the field of
German labor history.

35. For data on library expenditures on books and journals covering the period 1969–1973, see Fry and White (1975), especially page 61
for the change in the ratio. The ratio for Penn State's Pattee Library for
1991/92 is 1:4. Okerson and Stubbs (1991) note that serials prices rose
by 51 percent over the period from 1985-86 to 1989-90; they also report
on some of the trends toward cancellation of subscriptions now under
way. Among members of the Association of Research Libraries, 52 percent
indicated in response to a survey in late 1990 that they have already
begun to reduce their journals subscriptions. The University of California at Berkeley, for example, has canceled subscriptions amounting
to more than $400,000 in recent years. Penn State announced early in
1993 that its library had canceled about eight hundred subscriptions
worth over $200,000 for the current fiscal year.

36. For discussion of this looming crisis, see Thatcher (1990).

37. The increasingly important role played by the independents is
emphasized by Joseph Barbato in a letter to the *New York Times* on
April 9, 1990, in which he observed: "Serious American book publishing is no longer the sole domain of Random House and other major
trade houses. Last year, *Publishers Weekly* . . . gave its Carey-Thomas
Awards for creative publishing not to multi-million-dollar conglomerates, but to Thunder's Mouth Press, Curbstone Press, Seal Press, and
Eridanos Press—small publishers devoted to alternative fiction, Latin
American writing, feminist literature, and foreign literary classics." The
contribution the independents could make was enhanced further when
the Mellon Foundation gave grants of $50,000 to each of nine small
literary presses in December 1990 and the Lila Wallace–Reader's Di-
gest Fund followed in March 1991 by awarding a $3 million grant to
help such presses develop their marketing programs. See *Publishers
Weekly*, March 22, 1991, p. 11.

38. For example, see the remarks by Kenneth Arnold (1987), director of Rutgers University Press, and the "My Say" column in *Publishers Weekly* by L. E. Phillabaum (1989), director of the LSU Press.

39. For comments from various press directors about publishing fiction and poetry, see "University Presses: A Changing Role" in *Publishers Weekly*, September 23, 1988, p. 19. For an excellent history of poetry publishing at university presses, see the introduction in Wallace (1989).

40. The results of an extensive survey of the competitive practices of university presses are reported in Thatcher (1980).

41. For some observations about the practice of multiple submissions, see Powell (1985, p. 229), who points out: "But unpublished authors must recognize that, if they choose to send their manuscripts to many houses at once, they are probably hurting their chances of publication at each individual house."

42. Authors of books submitted for approval by the editorial board of the Penn State Press at one meeting not long ago included scholars based at the Memorial University of Newfoundland, Rocky Mountain College, Butler University, the University of North Carolina at Greensboro, and Western Louisiana University. Scholars not affiliated with universities with whom I have worked include Nicole Ball (then at the National Security Archives), Louis Fisher (of the Congressional Research Service), Joel Goldstein (a lawyer), Pedro-Pablo Kuczynski (president of the First Boston investment banking house), Joan Nelson (of the Overseas Development Council), William Odom (a military attache at the U.S. Embassy in Moscow at the time, later director of the National Security Agency), and Andrew Pierre (then at the Council on Foreign Relations).

43. Before the change in NEH's criteria, however, I would not have considered applying for a subsidy for a book with trade potential like Thomas Sowell's forthcoming *Race and Culture*, which was awarded an NEH grant in 1991 (but won't be published at Penn State owing to a dispute with the author over copyediting of his manuscript).

44. See the reports on Bertelsmann's operations in *Publishers Weekly*, October 20, 1989, p.14, and September 21, 1992, p.8.

45. For details of this project, see *Publishers Weekly*, June 7, 1991, p. 41.

46. The ARL *Directory of Electronic Journals, Newsletters, and Academic Discussion Lists* included over nine hundred entries in its 1992 edition.

47. Some librarians have been trying to persuade their colleagues that providing access to information wherever it can be obtained is the role that university libraries should be seeking to fulfill now, rather than continuing to develop collections of materials on site. For two statements from advocates of this philosophy of librarianship, see

Dougherty (1991) and Gherman (1991). According to Gherman, "the bottom line is that we will be spending more of our budgets for access to information and less on ownership of information."

48. See also Atkinson (1992) for a vision of the librarian's role in the age of the "electronic library."

49. For more about the future of scholarly publishing as it faces these challenges and problems, see two articles I wrote after this essay (Thatcher, 1992, 1993a) and also a long interview I had with two Penn State librarians in April 1992 (Thatcher, 1993b).

References

Arnold, Kenneth. 1987. "Reflections on the Future of University Publishing." Address delivered at the annual meeting of the Association of American University Presses, June 15.

Atkinson, Ross. 1992. "The Acquisitions Librarian as Change Agent in the Transition to the Electronic Library." *Library Resources and Technical Services* 36 (January): 7–20.

Bailey, Herbert S., Jr. 1989. "Einstein's collected papers: planning and development." *Scholarly Publishing* 20 (July): 203–217.

———. 1991. *On Style in Publishing*. University, Ala.: University of Alabama Press.

Battin, Patricia. 1984. "The Library: Center of the Restructured University." *College and Research Libraries* 45 (May): 170-176.

Dougherty, Richard M. 1991. "Research Libraries Must Abandon the Idea That 'Bigger Is Better.'" *The Chronicle of Higher Education* 37 (June 19): A32.

Frugé, August. 1984. "The Metamorphoses of the University of California Press." *Scholarly Publishing* 15 (January): 161–176.

Fry, Bernard M., & Herbert S. White. 1975. *Economics and Interaction of the Publisher–Library Relationship in the Production and Use of Scholarly and Research Journals*. Washington, DC: Office of Science Information Services, National Science Foundation.

Gherman, Paul M. 1991. "Setting Budgets for Libraries in Electronic Era." *The Chronicle of Higher Education* 37 (August 14): A36.

Goellner, J. G. 1990a. "The Editorial Board: Friend of Frustration." *Scholarly Publishing* 21 (April): 184–188.

———. 1990b. *Who Will Keep the Gates?* University, AL: University of Alabama Press.

Harman, Eleanor, & Ian Montagnes, eds. 1976. *The Thesis and the Book*. Toronto: University of Toronto Press.

McClung, William J. 1969. "The Short Book." *Scholarly Publishing* 1 (October): 45–52.

Okerson, Ann, & Kendon Stubbs. 1991. "The Library 'Doomsday Machine.'" *Publishers Weekly* 238 (February 8): 36–37.

Parsons, Paul. 1989a. "The Editorial Committee: Controller of the Imprint." *Scholarly Publishing* 20 (July): 238–244.

———. 1989b. *Getting Published: The Acquisition Process at University Presses*. Knoxville: University of Tennessee Press.

———. 1991. "The Evolving Publishing Agenda of University Presses." *Scholarly Publishing* 23 (October): 45–50.

Phillabaum, L. E. 1989. "The University Press and Suitable Priorities." *Publishers Weekly* 236 (May 26): 39.

Powell, Walter W. 1985. *Getting into Print: The Decision-Making Process in Scholarly Publishing*. Chicago: University of Chicago Press.

Smith, Eldred. 1991. "A Partnership for the Future." *Scholarly Publishing* 22 (January): 83–92.

———. 1992. "The Print Prison." *Library Journal* 117 (February 1): 48–51.

Solotaroff, Ted. 1991. "The Paperbacking of American Publishing." *The Nation* 253 (October 7): 399–404.

Thatcher, Sanford G. 1980. "Competitive Practices in Acquiring Manuscripts." *Scholarly Publishing* 11 (January): 112–132.

———. 1990. "Scholarly Monographs May Be the Ultimate Victims

———. 1992. "Towards the year 2001." *Scholarly Publishing* 24 (October): 25–27.

———. 1993a. "Latin American Studies and the Crisis in Scholarly Communication." *LASA Forum* 63 (Winter): 10–14.

———. 1993b. "An Interview with Sanford G. Thatcher, Director, The Penn State University Press." *Library Acquisitions: Practice and Theory* 17 (June): 203–225.

Wallace, Ronald, ed. 1989. *Vital Signs: Contemporary American Poetry from the University Presses*. Madison: University of Wisconsin Press.

Wanek, Diane. 1990/91. "Nebraska Assists Czech University Press." *The Exchange* 63 (Winter): 2.

Weisberg, Jacob. 1991. "Rough Trade." *The New Republic* 203 (June 17): 16–21.

Index

✳

About the Contributors

✳

Carole S. Appel. M.A. (linguistics), University of Michigan; senior editor and journal manager, University of Illinois Press, Champaign-Urbana, Illinois; author of "Women's Studies at the University of Illinois Press," *Women and Politics*, 1, no. 1 (1980).

Charles M. Bonjean. Ph.D. (sociology), University of North Carolina; vice president of the Hogg Foundation for Mental Health and Hogg Professor of Sociology, The University of Texas at Austin; editor of *Social Science Quarterly*, the Hogg Foundation Monograph Series, and consulting editor in sociology for Wadsworth Publishing Company.

Fred Cohen. J.D., Temple University, LLM, Yale Law School; professor of law and criminal justice at the School of Criminal Justice, The State University of New York at Albany; editor-in-chief of the *Criminal Law Bulletin*.

Leonard W. Doob. Ph.D. (psychology), Harvard University; Sterling Professor Emeritus of Psychology, Yale University; editor of *Journal of Social Psychology*, coeditor of *Journal of Psychology*; associate director, Southern African Research Program.

Melvin J. Dubnick. Ph.D. (political science), University of Colorado; professor of public administration at Rutgers University, Newark; managing editor, *Public Administration Review*, specializes in intergovernmental relations, bureaucratic politics, and accountability theory.

James J. Fyfe. Ph.D. (criminal justice), State University of New York at Albany; professor of criminal justice and Senior Public Policy Research Fellow, Temple University; former editor of *Justice Quar-*

terly; coauthor with Jerome Skolnick of *Above the Law: Police and the Excessive Use of Force* (Free Press, 1993).

Avery M. Guest. Ph.D. (sociology), University of Wisconsin; professor of sociology and geography at the University of Washington; former editor of *Demography*; recent research has focused on the social process of integration into communities in the early postmigration months.

Michael Lewis. Ph.D. (sociology), Princeton University; professor of sociology, University of Massachusetts, Amherst; former editor of JAI Press, *Research Annual in Social Policy*; author of *The Culture of Inequality* (University of Massachusetts Press).

Larry Neal. Ph.D. (economics), University of California, Berkeley; professor of economics, University of Illinois, Champaign-Urbana; editor, *Explorations in Economic History*; author of *The Rise of Financial Capitalism, International Capital Markets in the Age of Reason* (Cambridge University Press, 1990).

Samuel C. Patterson. Ph.D. (political science), University of Wisconsin; professor of political science at Ohio State University; former editor of the *American Political Science Review*; coauthor of *The Legislative Process in the United States* (4th ed.) (Random House, 1986).

David H. Rosenbloom. Ph.D. (political science), University of Chicago; Distinguished Professor of Public Administration at The American University; editor of *Public Administration Review*; research and teaching focuses on the intellectual history of public administration and the politics, law, and personnel of public bureaucracies.

Richard C. Rowson. M.I.A. (international affairs), Columbia University; publisher of the Woodrow Wilson Center Press; former and founding director of The American University Press; director of Duke University Press; president of Praeger Publishers; executive with Radio Free Europe.

Rita J. Simon. Ph.D. (sociology), University of Chicago; University Professor of Public Affairs and the College of Law, The American University; former editor of *The American Sociological Review, Justice Quarterly*, and sociology editor for JAI Press; author of studies on transracial adoption, public opinion and immigration, and women's movements.

Theresa A. Sullivan. Ph.D. (sociology), University of Chicago; professor of sociology and law, Faculty Fellow in Law, and chair of the Sociology Department, University of Texas at Austin; former editor of the Rose Monograph Series.

Sanford G. Thatcher. B.A. (philosophy), Princeton University; former editor-in-chief at Princeton University Press; director of the Pennsylvania State University Press; expert in copyright law, and current chair of the Copyright Committee of the Association of American University Presses.